Praise for *The Opposite of Fate*

"Tan lays out the truth about her life and career. . . . Alternately humorous and deadly serious, *The Opposite of Fate* is a portrait of a writer in midlife and midcareer. Tan has set her own record straight."
—*The Oregonian* (Portland)

"Artfully written. Tan's incisive wit and refreshing take on life are winsome. Even in her musings about her darker moments, her writing is keenly felt. Like her bestselling novels, her essays promise to delight, sadden and astonish. Readers, loyal and new, will find much to admire in Tan."
—*The Cleveland Plain-Dealer*

"A must-read memoir."
—*Marie Claire*

"Fans of Tan will cherish this collection."
—*US Weekly*

"Great fun. Readers of Tan's novels will enjoy frissions of recognition."
—*Newsday*

"A window into a candid, funny and engaging mind, as well as a provocative meditation on the way stories—and how we tell them—can shape our lives."
—*The Columbus Dispatch*

"A powerful collection that should enthrall readers of *The Joy Luck Club* and Tan's others novels."
—*Publishers Weekly*

"Tan is mischievously hilarious and intensely moving. No matter how much readers already revere Tan, their appreciation for her will grow tenfold after experiencing these provocative and unforgettable revelations."
—*Booklist*

"Excellent. Highly recommended."
—*Library Journal*

"Tan offers a wry but bracing take on life and writing. An examined life recalled with wisdom and grace."
—*Kirkus Reviews*

PENGUIN BOOKS

THE OPPOSITE OF FATE

Amy Tan is the author of *The Joy Luck Club*, *The Kitchen God's Wife*, *The Hundred Secret Senses*, *The Bonesetter's Daughter*, and two children's books, *The Moon Lady* and *The Chinese Siamese Cat*, which has now been adapted as a PBS production, *Sagwa*, for which she is a creative consultant and writer. Tan was also a coproducer and coscreenwriter of the film version of *The Joy Luck Club*, and her essays and stories have appeared in numerous magazines and anthologies. Her work has been translated into more than twenty-five languages. She lives with her husband in New York and San Francisco.

THE OPPOSITE OF FATE

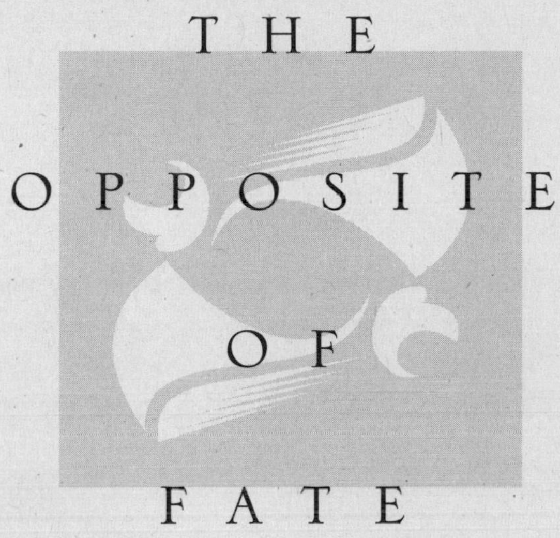

memories of a writing life

AMY TAN

PENGUIN BOOKS

PENGUIN BOOKS

Published by the Penguin Group
Penguin Group (USA) Inc., 375 Hudson Street, New York, New York 10014, U.S.A.
Penguin Group (Canada), 10 Alcorn Avenue, Toronto,
Ontario, Canada M4V 3B2 (a division of Pearson Penguin Canada Inc.)
Penguin Books Ltd, 80 Strand, London WC2R 0RL, England
Penguin Ireland, 25 St Stephen's Green, Dublin 2, Ireland (a division of Penguin Books Ltd)
Penguin Group (Australia), 250 Camberwell Road, Camberwell,
Victoria 3124, Australia (a division of Pearson Australia Group Pty Ltd)
Penguin Books India Pvt Ltd, 11 Community Centre, Panchsheel Park, New Delhi – 110 017, India
Penguin Group (NZ), cnr Airborne and Rosedale Roads, Albany,
Auckland, New Zealand (a division of Pearson New Zealand Ltd)
Penguin Books (South Africa) (Pty) Ltd, 24 Sturdee Avenue,
Rosebank, Johannesburg 2196, South Africa

Penguin Books Ltd, Registered Offices: 80 Strand, London WC2R 0RL, England

First published in the United States of America by G. P. Putnam's Sons,
a member of Penguin Group (USA) Inc. 2003
Published in Penguin Books 2004

1 3 5 7 9 10 8 6 4 2

Information on previous publication history appears on page 400.

THE LIBRARY OF CONGRESS HAS CATALOGED THE HARDCOVER EDITION AS FOLLOWS:
Tan, Amy
The opposite of fate : a book of musings / Amy Tan.
p. cm.
ISBN 0-399-15074-9 (hc.)
ISBN 0 14 20.0489 8 (pbk.)
1. Tan, Amy. 2. Novelists, American—20th century—Biography.
3. Chinese Americans—Biography. 4. Fiction—Authorship. I. Title.
PS3570.A48O67 2003 2003047190
813'.54—dc21
[B]

Printed in the United States of America
Designed by Claire Naylon Vaccaro

GRATITUDE

I owe thanks to many for the existence of this work: among them, Sandy Dijkstra and Carole Baron for suggesting the book when it seemed impossible for me to write another sentence; Aimee Taub for guidance, organization, and cheerfulness in making the overwhelming merely whelming, even fun; Anna Jardine for saving me from public disgrace; Raphael Stricker, M.D., for restoring my brain to sentence-writing strength; and Faith Sale and Daisy Tan, eternal muses, for inspiration, insight, and sense of purpose.

With love to Lou DeMattei,
who knows the fiction and nonfiction of my life,
as well as all that cannot be put into words.

CONTENTS

American Circumstances and Chinese Character

Strong Winds, Strong Influences

Luck, Chance, and a Charmed Life

A Choice of Words

Hope

THE OPPOSITE OF FATE

A NOTE TO THE READER

These are musings on my life, including the metaphors I used as an eight-year-old child, sensing books as windows opening and illuminating my room, and the thoughts I had as I wrote my mother's obituary, trying to sum up who she was and what legacy she had bequeathed to me.

I call this a book of musings because the writings are mostly casual pieces rather than formal essays. Some are long, versions of conversational talks I gave at universities. Others are short, particular to the desperate hour in which I wrote them, for example, the eulogy for my editor, the incomparable Faith Sale; or the e-mail sent to friends after an unexpected disaster resulting in my near-demise made the national news. There is also a love poem to my husband, which counts as my most difficult exercise in brevity.

I have included such longer pieces as my ruminations about the making of the film *The Joy Luck Club*. A reporter had faxed me questions, and I sent back the answers, written off the top of my head, ending with my wondering what would happen next; in a footnote, I explain what did. I offer as well a portion of my journal entries from a 1990 trip to China in which I was smothered in the bosom of family and had to acquiesce rather than follow my typical American ways. I offer it here for fun, and because it shows how nearly everything in my life turns into obsessive observation, images, questions, and if I am lucky, the beginnings of stories, however ragtag they may be. The last reflection in this book was written only recently, and for a fateful but hopeful reason.

Some of the pieces have ignominious origins. "Mother Tongue" was written hastily, as an apologia the night before I was to be on a panel with people far more erudite than I on the topic "The State of the English Language." The speech was later published in *The Threepenny Review* and then selected for inclusion in the anthology *The Best American Essays 1991*—leading me to wonder whether all my essays should be written at two in the morning in a state of panic. A version of "Mother Tongue" has also been used for the Advanced Placement SAT in English; this unanticipated development delights this author to no end, since her score in the 400s on the verbal section of the SAT made it seem unlikely, at least in 1969, that she would even think of making her living by the artful arrangement of words.

In gathering these pieces for the book, I made a new realization, so obvious that I was stunned I had not seen the pattern a hundred times before. In all of my writings, both fiction and nonfiction, directly or obliquely but always obsessively, I return to questions of fate and its alternatives. I saw that these musings about fate express my idiosyncratic and evolving philosophy, and this in turn is my "voice," the one that determines the kinds of stories I want to tell, the characters I choose, the details I decide are relevant. In my fictional stories, I have chosen characters who question what they should believe at different moments in their lives, often in times of loss. And while I never intended for the pieces in this current nonfiction book to explain my fiction, they do.

Thus, although each of these writings came about for its own reasons, collectively they hold much in common, and at times they overlap in my mention of ideas, people, and pivotal moments. They are musings linked by my fascination with fate, both blind and blessed, and its many alternatives: choice, chance, luck, faith, forgiveness, forgetting, freedom of expression, the pursuit of happiness, the balm of love, a sturdy attitude, a strong will, a bevy of good-luck charms, adherence to rituals, appeasement through prayer, trolling for miracles, a plea to others to throw a lifeline, and the generous provision of that by strangers and loved ones.

I see that these permutations of changing fate are really one all-encompassing thing: hope. Hope has always allowed for all things. Hope has always been there. My mother, who taught me the many permutations of fate, was hope's most stubborn defender. If fate was the minute hand on a clock, mindlessly moving forward, she could find a way to force it to go back. She did it often. She, who adamantly believed I would grow up to be a doctor, would later brag to anyone who listened, "I always know she be writer one day." And in so saying, fate was changed and hope was fulfilled. And here I am, a writer, just as she predicted.

FATE AND FAITH

My mother believed in God's will for many years. It was as if she had turned on a celestial faucet and goodness kept pouring out. She said it was faith that kept all these good things coming our way, only I thought she said "fate," because she couldn't pronounce that "th" sound in "faith."

And later, I discovered that maybe it was fate all along, that faith was just an illusion that somehow you're in control. I found out the most I *could have was hope, and with that I was not denying any possibility, good or bad. I was just saying, If there is a choice, dear God or whatever you are, here's where the odds should be placed.*

· The Joy Luck Club

· the cliffsnotes version of my life ·

Soon after my first book was published, I found myself often confronted with the subject of my mortality. I remember being asked by a young woman what I did for a living. "I'm an author," I said with proud new authority.

"A contemporary author?" she wanted to know.

And being newly published at the time, I had to think for a moment before I realized that if I were not contemporary I would be the alternative, which is, of course, dead.

Since then I have preferred to call myself a writer. A writer writes—she writes in the present progressive tense. Whereas an author, unless she is clearly said to be "contemporary," is in the past tense, someone who once wrote, someone who no longer has to sharpen her pencil, so to speak. To me, the word *author* is as chilling as rigor mortis, and I shudder when I hear myself introduced as such when I lecture at universities. This is probably due to the fact that when I was an English major at a university, all the authors I read were, sad to say, not contemporary.

What compels ardent readers of my work to ask me questions concerning my time-limited authorhood? In lecture halls and on live radio shows, I have been stunned by questions as deadly as these: "What would you like written on your tombstone?" "Which book would you like people to remember you by?" "Does it make you feel honored that your books probably will be in circulation at the library long after you're gone?"

I don't find those questions nearly as appalling as this one: "Are you loaded?" which is what a nine-year-old girl in Nashville once asked me at a book signing. I wondered whether the child might have just come from a school program on crime prevention or substance abuse and was now worried that all adults carried loaded weapons or were loaded on drugs. I said to her gently, "What kind of loaded are you worried about?"

"You know," the girl snapped, "loaded like filthy rich." I glanced over to her mother, expecting that she would reprimand her daughter. And the mother looked right at me and said, "Well, *are you?*"

I've grown accustomed to public scrutiny. Yet nothing prepared me for what I consider the ultimate reminder of an author's mortality. It happened when I was at yet another bookstore, about to give yet another reading. I was waiting in the wings, as the store manager delivered a long introduction on my credentials as an author. Glancing to my side, I saw a wire book rack crammed with cheap and familiar booklets. They were CliffsNotes, self-proclaimed as "your key to the classics."

As we all know, CliffsNotes have served as the midnight salvation of many a literature student, and if the sad truth be known, this former honors English major used them to write incisive papers on—dare I say it?—*Ulysses, Lord Jim,* and *Hamlet.*

Imagine: There I was, in a bookstore, recalling these past sins, about to read from my own published work. I gave a silent apology to my fellow authors Jim Joyce, Joe Conrad, and Bill

Shakespeare, may they rest in peace. And then my eyes landed on another familiar title: *The Joy Luck Club.* I stared at those CliffsNotes, thinking to myself, *But I'm not dead yet.*

I flipped through the pages and found an obituary-like biography of the author, me, Amy Tan. I was shocked to learn that I once had carried on "a relationship with an older German man, who had close contacts with drug dealers and organized crime."

Could this possibly be describing *my* Franz? True, he was older than I was, twenty-two years to my sixteen when we met. And yes, he was friends with a couple of Canadian hippies who sold hashish, but I don't remember them being *that* organized about it. Whatever the case, does my personal history of having once dated a loser constitute the sort of information needed by "serious students," as Cliff refers to them? Will this make them "secure in the knowledge that they have a basic understanding of the work"?

In page after chilling page, I saw that my book had been hacked apart, autopsied, and permanently embalmed into chapter-by-chapter blow-by-blows: plot summaries, genealogy charts, and—*ai-ya!*—even Chinese horoscopes. Further in, I was impressed to learn of all the clever nuances I'd apparently embedded into the phrase "invisible strength," which is what a mother in the book taught her chess-playing daughter, Waverly. According to Cliff, I meant for "invisible strength" to refer to the "human will," as well as to represent "female power" and "the power of foreigners." It was amazing what I had accomplished.

The truth is, I borrowed that phrase from my mother, who used to say something like it to me whenever I was whining out loud. She'd say, *"Fang pi bu-cho, cho pi bu-fang,"* which is commonly uttered by Chinese parents, and which translates approximately to: "There's more power in silence."

What *my* mother intended that I understand, however, was precisely this: "No one wants to hear you make a big stink over nothing, so shut up." The strict linguist might want to note that the literal translation of that Chinese phrase runs along these noble lines: "Loud farts don't smell, the really smelly ones are deadly silent."

Anyway, that's the sort of literary symbolism I use with phrases like "invisible strength"—*not* the sort of analysis you find in CliffsNotes, I might add.

At the end of the booklet was a list of questions. I read one: "Which daughter in the book is most like Amy Tan? Why?" What luck. This very question was often asked of me in interviews, and I had never known what to say. Here in my quaking hands, just one page turn away, was the definitive answer. But one page later, I discovered these were just discussion questions, no answers were given, and thus I was left to ponder my existential angst in the usual fashion.

In spite of my initial shock, I admit that I am perversely honored to be in CliffsNotes. Look at me: I'm sitting in the $4.95 bookstore bleachers along with Shakespeare, Conrad, and Joyce. Now, I'm not saying that I've reached their same literary status. I acknowledge there is a fundamental difference that separates us. I am a contemporary author and they are not. And since I'm not dead yet, I can talk back.

One of the problems of being a contemporary author is that you are confronted with frequent opportunities to see what people have written about you in the way of reviews, profiles, or student theses. It's all rather appalling. Good, bad, or ugly, there before your very eyes is an analysis of you, your intentions, and the deeper, more subterranean meanings of your books—say, the dichotomy between two cultures and two generations, or the sociopolitical concerns of immigration and assimilation—the subject matter that makes you sound high-minded when, really, your reasons for writing were more haphazard and personal.

The truth is, when I write, I begin with a simple question: How do things happen? Early in life, what I thought about that affected what I should hope. And in my family, there were two pillars of beliefs: Christian faith on my father's side, Chinese fate on my mother's. Picture these two ideologies as you might the goalposts of a soccer field, faith at one end, fate at the other, and me running between them trying to duck whatever dangerous missile had been launched in the air.

My father's faith had been nurtured by his family. He was born in 1913, the oldest of twelve children, to a mother who was a Chinese traditional healer and a father who was a Presbyterian minister. My grandfather Hugh Tan had been converted by missionaries in Canton and educated in their English-speaking schools. His education was so thoroughly Western that he could read and write English before he could his native tongue of Cantonese. He wrote me a letter once, shortly before he died of a stroke in Shanghai. His English was impeccable, and he prefaced his remarks with Christian feeling: "We thank the good Lord we are still in good health."

The Christian influence ran so deep and strong in the Tan family that all twelve children became evangelists of one sort or another. My father was a latecomer to the ministry, but at the age of thirty-four, he suffered a crisis of morals. A few years earlier, he had fallen in love with a beautiful woman who was unhappily married and had three young children. They started an affair, which led to the woman's being thrown in jail for adultery. Shortly afterward, my father left China for the United States, where he had been offered a scholarship to study at MIT.

Upon arriving in San Francisco, he lived at a YMCA and joined the First Chinese Baptist Church on Waverly Street. At night, he wrote in a black leather diary, and sometimes he pondered his sins and weaknesses. He and the woman had committed adultery. Now the woman was being punished in jail, while he was in San Francisco taking square-dancing lessons. Oh, the terrible inequity of it all. He berated himself until God answered with an epiphany that he should devote himself to saving others. He gave up his scholarship to MIT, and joined the ministry by enrolling in the Berkeley Baptist Divinity School.

For the rest of his life, my father would place his faith in God to provide the right answers. His faith was absolute. Among most people I know, a bit of wiggle room is expected in how your prayers might be answered. You might pray, for instance, for the love of your life, and God will land you a volunteer position at the local animal shelter, where saving animals becomes the love of your life. God, like your parents, Santa Claus, and perhaps your psychiatrist or editor, knows best how to funnel your desires into more likely and beneficial outcomes.

But my father's faith, as I said, was absolute. Through God's prayer he could be granted exactly what he wanted. He prayed that his sweetheart be freed, and sure enough, she was released from prison. Then she cabled my father and asked whether he wanted her to come to America. Shanghai would soon be taken over by the Communists, and his answer had to be now or never.

According to family lore, he immediately cabled her back, saying, "Yes, come!" Yet I imagine he must have taken a few minutes or even hours to weigh his obligation to her and his future obligations to the ministry. Could he marry the woman with whom he had committed adultery? Could he, a moral example to his flock, bear to be reminded of their sin for the rest of his life? And what would his parishioners think if his wife was a divorced woman? And how could she, his pampered beloved, who was accustomed to servants, to a sable coat, to smoking cigarettes, take on the austere existence of a poor minister's wife? I imagine him praying for God to "shine Your answer upon my face."

He may have turned to God also for guidance on how to break the news of his impending marriage to the young women friends he escorted to church picnics and on private outings. Lucky for me, he documented those friendships well. He was an amateur photographer who prized his Rollei and spent hours in the darkroom. He liked to pose his subjects, telling them to lean against a wall and tilt their head up toward the sunlight, to drape an arm over a wooden rail and cross their ankles and point their toes—the same directions he would give me when I was a child. The photos were meticulously pasted into an album, which I would later peruse. Some of the pages, however, had no photos inserted in the black corner tabs. The photos had been removed and discreetly placed in a shoe box, which I also found—such as the close-up of a young woman lying in the grass, another one artfully running her fingers along her feet, encased in small embroidered shoes. There was nothing lewd about these poses, nothing to suggest that this outing was more than a simple photography shoot. Yet the expression in their eyes is pure adoration. I sense them holding their breath in anticipation as my father looks at them through the viewfinder.

What do they see? He is handsome, a snazzy dresser. He knows exactly what words to say to put them at ease. He is more than your basic nice guy. Despite the fact that he is a an impoverished student at the divinity school, he is a good catch: a superb dancer, a witty conversationalist, a man given to romantic gestures and eternal pledges, plus he is about to become a minister, a man who will be certifiably of the highest morals, greatly respected, a leader. In the summer of 1949, when the minister of his church announced to the congregation that John Tan's bride-to-be was coming from China, several young women gasped and fled the church hall in tears.

From time to time, I have wondered how I might have turned out had my father married one of these other women. They were single, had unencumbered pasts—no sociopathic husbands or wailing abandoned daughters in the background. They were also college-educated and spoke English as well as any other American. I must have met them among the various aunties who attended the same church for more than fifty years: accomplished, kind, levelheaded women now in their seventies and eighties.

My father sent the cable saying, "Yes, come!" to the woman who would be my mother, the Shanghai divorcée who had just been released from prison. And that was how my mother came to the United States and married my father. It was God's will and some other woman's bad luck.

According to my mother, though, God had less to do with it

than fate. Consider how she and my father met, she would remind me. It was around 1941, during the war. She was on a boat, making her way to the city where her husband, a Kuomintang army pilot, was based. My father and his brother were on that same boat. She and my father chatted in a friendly way. They were attracted to each other, although they did not acknowledge this. The boat docked a few days later, and they went their separate ways.

That right there could have been the end of the egg and the sperm that would have made me. Instead four years passed. The war ended. My mother by then had tried numerous times to leave her abusive husband. "That bad man" was how she always referred to him. That bad man once put a gun to her head to force her to sign fake divorce papers. She gladly did this, no gun to her head was necessary, but immediately after she signed, he raped her.

Meanwhile, my father was gadding about in some other part of China, happily single. Many a pushy Chinese mother tried to engage his interest in her daughter. One mother had three daughters, all of them beautiful, talented, and photogenic. I saw the pictures. Because of his excellent language skills in English, Cantonese, and Mandarin, my father was able to work for the U.S. Information Service. He wore a U.S. Army uniform and visited local newspaper stalls and bookshops, gathering any magazines or reports that made mention of the United States, good or bad. One of my uncles told me that my father was recruited by the United States to be a spy. He also said my father used to smoke and drink and was quite the playboy in China. My mother laughed off those assertions. (To this day I wonder who was right. What about the visa to the United States that I found among my father's belongings? It said he was already married. Did he have another wife? Will I one day receive a letter announcing: "Surprise! I am your long-lost sister. Your other seven sisters and I arrive tomorrow and will stay at your house for a month or two, unless you would like us to visit longer. . . .")

But let us go back to 1945 and assume my mother's version of the story is true. My father, now in his early thirties, is still single. He is working in Tientsin, in the north, thousands of miles from the southwestern river where he and my mother first met.

My parents, John Tan and Du Ching (Daisy), Tientsin, China, 1945.

My mother happens to be in Tientsin visiting her brother and sister-in-law, who are working underground for the Communists. She is going up the street the very moment my father is coming in the opposite direction. They bump into each other. They confess it was instant love when they met four years before, because that love has only grown stronger all this time they have been missing each other.

This was not chance that they met twice, my mother would tell me whenever she recounted this story. It was fate. Love proved that it was. So that is how I was born to a mother with a convoluted secret past. I became the daughter of a woman who believed I was part of her fate.

Thanks to my mother, I was raised to have a morbid imagination. When I was a child, she often talked about death as warning, as an unavoidable matter of fact. Little Debbie's mom down the block might say, "Honey, look both ways before crossing the street." My mother's version: "You don't look, you get smash flat like sand dab." (Sand dabs were the cheap fish we bought live in the market, distinguished in my mind by their two eyes affixed on one side of their woebegone cartoon faces.)

The warnings grew worse, depending on the danger at hand. Sex education, for example, consisted of the following advice: "Don't ever let boy kiss you. You do, you can't stop. Then you have baby. You put baby in garbage can. Police find you, put you in jail, then you life over, better just kill youself."

The consequences of not heeding my mother's advice were grave. When I was six years old, she took me to the funeral of my playmate Rachel from down the street. As I stared at Rachel's sunken eyes, her bloodless hands crossed over a Bible, my mother whispered to me: "This what happen you don't listen to mother." My mother went on to say that Rachel died because she had not washed her fruit—a health precaution I ignored too often. (Years later, when pesticides on fruit were proven to cause cancer, I learned that my mother's warning had not been off base after all.)

I remember a day not too long after Rachel died, when I was sitting on the piano bench, sulking. My mother was scolding me for not practicing enough, for being lazy. She went on and on about how much the lessons with Miss Towler cost, how Daddy had to work overtime. And for what—so she could listen to me make the same mistakes? She then posed an important question: "What you rather do: play piano and become famous, or play outside and become nobody?" Guess what I said.

She was quiet for a moment and then said, "Okay, go play." As I happily slid off the bench, I heard her mutter that from now on I could do whatever I wanted. She would no longer tell me what to do. If I didn't want to play the piano, fine. "Forever no more obey," she said. "Don't matter. Soon, maybe tomorrow, next day, I dead anyway."

By then, I knew what dead meant, or at least what it looked like. But I didn't yet know that my mother's mother had killed herself in 1925. I didn't know that my mother had seen this happen, when she was nine years old, that thereafter she would see suicide as the answer to any kind of unhappiness, that she would routinely threaten to die, sometimes weekly, sometimes daily, whenever she was displeased with me or my father or my brothers, whenever she felt slighted by her friends, whenever the milk spilled or the rice burned. I didn't know that later her emotional terrorism would alternate between threats to kill herself or return to China and that this would lead me to think that China, like death, was an unpleasant place to go. On that day at the piano, when I was six and she first mentioned she was going to die soon, all I knew was fear.

Because of my mother's moods, I lived in a state of high suspense. I often thought about death, about Rachel being lifeless, about my mother's promise that soon she would be too. I also pictured in my mind the rat my father had recently shown us wide-eyed kids in the middle of the night: the rodent's bloody body smashed in the trap, black eyes bulging. "See," my mother had soothed, "now you no longer be scared what will eat you." Until then, we had imagined the rat in our house resembled a cheery creature like Mickey Mouse.

Since death was on my mind a lot as a child, I naturally wondered about ghosts as well. In our house, we had two kinds. First, there was the one we could talk about in front of others; that would be the Holy Ghost. My father, after all, was an ordained Baptist minister. True, by the mid-1950s he had returned to electrical engineering so he could make a living wage, but his avocation was still the ministry, and he encouraged daily devotion in the family. We children were taught to believe the Holy Ghost sat at our dinner table and ate Chinese food. We laid out chopsticks and a bowl for our unseen guest at every meal.

The second kind of ghost belonged to my mother. These ghosts were Chinese. We were not supposed to talk about them, because they were bad, of a different religion, and were specifically banned by the laws of the Holy Ghost. Yet they were there. I could sense them. My mother told me I could. One time when I was about four, I remember, she ordered me to go to the bathroom to brush my teeth and wash my face. Guests had arrived and I didn't want to go to bed, so I said, "I can't go in there."

Why, my mother demanded to know.

"I'm scared," I lied.

Why?

"There's a ghost in there."

Like most mothers might do, she grabbed my hand firmly and guided me to the bathroom. Most mothers would have flipped on the light switch and said, "See, there are no ghosts here—now brush your teeth." My mother stood at the doorway and said in a voice tinged with hope and excitement: "Where are they? Show me."

Much to my distress, for the rest of her life she continued to believe I had a talent for seeing ghosts. When I was older, she recalled this same bathroom incident: "I never teach you this word 'ghost.' So must be true. You see ghost!" It didn't matter that I insisted I could not see or hear or feel anything. She thought it admirable that I was lying to protect my invisible friends.

She had other proof that the ghosts came to me: the fact that I knew things I wasn't supposed to know. I don't remember what I said or did to her to make her think this. Perhaps it was the way I said a certain name. Or maybe it was my likes and dislikes of a certain dish she cooked. My mannerisms, my preferences, my tone of voice were exactly that of someone else—that person being dead, and having died in mysterious circumstances. My mother believed in reincarnation and she believed I was someone from her past, a woman she had obviously wronged. Why else had I come back as her daughter to torment her so?

I did not want to think of myself as a dead person. But I was also afraid to contradict my mother, for that would send her tumbling into one of her pitch-black moods, those times when she threatened to kill herself. I had already seen her try—as when she opened the car door while we were zooming down the freeway and my father had to yank her back. I was afraid that if my mother died, I would then see a real ghost.

These were matters I could not talk about with my father. I adored him, and he adored me, but he also both adored and feared my mother. He was much more easygoing than she, and not easily riled. He told multilingual jokes and roused friends into singing after dinner. He read bedtime stories to me and my brothers with great expression. He did the *Reader's Digest* "Word Power" quiz with me, making it seem the most fun a body could have. He read his sermons to me so I could serve as his best critic. He showed me his engineering homework when he was studying for his master's, as though I could instantly absorb the intricacies of symbols and formulas. He was hardworking and loved his work, which went on seven days a week. He was an engineer, a volunteer minister, a graduate student, and the entrepreneur of an electronics business he conducted in our family room, winding electromagnetic transformers the size of LifeSavers. Only twice that I recall did he take time off, and then for only a few days, to go with us to Disneyland and Knott's Berry Farm, and he still managed to perform a wedding along the way and visit an electronics firm that might be interested in buying the transformers he built in his "spare" time.

As smart and strong as he was, he always gave in to my mother's demands. That meant that every six to twelve months we had to move to another house. Whenever my mother became unhappy, she wanted to move. And once she locked on to an idea, she could not let it go, until her unhappiness permeated the entire house and she made us ill with her nonstop complaints.

By the time I graduated from high school, I had attended eleven schools. I had learned to lose friends, to remain the loner until I finally found new ones. Each time I started at a school, I had to sit back quietly for the first month or so and observe who was popular, who was not, who was smart, who was the smart-ass. I had to show my new teachers that I was a good student, that I knew how to draw realistically. But I also knew not to do anything to stand out in any other way, lest I join the ranks of the pariahs. I understood that I had to be a chameleon to survive, that I should fit in quietly, and watch.

In hindsight, I see that this was excellent training for a budding writer. It sharpened my skills of observation. It deepened my sense of alienation, which, while not a prerequisite for a writer, is certainly useful as an impetus for writing. Many of the great novels of our time are based on alienated narrators. And yet I hated those feelings of loneliness. I cried every time my father announced that we were moving. He may have prayed to God for general direction in his life, but he received the specifics from my mother to move to Oakland, Hayward, Santa Rosa, Palo Alto, Santa Clara, Sunnyvale.

Throughout my father's life, he remained devoted to his beliefs in God the Father, Son, and Holy Ghost. He practiced what he preached. He tithed ten percent. He didn't smoke or drink or say "gee," "gosh," or "golly." He prayed when he became impatient or lost his temper. He practiced charity to others. He made me feel good for giving away my best dolls to my poor cousins in Taiwan, the same cousins who today are millionaires. My father put his life in God's hands, and he encouraged us, his children, to believe that if we had absolute faith, God would take care of the rest. Miracles would happen.

About ten years ago, I found some of my father's diaries. In one of his last entries, written at the end of May 1967, he stated that he still firmly believed that God would grant him a miracle and save his sixteen-year-old son from dying of a brain tumor. He had absolute faith. By my father's own handwritten definition: "Faith is the confident assurance that something we want is going to happen. It is the certainty that what we hope for is waiting for us even though we still cannot see it ahead of us."

He wrote this less than two months before my brother Peter died, and shortly after, he stopped writing. But this was due to loss of ability rather than loss of faith. By then, my father couldn't hold a pen well enough to comment on the strange coincidence that he too, the father of the son who had become a ghost, had been stricken with a brain tumor.

These days I realize that faith and fate have similar effects on the believer. They suggest that a higher power knows the next move and that we are at the mercy of that force. They differ, among other things, in how you try to cull beneficence and what you do to avoid disaster. Come to think of it, those very notions are the plotlines of many novels.

Throughout their marriage, my mother, the minister's wife, publicly avowed her trust in God. The other day I came upon a letter she wrote to a family friend in 1967, in which she commented about my father's faith during his illness: "Most of the time, he spent in search of God, trusting deeply that God would take care of him. We were both easily moved to tears, for we felt deeply and were warmly touched by the warmth of the love that so many friends freely gave to us. We know from this that it is a blessing that is overflowing from our Lord."

The words are actually not my mother's writing. They are

mine, written as a fifteen-year-old girl taking dictation, rendered with almost as much repetition as my mother provided to me, her reluctant scribe. Our sessions would go something like this: "Amy-ah, put this down. Say you daddy all the time, searching searching searching God, why this happen? Amy-ah, you searching too? Why this brain tumor second time? No, don't write this down, I just asking you. Why so many bad things happen? . . . What you mean, don't know? You don't think! You don't care! And why you don't cry? You daddy, me, we cry so much. But you—look you face—no feeling! What's wrong with you, you don't cry? And why you make you hair that way? You look like Japanese girl. Ugly . . . Okay, put this down . . . Friends they so good to us. You daddy and I, we cry, tears so much overflowing, for sadness, for thanks so much."

It was torture to write those letters. I had to compose the thank-you notes to friends for coming to the hospital, the cards acknowledging them for coming first to my brother's funeral and then to my father's. Extra-long letters went to those who sent memorial donations.

After my father died, my mother no longer prayed to God. This was strange to me at first, because we had once been a family who prayed at every meal, before every important occasion. Now when the meal was served, we ate in silence. Or rather, it was silence if we were lucky. At times, my mother would go into obsessive monologues about our tragedies, about the curse, punctuating with her laments every bite we took: "Why two brains tumors? Why same family? Why same time? Who else die? If someone next, let be me." (Little did my mother know then that she may have already had a brain tumor. We learned of it in 1993 after she fell and suffered a suspected concussion. An

MRI showed that she had a meningioma, a benign tumor, which, the neurologist said, had been growing probably for twenty-five years, meaning since 1968 or so, around when my brother and father had died of their brain tumors.)

To counter the curse, my mother began to call openly on the ghosts of her past. She prayed to a painting of her mother. She hired a geomancer to inspect the spiritual architecture, the *feng shui,* of our suburban tract house. What forces were aligned against us? She sought faith healers who taught her to speak in tongues, a gibberish that convinced me she was insane. She blamed herself for not moving from our current house, the one we had lived in longest, two years. In that neighborhood, she now realized, nine bad things had already happened. She counted them out on her fingers: The man down the street had had a heart attack. This one lost his job. That one was getting divorced. Every day, my mother would count these disasters out, asking herself uselessly why she had not seen them clearly before.

When my father died, more phantoms sprang from my mother's past: ideas about karmic retribution, reincarnation, and the presence of ghosts as signaled by our barking dog, a misplaced object, a door slamming when a certain name was spoken. My mother was sure that what was uncertain in the real world could be accounted for in the supernatural one. There the possibilities of what happened and why were boundless. And because my mother still believed I was sensitive to the other world, she often asked me to use a Ouija board to communicate with the ghosts of my father, my brother, and sometimes her mother, my grandmother.

I had never met my grandmother. In 1925 she swallowed a large amount of raw opium, and my mother, then a girl of nine, watched her die. Yet in another sense I saw my grandmother every day. She was in our living room, in the form of an oil portrait my mother had commissioned, based on a sepia-toned photograph. In this portrait, my grandmother's face was larger than life. She was a beautiful young woman in her thirties with straight-cut bangs and a neat bun. Her dress was blue with a high collar. Her expression was enigmatic, her gaze ethereal, eyes focused on a spot beyond the artist, out into the future. The painting hung near the piano, where I practiced every day for one hour, with my grandmother peering over my shoulder.

This was the face I also saw in my mind as I sat before the Ouija board. My fingers would be poised on the planchette, my tearful mother opposite me. She was always hoping for one last good-bye, one more message of love. "Do you still love me? Do you miss me?" It was heart-wrenching even to me, the heartless teenager who would not permit herself to show any kind of emotion. I would give the answers my mother hoped for: *Yes. Yes.*

Pragmatic woman that my mother was, she would eventually seek advice about daily living. For some reason, she thought the ghosts had as much interest as she did in the Dow Jones. "IBM or U.S. Steel?" she would say, hoping for insider-trading tips of the best kind. And I, the supposed purveyor of these spiritual answers from Wall Street ghosts, pushed the planchette to whatever came to mind just to get the ordeal over with. *Buy. Sell. Yes. No. Up. Down.* Upon reflection now, I see that my spurious advice was probably no worse than that of most stockbrokers. My mother did amazingly well in building up her modest portfolio.

She turned to the ghosts for child-rearing advice too: "Amy treat me so bad," she once said as I prepared to divine the answer. "What I should do—send her Taiwan, school for bad girls?" The planchette deftly scooted to the correct answer: *No.*

Another time my mother wanted to know whether she should open a Chinese restaurant. Everyone loved her potsticker dumplings, and she dreamt she could make a million selling them. I pictured myself washing heaps of greasy bowls and pans with burnt dough stuck to the bottom. *Bad idea,* came the Ouija's answer. *Lose money.*

In my memory, which I admit can be subjectively poor and riddled with a wild imagination, I recall that our sessions with the Ouija board were often accompanied by eerie signs that ghosts were indeed in the room. It would suddenly become not just cold but windy. A flower would snap from its stem as if in answer to an important question. A sound would be heard in the distance—first by my mother, then by me—seemingly the voice of a crying woman. And once the board rose in the air several inches, my fingers still attached to it, then crashed to the floor. That is what I remember, although logic tells me it was the result of either hysteria or peanut butter stuck to my fingertips.

Besides using the Ouija board, my mother continued to find advice in other, less traditional places. One time she looked under the kitchen sink, where she stored cleaning products. She was cleaning the kitchen after dinner, and my little brother and I were watching TV nearby. I saw her pick up a can of Old Dutch cleanser and stare at it as if it possessed the lucidity of a crystal ball. "Holland," she announced to us. "Holland is clean. We moving to Holland."

A few months later, my mother, my brother, and I boarded the SS *Rotterdam*. Our mother had sold the ranch duplex, the maple colonial furniture, and the Plymouth, and otherwise reduced our worldly possessions to the contents of three new Samsonite suitcases and a huge duffel bag. Once in Holland, my brother and I realized our mother had absolutely no plan. We stayed in The Hague, then Amsterdam, then Utrecht. In each city, my mother used idiosyncratic sign language to inquire after the nearest Chinese restaurant. We would find these miserable way stations, and there she would eat with the hunger of the starved, Chinese food tinged with Indonesian ingredients and prepared for a Dutch palate. Awful, my mother would pronounce, and drink copious amounts of tea to wash away the bad taste. (This would be her pattern in every city, town, and hamlet we visited in Europe over the next year—this hopeful search for Chinese food, her disappointment in every dish she tasted.)

We located an international school in a small town called Werkhoven, as well as lodging in a woman's house. This landlady did not allow us to keep our lights on beyond nine at night, making it difficult for my brother and me to finish our homework. Equally bad, her housekeeping skills did not satisfy my mother's notions of Old Dutch cleanliness.

After two weeks in Holland, we took a train to Germany and landed in Karlsruhe, where we lived as guests of a U.S. Army chaplain, an old friend of my father's. We attended an American school, where students thought it a fun prank to aim lit Bunsen burners at one another. This, I told my mother, was not the kind of education she had had in mind when she had envisioned us studying abroad. With that, she bought a Volkswagen Beetle and a handbook of English-speaking schools, and off we went, heading south, letting ourselves be guided purely by the twists and turns of European highways.

By such maps of fate, we wound up in Montreux, Switzerland, at the shores of Lake Geneva. In this resort town, my mother quickly found our new home, a fully furnished chalet, complete with cuckoo clock and feather-tick beds, renting for the equivalent of one hundred U.S. dollars a month. The largest room served as living room, dining room, and my brother's bedroom, and its entire length was lined with mullioned windows showcasing a spectacular view of the lake and the Alps. Every day, I would stare at this amazing scenery and wonder how I came to be so lucky. I would then remember that my father and older brother were dead, and that was the reason I was here.

Half a mile from our chalet, down a cobblestone path, lay an international school. It was within eyesight of Château de Chillon, where the dashing Lord Byron was said to have chained himself to write his poetry in religious agony. By happy chance, there were two openings for day students. My mother weighed the benefits of a four-to-one pupil–teacher ratio, the mandatory ski outings as physical education, the private piano lessons and one-to-one drawing classes, the Spanish teacher from Spain, the French teacher from France, and English teachers from England, and decided it was all worth the extravagant cost of six hundred dollars per year.

This marvelous school was attended by the sons and daughters of ambassadors and company presidents, rich kids the likes of whom I had never known. One girl wore a lynx coat atop a bikini to class, much to the amusement of the young male teachers. There were two Persian kids in the lower grades, a six-year-old boy and his nine-year-old sister, who were followed everywhere by bodyguards. The girl who became my closest friend had also recently lost her father, and she had a clothing allowance of a thousand dollars a month—this was in 1968, mind you—yet she was forever broke and showed no shame in bumming cigarettes and a few francs off me on a regular basis.

The male teachers were handsome, not that much older than the junior and senior students. I promptly fell in love with one of them. I was by then a somewhat pudgy girl, usually blind because I would not wear my glasses. I had thick glossy hair that fell to my waist, which complemented my flower-power minishimmy. Whenever I had to go to the piano practice room, I would sit on the window ledge there and smoke cigarettes, watching the swans and geese at the lake, thinking my cynical and silly thoughts, most of which concerned ways to sneak off to meet my boyfriend. In America, I had been a dateless dork, the sisterly friend to boys I had crushes on. In Switzerland, I was an *exotique,* sought after by the regular customers in the café, the young drifter from Italy, the factory worker from Spain, the radicals from Germany. At last, I was a popular sex object. Life had begun! This, sad to say, was the quality of my thoughts.

My boyfriend was the "older man," as CliffsNotes described him. Franz was, in fact, the first boy who ever said he loved me. He wrote me a twenty-four-page love letter, all in German, of which I was able to translate the first line: "My darling Angel, who dims the heavens above me . . ." Who wouldn't fall for that? He was a frizzy-haired hippie whose father had been a Nazi officer. Franz had deserted the German army and fancied himself a revolutionary along the lines of Che Guevara. He smoked Gauloises incessantly, and he despised the small-mindedness of people who thought one had to work to have a worthy occupation. He, in contrast, occupied his time listening to The Rolling Stones. He had plenty of friends, whom he met at the café, where they played foosball, a form of table soccer operated by moving two sets of handles with rapid adjustments and twists of the wrist. Since Franz played for hours every day, he was spectacularly good, rather like an international soccer champion, had anyone been wise enough to honor people who play table soccer in cafés. To a teenage girl in the late 1960s, nothing could be more romantic than the combination of attributes that Franz possessed.

I found out later that my *Liebling* had deserted the German army all right, but from its mental hospital. Oh, well. Mental illness was romantic and even revolutionary in its way.

My mother was, shall we say, less open-minded. It didn't help matters that Franz once flipped her off, which she misinterpreted as his showing his fist in a threat to beat her up. I thought about telling her what the gesture really meant, then deemed it better that she think he was merely violent rather than disrespectful.

For the months Franz and I were together, ours was a romance of stolen kisses—and kisses only, I might add, although my mother was certain he had defiled me. She wore my ear down, telling me how lazy he was, that his breath stank, that he had no future. My little brother chimed in to say that he looked like Larry of the Three Stooges. My mother took to yelling at me, locking me in the bedroom, and slapping me. She grew frantic, then hysterical, and talked of killing herself so she would not have to see me destroy my life.

One day, sick of my mother's tirades, I decided I should break up with Franz. Or was it that I was weary of Franz and wanted to use my mother as my excuse? In any case, I remember that our breakup came on the night before some big examinations. Until then I had been a straight-A student. Though I was a junior, I was graduating early and applying to colleges, so these exams were very important. I was looking forward to college, for therein lay the means by which I could escape my mother. Having a ne'er-do-well boyfriend did not fit into my new life as a serious college student. That was not what I told Franz, of course. I blamed my mother for the breakup.

That night, after I made my announcement, Franz threw himself on the train tracks and vowed he would let the next train from Lausanne squish him to pieces if I did not immediately change my mind, hop aboard the next train to Austria with him, and elope. I pleaded with him for an hour and more to please not do this. Then came the warning call of the train. *Whoo-whoo!* Which would it be—marry him or bury him?

A minute later, after a tearful embrace, we both hurried to the station. While waiting for the train to Vienna, I had a chance to ask myself whether I really wanted to be married to a man whose sole occupation was being the unofficial international champion of foosball. I found a pay phone and called my mother. I did what was only considerate, and let her know I wouldn't be home for breakfast. Why? Oh, didn't I tell you? Franz and I are at the train station, about to elope. Before the train took off, bearing me to a fate of certain marital unhappiness, my mother and the police arrived. And so I did not get married, but because of sheer mental exhaustion from a sleepless night of high drama, I flunked my exams.

After this escapade, my mother decided enough was enough. She hired a private detective, who was also the town mayor. Unbeknownst to me, my mother confiscated my diary, which I had written in Spanish, and the detective-mayor had it translated into French. The unintended confession provided in novelistic detail all the evidence the detective needed for the biggest drug bust in Montreux's history.

This is not to say it was that big—only a small stash of psychedelic mushrooms was found, in a Volkswagen van belonging to some Canadian hippies. The largest part of the illegal goods, four kilos of Moroccan hashish, had already been tossed into Lake Geneva, where, I was told, it was joyfully devoured by the resident geese, which later that day were seen to be flying high.

Franz and his friends were jailed, then deported. Because of my young age, I was not, but I had to appear before a magistrate in Bern and promise I would not do anything bad ever again in my entire life. I would not smoke, not even one cigarette. I would always obey my mother, give her not even one word of defiance.

A few months later I graduated from high school, in my junior year. I returned to the States and in the fall started my freshman year in college as an American Baptist Scholar, chosen for my high morals.

That was my childhood. Told as is, it would not make for good fiction. It is too full of coincidences, too full of melodrama, veering toward the implausible in both tragedy and comedy. But my life is, I believe, excellent fodder for fiction. Memory feeds imagination, and my imagination is glutted with a Thanksgiving of nightmares.

Looking back, I'm convinced it was also my mother who affected my imagination to such a degree that I now hear and see things that others do not. I see connections in coincidences, ironies in lies, and truths in contradictions, all sorts of things that others do not.

But I also see and hear—how shall I say it?—the inexplicable: noisy apparitions, mysterious electrical phenomena, prophetic dreams, bodiless laughter, and the abrupt disappearance of objects more significant than the mates to socks. How would *you* explain it if you heard the *Jeopardy!* tune being whistled behind your back when you were alone at home; if paper plates at a funeral reception wafted up and down whenever the name of the deceased was mentioned; if your television set turned on by itself in the middle of the night, tuned to a religious channel; if your phone disconnected, but only when you were talking to your mother?

I've had discussions with my husband about this. I told him about hearing footsteps running up and down the stairs, doors slamming, and what resembled the raucous pounding of a couple taking lambada lessons in our bedroom. My husband said our house was old, it had funny acoustics. I brought up the fact that electrical equipment often shorted when I talked about my grandmother. I reminded him that some of these mysteries had followed me across the continent, to Denver, Austin, Atlanta, and New York, and even across the ocean, to London, Amsterdam, Milan, and Munich, where tape recorders and video equipment had malfunctioned, TV and radio stations had gone off the air—all while I was being interviewed. To all that, my husband shrugged. (What do you expect from a man who is a tax attorney? It's his *job* to write things off.)

My mother, on the other hand, assured me that I was not crazy, that it was not my imagination or bad structural engineering. There were ghosts in my house, she said, in fact one that lived in the computer. Her proof was the first book I wrote, *The*

Joy Luck Club. Contrary to what CliffsNotes and reviewers had to say, she did not believe that I wove "intimate knowledge of [my] culture into a Chinese puzzle box." No such thing. The way she saw it, in matters Chinese, I was an idiot. Only after I was published did my status rise to that of idiot savant.

This is how and why her opinion changed: While I was writing *The Joy Luck Club,* I asked her to tell me more about her parents, both of whom had died when she was a child. My mother revealed that my widowed grandmother had remarried—a disgraceful thing to do, my mother said, but at least she became the first wife to a rich man. Later my grandmother gave birth to a son; two months after that, she accidentally died, from eating opium while having too much of a good time.

When I wrote the story "Magpies," I changed the details a bit; the young widow is raped by a rich man and becomes his fourth wife, a lowly concubine who gives birth to the man's first son, the result of the rape. The baby is claimed by a higher-ranking wife, and this so enrages the fourth wife about the worthlessness of her life that she dies, not accidentally while having fun, but with the vengeance of suicide.

When my mother read this story, she asked me, "How you know you grandmother really the *fourth* wife? How you know what really happen? Why you can write about things you don't know?" And then she remembered: I had always been able to talk to ghosts.

As a result of the truth of this fiction, my mother came to believe that my dead grandmother had served as my ghostwriter. Sometimes she would greet my computer as if her mother were listening. "Hey, it's me," she'd call in Chinese. "Are you there? Do you miss me?" And at times I too have thought that my computer was equipped with a grandmotherboard of sorts, that my keyboard was a high-tech Ouija board, that I was simply downloading stories from the Nirvana Wide Web. Because I too have wondered why I can write about what I don't know.

Yet I do know things. I have always known them, I realize. I've known them from childhood, perhaps from listening to my mother and my aunties gossip about their secrets as they shelled the fava beans and pummeled the dumpling dough at the kitchen table. They spoke in Shanghainese, a language I now, as an adult, cannot speak. I must have intuitively understood it as a child. I must have paid close attention when their voices lowered and the rush of shameful words streamed out. How else is it that I know their secrets?

Or is it that I've known things because of all those suicidal threats my mother made when I was a child? I paid attention to her laments, what she said she wanted to forget. I've known things because we had to move so often, and I had a mother who believed happiness was a place she had never been. I've known things from listening to her talk about dangers of every form, unwanted babies, a man who will kiss you and ruin your life. She helped me imagine fully the unhappy consequences in all their gory details—what can happen if you don't have a mother to listen to.

Today my mother is gone, but I still know certain things. They are in my bones.

There is a morbid fantasy I play with myself from time to time. I sit at my desk, trying to write a story. How do things happen?

And then I consider that I may not be who I think I am. I am not this person Amy Tan in CliffsNotes. The sad truth is, my mother's gruesome worries were fulfilled when I was six or so, when I ran into the street and was smashed flat or when I ate unwashed fruit, I forget which, but the result was that I died or fell into a coma—it's hard to say which, and which is worse. Whatever the case, this is the state I have been in since, this cocoon of a world where I dream that anything can happen. In this altered reality, I have dreamt everything that I think has happened to me from age six to the present. And now I am only dreaming that I am a writer.

To convince myself that this is not true, that I truly am alive, I do what writers do to make the fiction come true. I begin to recount all that has happened in my life, the smallest details, as if this memory of the order of my life will prove it is a real life, a life so fraught with complications and the mundane that it could not be anything but real.

I see my conception, my father's and mother's DNA combining into a hybrid form of fate and faith held together by a suspension of disbelief. I picture this newly created genetic code as mah jong tiles lined up one after another, curving this way and that, standing precariously in place, always on the verge of falling over to reveal the whiplike pattern of a dragon's tail. That is what I was born, a water dragon, to my mother, a fire dragon. Is this a coincidence, or is this fate?

I let the pieces fall. I look back at the pattern that was created, the whole concatenation of events. And then I begin to sort the pieces according to my own design, asking myself: How are they connected? Which pieces should I choose? Which ones should I discard? How does each piece lead to another, from a street in

Tientsin, China, to this moment in San Francisco, where I am sitting at my wooden desk, in a wood-lined room, in a wood-shingled house, wondering how things came to be?

How is it that I am so lucky to be a writer? Is it fate? Is it a miracle? Was it by choice? Is it only my imagination? Yes, yes, yes, yes. It is all those things. All things are possible.

· how we knew ·

One August afternoon, soon after we met on a blind date, we drove fifty miles to San Juan Bautista, a time-warped town with a mud-walled mission, false-front buildings, and a former dormitory for unmarried Indian women. As we wandered, we became the ghosts, he the vaquero who slept on a cot in the stable, I the Mutsun maiden who had slipped out of the dormitory window, leaving behind her button shoes and pinch-waist corset. We ran freely, stopping to kiss in cool, dark adobe corners.

At sunset, we walked toward the dance hall and saw a crowded wedding party. The mariachi band was blaring, the bride and groom were drunk with happiness, and they shouted for us to join them, pulled us in. Arms on shoulders in a chorus line, we pranced and yipped like coyotes. Later we tumbled out and lay on the grass, staring upward. Eternity, we were part of it. As if to celebrate our joy, stars streaked across the sky—"There!" "There!" "There!" it was the Perseid meteor shower, a billion-year celestial event put on annually by the universe.

It was also our proof that we had lain here before, when he was the vaquero and I the Mutsun maiden, lovers who believed their passion was strong enough to survive scandal, pure enough to bind them into the next lifetime, two hundred years from now.

We are they now, in love, in awe.

· *a question of fate* ·

This is a true story.

Hours after my twenty-fourth birthday, my life began to change with strangely aligned events that today make me wonder whether they did not spring from the fictional leanings of my mind.

It was the Year of the Dragon, when my life's tide was said by Chinese astrologers to be at its most powerful, when change was inevitable. But all this was nonsense to me, for I was an educated person, a doctoral student in linguistics at UC Berkeley.

I tell you what my major was, because it reveals, I believe, what my mental inclinations were at the time. I was in a field of heady theories, seeking random and fortuitous evidence. As linguists we could not prove much in any terribly convincing scientific way, for instance, that grammar is innate and organized in the brain. But we could convolute ad infinitum on why that was possible and then search for empirical findings that suggested the science. Our methods were descriptive, the everyday use of everyday language by everyday people, the best examples being those that made one ponder such inanities as how the *p* sound came to be in the word *warmth* and what rules led people to innovate words like *hodgepodge*, *hocus-pocus*, and *hanky-panky*. Intricate convolution was also how I liked to occupy my mind when it came to worries about myself and, in particular, about how I showed my ineptitude when compared with other students.

Early that year, I had been married for nearly two years. Although I knew I was with the right person, I had the usual angst of a young woman who felt she had traded her soul's identity for a joint return. Lou and I lived in Danville, California, in a brand-new two-bedroom apartment with gold shag carpeting, a burgundy velour sofa, and a rotating variety of uncuddly pets, including a bull snake that was an escape artist and a tarantula that required a diet of live crickets.

Lou DeMattei and me, 1974.

To help us pay the rent, we had a roommate, Pete, a young man who was around our age, a bioengineering student also at Berkeley. He had pale blond hair, an amblyopic eye, and a Wisconsin accent. We had met him two years before, when we all worked at a Round Table pizza parlor in San Jose. We continued to work at Round Tables in Berkeley and Danville, where we often took the closing shift and wound up sharing conversations over after-hours pitchers of beer.

Pete liked to argue about what was impossible to know, from conspiracies to eternity. His philosophical meanderings depended on how much beer he had imbibed, and were often related to the intersection of philosophy and science—the physics of infinity, say, or the ecology of ideas. He had a particular fascination with the I Ching, that art of tossing three coins three times and divining a pattern out of heads and tails. Pete would begin with questions: What determined the pattern? Was it random? Was it a higher power? Was it mathematical? Wasn't poker based on mathematical probability and not just luck? Did that mean randomness was actually mathematical? And if the I Ching was governed by mathematics, hey, wouldn't that mean the I Ching was actually predictable, a prescribed answer? And if it was prescribed, did that mean that your life *followed* the I Ching, like some sort of equation? Or did the I Ching simply capture correctly what had already been determined as the next series of events in your life?

And so the circular discussion would go. Somewhere in this mystery, mathematics always held the answer. Don't ask me how. I am only describing what I remember, what I never understood. We had such conversations during backpacking trips, while climbing the backcountry in Yosemite. At night, when we were not arguing over questions of eternity, we read H. P. Lovecraft tales around the campfire, shooed away marauding black bears, and identified the constellations from our sleeping bags, our chilled faces to the sky. Those are elements that strengthen any friendship, I think.

I remember enjoying many long conversations about secular transcendentalism, that motley union of the psychedelic and the physical. We had the sense that we were talking about what really mattered, the hidden universe and our souls. But perhaps that was also the atmosphere of the times, the 1970s, when all things were possible, particularly after eating brownies laced with goodies other than walnuts, when unorthodox speculation could be answered sufficiently with a reverential "Wow."

Pete also talked a lot about his wife. She was a poet, naturally intuitive, a sexy earth-mother type. They were separated, the result of his own immaturity, he said, his predilection for recklessness and his not thinking enough about the consequences. He expressed hope that his wife might understand that he was sorry, and that they'd be together again one day. Several months after we met, while explaining how he had lost his wallet and hence his driver's license, he told us how he had lost his wife.

They had been traveling by car through Nevada on their first trip from Wisconsin to California. A nineteen-year-old hitchhiker offered to spell them from driving, and they gladly let him take the wheel. Just outside Lovelock, while they were speeding through the pitch-black desert, a rear tire blew, and as Pete turned to tell him to let the car drift to a stop, the hitchhiker instinctively slammed on the brakes, and the car began to roll over. It all happened gently enough, Pete told us, that first roll, the kind of flip you experience in an amusement-park ride, with the car landing on its wheels, righting itself. For a moment, it appeared that they might be able to continue their journey with the only alterations a replaced tire, a slightly dented roof, and one hell of an adrenaline rush. But in the next breath, the car flipped again, this time with the vigor of increased momentum and lift, and when it turned over, it crashed down hard, on its roof, bringing Pete to guess that the car was now totaled. If they were lucky, they might get by with a few injuries, although broken bones seemed likely. And then the car sailed into its third roll, crunched down with the certitude of finality, and slid belly-up into clouds of dust and uprooted sagebrush. When all was quiet, Pete patted himself and found that he was alive and, even more miraculous, uninjured. In the next second, he felt around in the darkness and ascertained that his wife and the hitchhiker were alive as well, breathing hard and fast. But then they let out a final exhale, first the hitchhiker, then Pete's wife, and he was alone. When the police and ambulance crew arrived and asked for his driver's license, he realized that he had lost his wallet.

Two years after the accident, Pete reconciled with his wife in a dream. In fact there were two dreams, a week apart. In the first, which he related to Lou and me, two men, strangers to him, broke into his room, overcame him, and slowly strangled him to death. He described the sensation of absolute terror and the pain of not being able to breathe, and then a tremendous release from struggle. When it was over, he found his wife waiting for him.

Pete went on to say that the dream felt like a premonition. It was scary as hell, but he was at peace with it. His wife would be there. If anything happened to him, he said, he would like Lou and me to distribute his belongings among various friends and family: his guitar to one brother, his camera to another . . .

Stop, I said. Stop being ridiculous. I thought that he, like Lou and me, was nervous about the death threats the three of us had received from a gang whom we had thrown out of the pizza parlor. Two attempts on our lives had already been made, knives and clubs had been drawn, punches exchanged, and my shin nearly broken by a kick with steel-toed boots. Pete had made the mistake of winning one fistfight and breaking his opponent's nose. The gang was now doubly committed to killing us. When we called the Danville police for help, they informed us that our personal thugs had arrest records for dozens of assaults, but there were no convictions, nor were any likely. The best way to deal with future attempts on our lives, someone told us, was to equip ourselves with guns, learn how to use them properly, and make sure that the bodies fell *inside* our door. Outside it was homicide, we were told, inside it was self-defense. Moving to another town was also not a bad idea.

The latter advice was ultimately what we decided to follow. A week after Pete had the disturbing dream he told us about, Lou and I helped him move to Oakland, into a studio apartment in an art deco building. We were placed on a waiting list for a one-bedroom apartment in the same building; for now we kept the apartment in Danville. Pete had few possessions: a bed, a TV set and a stereo, a small table and a chair, his guitar and camera, books, and an expensive calculator that he had purchased with my credit card. There was also a .22 automatic, which he had bought to defend himself in Danville.

Lou and I stayed at Pete's his first night in Oakland, in a sleeping bag on the floor. I recall Pete reiterating his feeling that something bad was going to happen, that someone might break in and kill him. We assured him that there was no way the thugs would know where he had moved. Nor were they industrious enough to want to follow us. Nevertheless, Pete placed the gun between the mattress and the box spring, within easy reaching distance. We kidded him for being paranoid.

The next morning was my twenty-fourth birthday. I can admit now that I was deflated that nothing special was mentioned or offered from the start: no profusion of beautifully beribboned presents, no announcement that plans had been made for going on a lark or winding up at a banquet. But perhaps this seeming lack of preparation really meant that an even more elaborate scheme was in the works, and I would have to be patient to see what it was. Lou suggested we go for a drive, and Pete declined the invitation. He was going to unpack, settle in, and nurse a cold he had just developed. A ruse, I thought. He would be behind the scenes, getting the surprise party under way. As we left, I mentioned we might stop by later, but we would be unable to call ahead of time, since he did not yet have phone service.

As it turned out, my twenty-fourth birthday was a cobbled assortment of activities, spontaneity being the key and "Why not?" being the answer. Lou and I had an impromptu lunch at a restaurant, a drive through the country later, and then we took up an invitation from a friend in Marin County to have dinner with her parents. We spent the night in their driveway, sleeping in our Volkswagen bus. So there was no grand party. The day had been pleasant, but not as eventful as I had secretly hoped.

The next day, back at the apartment in Danville, an acquaintance called. He lived in the building Pete had moved into—we had learned of the vacancy there from him. I greeted him cheerfully.

"Oh," he said flatly, "then you haven't heard the news."

What news?

"Pete's dead. Two guys broke into his place last night and killed him."

"That is the worst joke I've ever heard," I responded angrily. But later Lou and I learned that, indeed, two men had entered through the bathroom window; according to a witness's report, they did not resemble our thugs from Danville. These men had used Pete's .22 to bash him over the head, then hog-tied him stomach down, the rope lashed around his neck and ankles so that the soles of his feet faced the back of his head. When he could no longer hold his muscles taut, he let go and slowly strangled.

In one imagined version—I've played them a thousand times—the robbers stand and watch as Pete struggles to stay alive. That's the worst. In another version, they leave him while he is still struggling. The police arrive, but seconds too late. Actually, that is the worst. They are all the worst. As to what happened after Pete was tied up, I have only these facts: The two men ran out of Pete's studio with his gun and went to pound on the door of the apartment manager, demanding to be let in. When the manager refused, they blasted the door with bullets, then ran out of the building toward their car. A man on the sidewalk had the misfortune of being there; they shot and killed him on the spot. A newspaper story identified the man on the sidewalk as a business student from India who attended Armstrong College. I don't remember his name, and I regret that, for no one killed in that manner should be nameless and forgotten.

I've often thought of that young man from India, and of his family, who must think of his death, as I do, every anniversary of that February night in 1976. "Today," I imagine them saying, "our son would have been fifty years old. Can you imagine? That's older than we were when he died."

The next day, Lou and I went to the Oakland Police Department to identify Pete on behalf of his family in Wisconsin. The police showed us only photographs, but what I saw is too obscene to relay in words. Since then, whenever I read stories of wars, or earthquakes, or murders, I have imagined those who have seen what I have, the face of a loved one, not in peaceful slumber as morticians might have devised, but as it appeared at the moment of death, a body unwashed, ungroomed, not prepared, in any conceivable way, to be viewed by another human being, let alone someone who loved that person.

After collecting the Saint Christopher's medal that Pete always wore around his neck, we drove to his apartment to assist detectives in identifying what might have been taken. I remember seeing everything as in a TV documentary filmed in close-up, with no possibility of pulling away: the door, dusted for fingerprints, and the yellow tape; the opening of the door and my recoiling at the smell. It was the pungent scent of fear, a wild-animal smell of nervous sweat, and it was as potent as if Pete and his assailants had still been in the room, the torment happening in front of me. To the right was further evidence of who had been there, the powdery impressions of fingertips and palms on the doorjamb. Littering the floor were used tissues: so the cold had not been a ruse at all. On the table were the remnants of a dinner—a can of stew (what a poor last meal!)—and a bottle of NyQuil, half empty. Had he been too lethargic to hear the robbers breaking the bathroom window? Was he slow to react? Did he think it was Lou and I who were trying to get back in, looking for a place to stay after a night of birthday-partying? Why didn't he use his gun?

Also on the table was a letter he had written to a friend. I read the page facing up. In it, he described a dream he had had, similar to the one he had recounted the week before: He found himself enmeshed in wads of thick cotton. Soon it became as light as cotton candy, and when he broke free, he saw his wife and others, people whom he did not recognize but who seemed warmly familiar. It was a good dream, the letter said. It felt like a premonition. So that was the second dream. At last, Pete was reconciled with his wife.

When I turned to the left, I saw the rappelling ropes that had been used to strangle him, the bed with a large bloodstain from the blow to his head.

Lou and I listed what had been taken: a stereo; a small television set; a $600 Hewlett-Packard calculator, the prize of any bioengineering student; and a .22 automatic. I wondered whether a birthday present for me must also have been stolen. We were good friends, after all, and so of course he would have bought me something. But whatever it might have been, it was not there, and it pained me that I would never know.

When we returned to Danville that night, we held a wake with a small group of friends. We sat on the floor, on the gold shag carpet, and because we could not talk, we drank. I downed a lot of vodka to block out the images of death, the odor of fear. Soon I vomited, and when my mind became clearer, I heard Pete's voice. By that I mean that it sounded as if he were speaking out loud. It was no doubt grief preying on my imagination, drunken thinking taking voice. Yet I could not help relaying aloud what I had just heard: "The names of the guys who killed him are Ronald and John." My friends stared at me. "Pete just told me," I said. Cracked, their looks implied. She's really cracked.

Four days later, two men were apprehended in a robbery in Oakland. In the backseat of their car were items that had been taken from Pete's apartment, including the calculator that he had purchased on my credit card. The serial number on the receipt matched the one on the calculator. The police told us the names of the men in their custody: Ronald and John.

Lou and I were stunned to hear the names I had blurted the night before. The police guessed that the two had targeted Pete after watching him move into the apartment; robberies often occur around the time of such transitions, they said, as criminals size up victim and possessions. Other than that, the choice of Pete as victim was random, a bit of bad luck. Both men had long arrest records, for robbery, and assault and battery, and they had a nasty penchant for tying up people and beating them. The fingerprints taken at Pete's apartment, however, matched only one of the men arrested. Because of what I had heard or imagined Pete saying, I was certain both men had been in the room. The police were too, but for another, more earthbound reason: A neighbor had heard two men's voices in the hall just before they fired through his door. In the end, only one of the men, John, was charged with Pete's murder.

The police said that I would be called as a witness, because I was the owner of the credit card. They cautioned me that I would have to take the witness stand during the preliminary hearing and the trial itself, and I would be required to look at the morgue photos and once again identify the body. I was sickened even to think of the prospect.

The night before the preliminary hearing, I had a fantastical dream, the first of a series that would occur nightly until Pete's murderer was convicted several months later. The dreams may have been delusional, the result of emotional trauma at having seen the gruesome evidence of a friend's death. Yet even if that is the case, it does not diminish the importance of those dreams to me or what I learned and did as a consequence. While I have always been a prolific dreamer, one who remembers up to a dozen dreams a night, I have never had dreams quite like these before or since. For one thing, these dreams followed a singular convention: I was always aware that Pete was dead and that I was alive, and that where we were meeting was the consciousness called dreams. In addition, each dream consisted of lessons in the form of metaphors that were obvious in their meanings.

In the first dream, I arrived at the place where Pete was now staying. It was—as dreams go—a surreal land with glorious green mountains, flowering meadows, and canyons flowing with waterfalls. Elephants, mastodons, and people flew about, as though a circus had been cast into a gravity-free environment. Only Pete and I were on solid ground.

"Hey," he said, "let's go flying."

"I'm not dead," I reminded him. "I can't fly."

"Oh, right. Well, see over there, that lady at the stand? She can rent you some wings."

He took off, and I turned toward the stand he had mentioned and duly procured a set of plastic wings for the bargain price of a quarter. I slipped them on, walked to the edge of a cliff, and took off soaring, but uncertain as to what I should do next. With the wings I was weightless and could move toward whatever I wished to see. All at once, I had a disturbing thought: How can a pair of cheap wings enable me to fly?

The next instant I was plummeting, the weight of my body pushing down, the wind pressing up, and I knew that soon I would be smashed to pieces. How could this be? Hadn't I been flying a moment ago? In the next instant, I was aloft once more, weightless. Relieved but still puzzled, I wondered again how I could be flying with wings that cost only a quarter—and abruptly, I was falling again. But I was flying a second ago, I said to myself. And immediately, I was aloft. . . . At the instant I realized the meaning of the dream, Pete spoke: "And now you see, it's your belief in yourself that enables you to do what you wish." With that, the dream ended.

The next night, a monster was set on me and I began to run. This was the boogieman I had known since childhood. I ran up a long stairwell, I ran through the dark streets. All the while, Pete was urging me to stop and turn around and look at what was chasing me.

"I can't," I cried. "If he touches me, I'll die."

"Turn around," Pete said firmly.

Finally I did. Before me was a monster, as I had expected, and yes, he was hideous in every respect: a huge, scaly creature with a venomous look. But he was also surprised that I stood there examining him. After a few seconds he started to shrink, and then he disappeared.

"You see," Pete said, "it's your own fears that give them the power to chase you."

And so the dreams went each night, a visceral truth played

out to heights of drama. I learned to make money come pouring out of pay phones that had been broken and never connected me to those I was trying to reach. I learned to fly down stairs in huge leaps, rather than being paralyzed with leaden legs and attempting only one small step at a time. I discovered that if I did not like what was before me, I had only to look at my shoes, then look up and walk ahead toward a fresher, more pleasant scene. During this time, my life changed—or rather, I changed my life, in ways I would previously have thought inconceivable. For one thing, I decided to quit my doctoral program.

This drastic decision was clearly born when the idealism of my twenties collided with the shock of tragedy. A valuable life had been lost, and to make up for it, I had to find value in mine. That was the gist of the feeling. The doctorate, I decided, would be a worthless appendage. Besides, there were no jobs in linguistics, and even if there were, how was I bettering the world by teaching others to examine the intricacies of dead languages and the like?

To leave academia was a terrifying idea, however. It meant abandoning the dream my parents had nurtured in me since the age of six, that I would become a doctor of some sort. Within that doctorate were all the embellishments of my ego, my sense of worth, my place in the world, and hence all my worries as well, the fear that I would never be good enough, that I would forever be struggling to hide that I was a fraud, doomed one day to fail and reveal how inadequate I truly was. But if I left the doctoral program, what could I do instead? What could I do that was worth anything to anyone, including myself? I could see nothing.

I remembered that Pete had once suggested that I apply my linguistics knowledge toward working with disabled children.

He had said this a month or so before he died. He himself had intended to make computerized equipment for people with disabilities. At the time, his suggestion held no appeal for me. I was not particularly fond of children, except as objects of research, and I knew nothing about disabilities.

But once I quit my doctoral program, I found a job listing for exactly what he had in mind: a language development specialist for a county program serving children, newborns to five years old, who had developmental disabilities. At the interview, it was as apparent to the administrator as it was to me that I was both overqualified and specifically unqualified for this job. When the interview ended and I stood to leave, I heard Pete telling me that I should simply tell this woman my motivations in applying for a job with exactly these challenges and unknowns. And out came my story of Pete's death and my pledge to do with my life what he had intended to do with his. Ten minutes later, I was hired.

It was my job to observe the children, informally assess their communication skills, and then work with parents and teachers to devise a plan and help them carry it out.

I remember the first talk on language development I gave for the parents. I mustered all my knowledge, prepared a detailed examination of the steps and processes entailed in language acquisition, and delivered an impressive one-hour lecture to a dozen parents, many of whom had just been told their babies had Down's syndrome, cerebral palsy, autism, or some rare congenital disorder that would lead to an early death. At the end of my talk, a mother came up to me and said, "You are *so* smart." I never felt more stupid. You just have to learn how to learn, I heard Pete say.

After that, I would listen to parents as they discussed their hopes for their children, and then together we would cry before we set out to find new hopes. With the kids themselves, I learned to play, to discover what made them laugh, what they could not resist watching or touching or reaching for. I found myself observing not deficits but the qualities of souls. Over the next five years, I had opportunities to work with more than a thousand families, and from them I sensed the limitlessness of hope within the limits of human beings. I learned to have compassion. It was the best training I could have had for becoming a writer.

Of course, not everything about me had changed for the better. I still worried incessantly about every detail of my life, twisting the permutations of these anxieties into knots. I remember one day, some six months after Pete died, when I was fretting over money, or rather, our profound lack of it. I was driving across the Bay Bridge in our rickety VW bus, coming home from my job, which netted me barely enough for rent, utilities, and food. Lou was in law school, and what little he earned went toward his tuition and books. But now we had a crisis: Our recently adopted cat, Sagwa, had gone into her first throes of heat the night before, and in searching for her Romeo, she jumped out of our fourth-story apartment window. Luckily, she lived, but fixing the resulting broken leg was going to cost us $383. How would we pay for it? We couldn't save that amount in a year. Why the hell did we get the damn cat?

I heard Pete say: "Come on, it was an accident. You worry about things over which you have no control." By then, I had heard his counseling voice many times. In the weeks right after his death, I had believed he was speaking to me across the divide. But now, with the natural waning of grief and shock, I had returned to thinking it was merely my imagination conjuring what he might have said.

"Easy for you to say," I responded. "You're dead. I have real bills."

I heard him laughing. "These things happen by themselves. They'll take care of themselves."

I was about to banter back when I felt something slam the side of the bus, and send me swerving across a lane of traffic on the bridge. I fought to regain control, finally pulled over, and got out of the car with shaky legs. A man rushed up to me.

"Are you all right? I'm so sorry. I don't know what happened. Thank God you're not hurt."

We went around to the side of the VW that he had rammed. At first I could see no sign of damage, but when we bent down and looked at the panel that curved under the bus, we saw it: a long gash, barely noticeable in a vehicle riddled with dings and oxidized paint.

"Get some estimates," the man told me. "Send them to my insurance company and they'll pay."

"It's not worth it," I said. "Even though it's not my fault, this will be reported to my insurance company and my rates will go up."

"I see what you mean," he answered. "Well then, just get one estimate and send it directly to me. Here's my card. I'm the vice-president of this corporation. I'll send a check to you directly."

Fair enough. I drove to the first body shop off the ramp. Ten minutes later, I heard Pete laughing as I stared at the written total for the estimate: $383.

I will relate only one more dream. It was the last.

On Lou's birthday that year, the trial ended, with a conviction on two counts. First-degree robbery. First-degree murder. That night, I dreamt that I met Pete in a garage, a rather prosaic location for a farewell meeting. He told me this was the last dream, now that the trial was over. I protested, "These are *my* dreams. I get to decide when they end." Pete ignored what I said, and went on: "You're going to meet my friend Rose—"

"Rose!" I sneered. "Fat chance. She hates me." When I had called her months before to tell her Pete was dead, she had been curt almost to the point of rudeness. Then again, I had been the same with the messenger who delivered the news to me.

"Rose is going to become very important to you," Pete said. "She's a writer, and she'll be helpful to you when you become a writer."

"Who said I was going to be a writer?"

"That's all I wanted to say," Pete told me, and then, as if going down to the corner store, he left me there.

After that, I still had dreams about him, but they were different, nothing at all like the dream-lessons. The new dreams conveyed the full horror of his death, for in them he was not dead, as I had feared, but alive, as I had hoped. Having survived near-strangling, he was brain-damaged, confused and suspicious, preferring to live as a beer-drinking recluse, unsure of who he was and uninterested in finding out.

Each year for seven years, on the anniversary of Pete's death, I lost my voice. It must have been a psychogenic gesture for the horror I could not talk about. And yes, eventually, Rose and I did connect with each other, tentatively at first, through brief letters, and then in lengthy missives, both of us grasping to understand the transcendental experiences we have had since his death.

If you've followed this story so far, you have already understood that Rose is indeed a writer, and that she was the first person to encourage me to write fiction, suggesting what I might read for inspiration and to which little magazines I might send my first attempts.

Enough time has passed that I can now more reasonably assess that period after Pete died. I have considered that those dreams were the subconscious by-product of trauma and grief, or the delusional thinking that enables a person to cope with horror. The metaphors were ones I have had all along, and through the need to survive, I brought out their meanings. Whatever they sprang from, the dreams were a lot more cost-effective than psychoanalysis. As to the counseling voice of Pete, guiding me toward the job with children, that was my own, pushed by fear of failure to the point that I made myself finally hear it. The coincidence of the $383? Well, that's odd, and hard to explain, except to say that when you are looking for coincidences, you will surely notice them. There are rational answers for everything. Sometimes I think about what they might be.

And yet no matter what these dreams and coincidences were, everything that happened during those months from my birthday to Lou's had a wondrous effect on me, on the shape of my life. It pushed me, enlarged my outlook, and sent me searching for what I should believe in. Does it matter what the origins were?

Today I am neither a believer nor a skeptic. I am a puzzler. I still puzzle over what Pete's story presents: what I fear, what I dream, what I believe. I ask myself: What's real? What's important? What do I gain in believing one reality over another? What do I lose? And if we understand the mysteries of the universe, if they end up being explained entirely by mathematics, as Pete said they could be, will they still bless us with the same amazing joy?

· faith ·

These are remarks I gave at the memorial of my editor, the late, great Faith Sale, who died on December 7, 1999.

The first time I talked to Faith on the phone, I was a publishing neophyte. I didn't know what serial rights were. I thought Faith's remark about "interest from the clubs" meant that places like Club Med might stock *The Joy Luck Club* in their beachfront stores. The year was 1988, and after talking about the book I was finishing and other literary concerns, I told Faith I was interested in attending a national book convention with a friend who had invited me. Faith immediately cut me off: "Oh, no! You shouldn't get caught up in all those publishing parties. They'll ruin you as a writer." Parties? I didn't know that book conventions held parties. Frankly, I was interested in going because my friend said I could score a lot of free books.

It wasn't until after I got to know Faith well that I realized how ironic it was that *she* warned me away from parties. Faith was, after all, the ultimate publishing party girl. And those who knew her well also know that I can say this without detracting whatsoever from her reputation as a serious and hardworking literary editor. In later years, whenever I went to the American

Booksellers Association convention with Faith, it took us two hours to go from one hall to the next. She knew everybody, had to talk to everybody, and I felt like the recalcitrant kid impatient to make her way to the amusement rides. She was late to almost everything as a result, late even to her own passing from a disease that commonly took people much earlier. And thank God for that. Thank God for her stubbornness, for her need to control every last detail before she could let go.

If Faith had stayed with us longer, I think she would have been seduced one way or the other by the Internet, as had been my plot. I know she touched her fingers to the keyboard at least a few times, once to send me an e-mail, other times to play solitaire and Freecell. And had she dabbled further, I think she would have discovered eBay, the great cyber bargain basement. We shared that—the art of the cheap deal. We used to go around the corner from her apartment on West Eleventh Street to an outlet called SubPrice, where we could buy stretch-velvet tops and leggings for five bucks.

That love of a bargain was still very much in evidence the day before her final operation. I was telling her that I, a New York carpetbagger, was going to hold a fund-raiser in my SoHo loft for a certain political candidate, about whom Faith held, shall we say, ambivalent feelings. The fund-raiser would probably take place in March, some four months away. "Do you want to come?" I asked, and I tried to sound casual. In hearing her answer, I figured I could gauge how she felt about the upcoming surgery and her chances of surviving it. Faith immediately said, "Of course. But I'm not going to *pay*."

In Faith, I had not only an editor and a cohort in bargain

shopping but a mentor and a friend, someone who knew my best intentions and intuitions as a writer and how these fit in with the rest of my life. She knew all the details of what I did, whom I saw, what happened on my vacation, what my mother said, what she didn't say. Faith also called me during the last hour that my mother was alive.

Faith Sale and my mother on a shopping spree in New York, 1992.

Whenever I gave Faith something to read, she'd ask me what I wanted from her as an editor. "Keep me from embarrassing myself in public," was my usual answer. And she did keep me from exposing the glitches in my prose, but she also prodded me to go deeper, to be more generous in the story I had to tell, to not hold back, to show what was most important in my life and on the page. She had an unerring sense of what mattered—to me. She could help me find it, though there were many ways in which we differed in taste and opinions. Olives, for example. She could not abide any dish littered with canned olives, a favorite of mine. And music—who would want to assault his or her ears with anything less than classical music or Broadway musicals or the rocker Michael Parrish, her son-in-law? Then there was the matter of ghosts. I was raised with them. She was not. But here Faith was diplomatic. She indulged me. She listened with genuine interest when I told her about unseen visitors whistling in my kitchen, about the TV's turning on by itself, about my version of ghostwriters, who, by the way, also provide research and editing on request. She was not going to argue scientific logic with me, since, delusion or not, ancestral spirits and reincarnation increased my material multifold. And for my part, I liked to remind Faith now and then that she, oh esteemed one, had after all served as editor for George Anderson, the world-famous talk-show host to the dead. And more than once I recalled for her benefit the time my mother had written her a note thanking her for "the book" and for helping her feel closer to "the other side." Faith was quite touched; she thought that my mother was referring to *The Joy Luck Club* and that her own help in publishing it had brought my mother fond memories of her family. I had to break the news to Faith that my mother was talking about George Anderson's book *We Don't Die*. I'm not done tormenting Faith about this. I plan to have regular séances with her in which we discuss how and why she was wrong in her opinion about an afterlife.

She was also wrong in one thing about me as a writer. She believed for some reason that writing came easily to me, that words poured onto the page with the ease of turning on a faucet, and that her role was mostly to help me adjust the outpouring toward the right balance. That belief had so much to do with her confidence in me. And I guess that is the role of both an editor and a friend—to have that confidence in another person, that the person's best is natural and always possible, forthcoming after an occasional kick in the butt.

I remember the proudest moment I had as her friend. We were at a medical clinic, and Faith was having her blood drawn. The nurse looked at Faith, then scrutinized me and said without any hint of the absurd, "You two are sisters, aren't you?"

And Faith looked at me without any hint of the absurd and said: "Yes. Yes we are."

CHANGING THE PAST

If you can't change your fate, change your attitude.

· The Kitchen God's Wife

To the missionaries, we were Girls of New Destiny. Each classroom had a big red banner embroidered with gold characters that proclaimed this. And every afternoon, during exercise, we sang our destiny in a song that Miss Towler had written, in both English and Chinese:

We can study, we can learn,
We can marry whom we choose.
We can work, we can earn,
And bad fate is all we lose.

· The Bonesetter's Daughter

· *last week* ·

In the last week of my mother's life, we were all there—my three half sisters and their husbands; my younger brother, John, and his fiancée; my husband, Lou, and I—gathered around the easy chair in which she lay floating between this world and the next. She looked like a waif in an oarless boat, and we were her anchors, keeping her from leaving us too soon for the new world.

"Nyah-nyah," she moaned in Shanghainese, and waved to an apparition on the ceiling. Then she motioned to me to invite her guests in and bring them refreshments. After I indulged my mother these wishes, I began to write her Chinese obituary, with the help of my half sisters, daughters from my mother's first marriage. It was a task that kept our minds focused, unified us, made us feel helpful instead of helpless.

"Daisy Tan," I started to write, "born Li Ching."

"*Not* Li Ching," someone interrupted. "It was Li Bingzi." That was Yuhang speaking, my sister from Shanghai. "Li Bingzi was the name our grandmother gave her when she was born."

How stupid of me not to know that. I had always thought

Bingzi was just a nickname my mother's brother called her. Yuhang watched me write her important contribution to the obituary. She is sixteen years older than I, a short, ever-smiling, chubby-faced version of my mother. She speaks no English, but has read my books in translation.

"Born Li Bingzi," I duly put down in English letters, "daughter of Li Jingmei . . ." And then Jindo, my second-eldest sister, chided in Chinese: "No, no, Grandma's last name was not Li. Li was the father's side. The mother's side was Gu. Gu Jingmei." Jindo, who most resembles our mother, proudly watched me write her addition.

By now, I sensed the ghost of my grandmother in the room. "*Ai-ya!*" she was lamenting. "What a stupid girl. This is what happens when you let them become Americans." I imagined other wispy-edged relatives, frowning and shaking their heads.

My third-eldest sister, Lijun, picked up the baton and added to the list of corrections: "After our grandmother die," she said in passable English, "our mother receive the name Du Lian Zen, to show she is adopt by Du family." Lijun was the one I relied on for rough translations, her English being on a par with my Chinese, the combination of which sometimes provided hilarious if not miserable renditions of what was actually meant. Her husband, Yan Zheng, wrote "Du Lian Zen" in Chinese characters, with the English next to that in the precise block script typical of architects.

"For Ma's school name," Yuhang continued in Chinese, "she chose Du Ching, the same name she kept after she married Wang Zo." I have long noted that my sisters never call this man "our father." They knew all too well that our mother despised "that bad man," as she called him, and they should act as if the paternal connection were accidental at best.

"Do you know why my father renamed her Daisy?" I asked my sisters. They were eager to hear. "Well, there was a funny song about a woman named Daisy and a bicycle built for two. In it, the man asks the woman, Daisy, to marry him."

My grandmother Gu Jingmei (left) and an unidentified relative, Shanghai, circa 1905.

"So our mother liked to ride a bicycle?" Yuhang asked.

I thought about this. "No," I answered.

"Did your father give her a bicycle when he asked to marry her?"

I laughed and shook my head. My sisters looked puzzled and confirmed among themselves that American names have no meanings.

I realized I had never told my sisters about the name Daisy Tan Chan—Chan being the name our mother took when she married for the third time, in her seventies; a year later she had the marriage annulled and reverted to Daisy C. Tan. But why bring that up now? As to her fourth "marriage," to T. C. Lee, the dapper eighty-five-year-old gentleman whom our family in Beijing feted when he and our mother "honeymooned" in China, well, the truth was, she and T.C. never really married.

"What!" cried my sisters.

"It's true," I told them, to explain why I was not mentioning him in the obituary. "They were living together and she was too embarrassed to say they were lovers, so she made me lie and tell Uncle they were married." My sisters guffawed.

My mother's many names were vestiges of her many selves, lives I have been excavating most of my own adult life. At times I have dreaded that I might stumble across evidence of additional husbands and lovers, more secrets, more ghosts, more siblings. I had once thought I was the only daughter, the middle child, a position I took to have great psychological significance. I then discovered I was really the youngest of five girls, one of whom had died at birth. Our mother had three sons as well, one who died at age two or three, and another, my brother Peter, who died at age sixteen. With all taken into account, I was demoted to Number Seven of eight children.

There was also a great deal of confusion about my mother's age. She had one birth date based on the Chinese lunar calendar.

By that method, she was considered one year old the day she was born. My mother had further explained to me that when my father transferred her Chinese age to a Western one, he made her *too* young—writing on her visa that she was born on May 8, 1917, instead of May 9, 1916. The age followed her into her naturalization papers, onto her Social Security card, all her official records. This was not a problem until she was about to turn sixty-four. That was when she told me she was really almost sixty-five. She insisted she knew for sure that she was older than her American age, because she was born in a Dragon Year, 1916, just as I was born in a Dragon Year thirty-six years later. There was absolutely no way she could confuse whether she was a Dragon, none whatsoever. My mother fretted over this mistake day after day, until my husband untangled bureaucratic knots and set the record straight just in time for her to retire and start collecting Social Security when she truly turned sixty-five.

But even that was not the end to her ever-changing age. My sister Jindo said that the international Chinese-language newspaper wanted to report her as being eighty-six instead of eighty-three, to account for the "bonus years" she had earned for living a long life. All the confusion about her age, her three or four marriages, her many names, and the order in which her children, living and dead, should be listed led us to nix the idea of a Chinese obituary. It simply wouldn't look proper if we told the truth.

In trying to write an obituary, I appreciated that there was still much I did not know about my mother. Though I had written books informed by her life, she remained a source of revelation and surprise. Of course I longed to know more about her, for her past had shaped me: her sense of danger, her regrets, the mistakes she vowed never to repeat. What I know about myself is related to what I know about her, including her secrets, or in some cases fragments of them. I found the pieces both by deliberate effort and by accident, and with each discovery I had to reconfigure the growing whole.

She had always been tiny. When she came to the United States from China in 1949, my mother recorded that she was five feet tall, stretching the truth by at least two inches. On the day she married my father, she weighed seventy-nine pounds. When she was nine months pregnant with me, she weighed barely one hundred—even more remarkable if you consider that I came into this world at nine pounds, eleven ounces.

By age ten, I was her equal in height, and I continued to grow until I reached an impressive five feet, three and three-quarter inches. Compared with my mother, I was a giantess, and this forever skewed my perception of myself. Although my brother John and I quickly grew bigger than our mother, she had never seemed fragile to us, that is, not until she began to lose her mind.

When failure to thrive set in and she began to lose weight rapidly as well, I offered her bribes: a thousand dollars for each pound she could gain back. My mother held out her palm in gleeful anticipation. Later, I raised the stakes to ten thousand. She never collected on a single pound.

In the last week of her life, she dwindled to fifty pounds, and although I had a chronic joint problem in my shoulders, my own pain disappeared whenever I needed to lift her from bed to chair or chair to bed. It seemed to me she was fast becoming weightless and would soon disappear.

Four years before all this, in 1995, my mother had been diagnosed with Alzheimer's disease. She was several months shy of her eightieth birthday. The plaques on her brain had likely started to accumulate years before. But we never would have recognized the signs. "Language difficulties," "gets into arguments," "poor judgment"—those were traits my mother had shown her entire life. How could we distinguish between a chronically difficult personality and a dementing one?

Still, I began to look back on those times when I might have seen the clues. In 1991, when we were in Beijing, she had declined to go into one of the many temples of the Summer Palace. "Why I go see?" she said, and retreated to a cool stone bench in the shade. "Soon I just forget I been there anyway."

My husband and I laughed. Wasn't that the truth? Who among us could remember the blur of tourist sites we had been to in our increasing span of years?

I recalled another time, a couple of years later, when we had gathered at the home of family friends to watch a televised interview of my mother, which had been taped earlier that day. The subject was the opening of the movie *The Joy Luck Club.* The interviewer wondered whether watching the film had been difficult for her, given how much of it was true to her life: "Did you cry like everyone else in the audience?"

My mother watched her televised self as she answered in that truthful, bare-all manner of hers: "Oh, no. My real life worser than this, so movie already much, much better." Those were my mother's words, but they were rendered into better English through subtitles. She was perplexed to see this. The son of our family friends called out to her, "Hey, Auntie Daisy, why are they translating what you're saying? Don't they know you're speaking English?" He had the misfortune of saying this with a laughing face. My mother became livid. Forever after, she would speak about this young man, whom she had always treated like a dear nephew, with only the bitterest of criticisms about his character.

I wondered: Was her grudge toward him a sign that she was already ill? Yet my mother had always borne grudges. She never forgot a wrong, even an accidental one, but especially not an arrogant one. When her brother and sister-in-law who were visiting from Beijing told her they needed to return to China sooner than expected because of an important government meeting, my mother tried to persuade them to stay longer in California. What was more important, she cajoled, the Communist Party or family? Her sister-in-law, who had enlisted with the party in the 1930s as a young revolutionary, gave the politically correct answer. My mother was shocked to hear it. She took this to mean that her sister-in-law considered her to be worth less than a speck of dirt under the toe of her proletariat shoes. Later that day, my mother recounted to me what her sister-in-law had said. She added to that a number of slights that her sister-in-law had apparently delivered in the past week, and complaints about how, the last time she had visited them in Beijing, her sister-in-law had cut off the sleeves of an expensive shirt my mother had given to her brother, so it would be cooler. On and on my mother went, until her stream of injustices eventually did the long march through the fifty-five years of a formerly harmonious relationship.

If we, her children, did anything to suggest we were not one hundred percent in her camp, if we tired of listening and suggested with weariness—or rather, genuine concern—that she try to "calm down for your own sake," she would become even more furious. "Not my sake," she'd retort, "*your* sake." Her face stiffened, her jaw quavered as she shouted and punched herself. Who cared what happened to her? Nobody! Her life was nothing. She was worthless.

Anger inevitably blended with anguish, and the helpless and lonely sorrow she had felt years earlier, during the illness and death of my brother Peter, and my father's death seven months after that, both of them succumbing to brain tumors. My mother had both of them put on life support, and because of that, she told me years later, she had to do the worst thing in her entire life, and that was to take them off life support. "Don't start," she advised, "then don't have to stop. No use anyway."

This double tragedy of brain tumors was so horrific that the neurosurgeon himself, in trying to soothe my mother as she poured out endless questions of why and how can this be, simply said: "Mrs. Tan, it's just bad luck, I'm afraid."

That official pronouncement of bad luck then set my mother into a protracted search for the reason we were cursed. Were the rest of us doomed to die as well because of this bad luck? She believed so. Thereafter my brother and I learned to hide our headaches from her, to curb ourselves from saying we were "tired," which was, of course, an excuse that all teenagers mindlessly blurt to get out of doing whatever they don't want to do. Tiredness had been Peter's earliest symptom that something was wrong. We had learned the consequences of saying we did not feel well: being hauled off to the hospital to undergo an EEG, an

X ray, and later, once we returned home, being subjected to our mother's endless and unanswerable questions. We saw her as our tormentor and not our protector against curses. Late at night, months after my father had died, she would moan, "Why? Why this happen?"

After my mother was diagnosed with Alzheimer's, I too was obsessed in knowing why. When did the disease begin? When had her logic become even more impaired than usual? It was important to know exactly when, for in that answer I would also know how much of her behavior, her tirades that had pained and inconvenienced us, her family, could now be viewed as illness and thus with a more sympathetic eye.

I recalled a Thanksgiving at her house when we had arrived late. It was my fault. I have always had a propensity for running at least forty-seven minutes behind schedule for anything and everything. "Why so late?" my mother said when I stepped inside. She took my tardiness as a personal insult, a sign of disrespect, tantamount to saying I did not think she was worth the time of day. She was sitting in her dining room, refusing to speak. This was the deadly silence we had known all our lives. The dark clouds were practically visible above her steaming head. Static was in the air we breathed. We told her to calm down—big mistake—and her silence exploded into threats to kill herself. There would be no Thanksgiving that year.

My little brother and I had heard similar threats all our lives. As a very young child, I also must have seen her try to cut her wrists with a knife. I assume this because I tried to do the same when I had a private moment of rage after being sent to bed. I was six at the time. Fortunately, I used a butter knife and was chagrined to learn that running a blade across one's skin actually hurt.

My mother's usual method of near-demise involved traffic. Her last attempt was typical. We were eating dinner in a restaurant, and she was obsessing about a family member whom she believed did not respect her. Lou, my brother, and I didn't exactly disagree with her; the trouble was, we didn't wholeheartedly *agree*. Her anger mounted until she leapt up from the table and ran out of the crowded restaurant with us chasing after her. Just before she dashed into a busy six-lane street, screaming that she wanted to die, Lou grabbed her, threw her over his shoulder, and carried her, kicking and sobbing, back to safety.

My mother's threats to "do it" rained so often that I developed an emotional shield. As a teenager, I pretended to be unaffected. She could rant and beat her chest. She could shower her fists on me. My face would remain maddeningly bland, as inscrutable as Westerners have always accused Chinese people of being. When she was not looking, I would walk briskly to the bathroom and have dry heaves. At times, I privately wished she would carry out her word. How peaceful life would be without her. This thought was immediately followed by fear that my secret wish would come true, and then I would be as guilty of murder as if I had killed her myself.

As my brother and I grew older, we supposedly grew wiser. Yet it did not matter that we were twenty, thirty, or forty. Whenever our mother beat her chest with her tiny fists, we knew what was coming, and were reduced to small children who trembled with fear that this time she might make good on her word.

As adults, we commiserated in anger and frustration over the fact that our mother could still make us feel manipulated, guilty, and fearful. Later we confided that we had grown to have her same furies. Sometimes, I have sensed the inescapable rush of a geyserlike rage, which soon would drench all reason from my mind and leave me with a self-destructive urge.

It wasn't until I was in my thirties that I learned that my mother, at age nine, had seen her own mother kill herself. I felt sorry for that nine-year-old child. I could now see that in many respects my mother had remained stuck at that age of her abandonment.

I recently learned that in China today, a third of all deaths among women in rural areas are suicides. Nationwide, more than two million Chinese women each year attempt suicide, and 300,000 succeed. And in contrast to any other country, more women than men in China kill themselves. I pondered this. Conditions for women in China have changed for the better in the last hundred years, and life in the countryside may not be egalitarian, but is it really so bad that women are willing to down a bottle of rat poison? And why is ingestion still the preferred method?

More than two million *reported* attempts. How many attempts are not reported? China as a society is loath to make shameful events public, so the real number is probably staggeringly higher. I found this all strangely comforting, as if in this context our family was practically *normal*. In Western terms, we were a dysfunctional family. From a Chinese perspective, however, my mother's urge to kill herself was understandable. It was part of a larger legacy passed from generation to generation, grandmother to mother to daughter. In lieu of the family silver, what was inherited was a suffering silence followed by sudden implosion, an urge to blot out all memory of existence.

My mother had always bragged about her memory. She never forgot anything. It wasn't that she remembered just dates or facts and figures. When she remembered an event from her past, especially a traumatic one, it was as though she had boarded a time machine and had been transported to the moment she was remembering. She was experiencing it again as she spoke of it.

Psychiatrists might call that a posttraumatic flashback, but to me, her memories were gifts. In 1990, before she became ill, I set up a videocamera and had her tell her story. I was concerned she might be self-conscious. And at first, she did speak carefully, looking shyly at the camera. But soon enough, she had gone back to her past and was re-creating it for me, as someone might who is under hypnosis. She was recalling her own mother's sadness after her husband died of illness, leaving her to care for two small children without any means of support. My grandmother's young son would take clothes to a pawnshop so the family could have a little money. "Can you imagine?" my mother would say to me, as she told her story. She would repeat this question often, making me work harder to imagine it.

Later, she enacted a day when her first husband returned home roaring with anger so he could make a big show in front of his friends. It happens afresh in her memory's eye: He pulls out a pistol and makes her kowtow to him. "What are you looking at?"

he bellows to the friends, who stand by the door, their mouths dropped open. They kowtow too. She is looking up at him, at the wild waving of the gun, getting ready to duck in case he shoots. But then "that bad man" begins to laugh. It's a joke, he made us do this as a joke.

In another memory, she is holding a baby in her arms, her first son. He has just died of dysentery, because her husband refused to interrupt his mah jong game with the doctor. I said to her as gently as I could, "What did you feel when the baby died? You must have been in so much pain."

She looked up blankly. "No pain, only numb. I said, 'Good for you, little one, you escaped. Good for you.'"

One time, several hours into one of her stories, she stopped talking and looked at me as if she had just woken from a dream. "Maybe you don't want this part on TV," she said. I was amazed to realize she was cognizant of the camera. "This part concerning sex . . ." The camera kept rolling, and she lowered her head to say conspiratorially, "He want sex, I go to bathroom, pretend use my chamber pot. Oooh, oooh, so sick, bad diarrhea. That night, no sex. So many nights, I pretend I go to my chamber pot." She was laughing when she told me this. The camera caught it all.

The more I heard, the more I wanted to know. I could not believe I had once taken no interest in these stories she tried to tell me for years. Now I wanted to go back to the past. I wanted to be there with her, to be her witness, to agree with her, "Your life was terrible." It was not too late to comfort her.

In 1991, I presented her with my second book, *The Kitchen God's Wife,* a story based on her life, one she had asked that I write. She began to read the first page, then said with consternation, "Helen? I never knew Helen in China." I reminded her that this was not *that* Helen, this was fiction and the characters were made up. "Ah, yes, yes," she said, then resumed reading, before soon stopping again. "I never live in pink house in San Francisco."

Months later, I asked whether she had finished reading the book. "No time," she said. Even later, her excuse was this: "Why I need finish? That's my story. I already know the ending."

I saw more things that she could not finish: Half-knit sweaters. Bills she opened but had not paid. Food she had defrosted but had not cooked. Her apartment was becoming untidy, not just cluttered in the way it had always been, but dirty. She forgot to lock her door and the security elevator. She forgot how to go in reverse and dented her car backing out of her garage. She later bashed it again, running into the back of a truck. And even stranger, she didn't seem very concerned that her car was full of dings.

I also noticed that my once fastidious mother was looking disheveled. She wore the same clothes every day, a purple sweater, a pair of black stretch pants. She was not bathing. Her hair was dirty and it smelled. One day when I suggested she wash her hair before we went to a dressy event, she commented that the shower knobs were broken.

I went to the bathroom to check. They were fine. It occurred to me that she did not know how to adjust them. As someone who goes on book tours and stays in a different hotel every night, I know how disconcerting it is to figure out how the water works without getting either scalded or doused with cold water. I turned on the water, adjusted the temperature, and ran a bath for my mother. Then I noticed that she was missing soap, shampoo, toothpaste. Why had she not bothered to buy these things? I made a mental note to do some shopping for her.

Sometime later, our family was gathered around the dining table for a Thanksgiving different from the disastrous one of a few years before. We were with my husband's family. The conversation touched on sports, the weather, politics, and then eventually on O. J. Simpson's acquittal. My mother had a comment to make there. "Oh, that man kill his wife," she said with great authority. "I there. I see it."

"You mean you saw it on television," I corrected.

"No!" my mother insisted. "I there. He hide in bush, jump out, cut the knife on that girl's throat. So much blood, you cannot believe so much. Awful."

My mother's English often left seeming gaps in logic. I frequently served as her interpreter, even in childhood, when I wrote my own letters to the principal, excusing my absence from school. I now attempted to clarify for the others what she meant: "Oh, you saw a documentary on what the lawyers *said* happened."

"Maybe you see documentary," my mother replied. "I see everything. I there."

"What do you mean?" I said. Lou put his hand on my arm. Those around us had grown quiet, sipping wine or chewing turkey in embarrassment. But I couldn't stop. I had to know what was going on. Did my mother think she had astrally projected herself?

She was oblivious of everyone's discomfort. "I hide in bush too."

"You saw him get in his car and go home?"

My mother nodded. "I follow."

"How? How did you get to Los Angeles?"

I couldn't shake her illogic. "I don't remember. Must be I drive."

"And you were in his bedroom when he cleaned up?"

She nodded confidently.

"You watched him get *undressed*?" I challenged, desperate to make her realize how crazy her line of thinking was.

"Oh, no!" she answered quickly. "I turn my eyes away."

That was the moment I could no longer deny to myself that something was terribly wrong. She was certainly at an age when Alzheimer's could be a possibility. On the way home, Lou and I agreed we needed to take her to the doctor.

To get her there would require subterfuge. I told her we were going for a checkup.

"I already checkup this year," she said.

"We need another one," I said, and then I took the plunge: "I think we should check out this problem with your memory."

"What problem?" my mother said.

"Well, sometimes you forget things. . . . It could be due to depression."

And my mother shot back: "Nothing wrong my memory. Depress 'cause can *not* forget." Then she started to recount the tragedies of losing her mother, my brother, my father. She was right. Nothing was wrong with her memory.

"Well, let's just go to the doctor to check your blood pressure. Last time it was high. You don't want to have a stroke, do you?"

A week later, we were in her internist's office. He asked her a few questions. "How old are you?"

"Oh, I already almost eighty-one."

The doctor glanced at my mother's chart. "She might mean her Chinese age," I said. The doctor waved away my explanation. What I wanted to tell him, of course, was the problem with her age, how it had always been a source of massive confusion and exasperation in our family. Her age was no easy answer. Even a person with all her wits about her would have had a hard time answering a question that sounded as simple as "How old are you?" But then I realized I was trying to protect my mother—or perhaps myself—from hearing the diagnosis.

The doctor posed another question: "How many children do you have?"

"Three," she said.

I puzzled over her answer. The doctor, of course, had no idea what the correct answer was, but neither did I, unless I knew what context my mother was using. Maybe the three referred to the children she had had with my father: two sons, one daughter, though one son had died in 1967.

"What about Lijun, Jindo, and Yuhang?" I gently prodded, reminding her of her daughters from her first marriage to the bad man. She had been separated from them from 1949 until 1978, so in some ways they had been lost to her as children. When they reappeared in her life, they were "old ladies" by her estimation, not children.

My mother recalculated her answer. "Five children," she decided.

And this was correct in one sense. There were five living children, three from her first marriage and two from her second. The doctor went on: "I want you to count backward from one hundred and keep subtracting seven."

My mother began. "Ninety-three."

"And seven from that?" the doctor asked.

My mother paused and thought hard. "Ninety-three."

I remember feeling bad that my mother, the one who scolded me for anything less than straight A's, was now failing miserably. While I knew she had a problem, I was not prepared to see how bad it truly was.

"Who's the president of the United States?" the doctor posed.

My mother snorted. That was easy. "Clinton."

"And who was the president before that?"

My mother crinkled her brow, before she answered, "Still Clinton." She was obviously referring to the previous year, not the previous president.

The doctor did a brief physical, testing my mother's reflexes, tapping her tiny knees, running his stethoscope over her doll-like body. The test was almost over, when the doctor made an innocuous remark, which I can no longer recall. Perhaps he apologized to my mother for putting her through so many questions, as if she were on trial. Whatever it was, my mother began to talk about O. J. Simpson's trial and how she knew he was guilty because she had been right there when he killed his wife. And in her mind, she again was right there, as she had been at the Thanksgiving table. She reenacted the scene: how she hid in the bushes, how she saw the blood "spurt all over the place."

The doctor gave me his diagnosis that day, although I did not really need to hear it to know it.

Some months later, I decided to throw a black-tie dinner in a nightclub for my mother's eightieth birthday. I invited family and all her friends. I hired a professional ballroom dancer because my mother adored dancing. In the invitation, I wrote a note about my mother's diagnosis. I explained what difficulties she might have, what changes might be noticed in the future. I said the best present anyone could give her was continued friendship.

I did not know the term for Alzheimer's disease in Chinese, nor did my sisters. They described it to my aunt and uncle in Beijing as "that malady in the head that affects old people," in other words, benign forgetfulness. I could tell by my sisters' attitude that they had no idea how serious this disease really was. To them, it was an illness of guilt, their guilt for having been inattentive, that had caused our mother to become inattentive to the world. My sisters blamed themselves for not visiting her more often. They prescribed favorite foods as a cure.

My auntie Su said her sister-in-law's mind had slowed because she didn't have enough people to speak to in Shanghainese, her native tongue. She promised she would take my mother out to lunch more often and talk to her.

My sister Jindo sent Wisconsin ginseng, the best kind, she said. "She will get better," she assured me. None of my sisters felt the numb shock I did in recognizing that our mother's brain was dying and thus she would disappear even before her death.

Yet as I discovered, her memory losses were not always a bad thing. For instance, she seemed to forget what had happened to my father and older brother. She no longer dwelled on their deaths as much. Instead, she began to talk about happier days, for instance the trips she and I had taken together. She counted them out on her hand: China, Japan, China again, New York, China again and again. She loved to tell people about the year we lived in Switzerland, when I was so bad and so was my boyfriend Franz. "So much headache you give me," she would claim proudly. It was astonishing how much she remembered, details about my misadventures that I had forgotten.

She recalled the night she drove my younger brother and me through the mountains in Spain: "You remember? We afraid to stop, because so many stories about bandits. So I drive, drive, drive all night, but too sleepy to keep my eyes open. I told you, 'Start fight about you boyfriend so I can argue, stay awake.'"

Oh yes, now I remember, I said. She could summon the past better than I. How could she have Alzheimer's? I fantasized that she did not have that dreaded disease at all. Her earlier confusion and delusions were due to a stroke or a tumor, perhaps vitamin deficiencies or severe depression. Soon, with medicine, she could be restored to her old feisty self, but as happy as she was now.

One day, she talked about the first time she met my father. What a joyful day that was. "You remember?" she said. "You with me."

"Tell me," I said. "Your memory is better than mine."

"We in elevator," she reminisced. "All a sudden, door open. You push me out and there you daddy on a dance floor, waiting. You smiling whole time, tell me go see, go dance. Then you get back in elevator, go up. Very tricky, you."

Instead of being saddened by her delusion, I was choked with happiness. She had placed me in her memory of one of the best days of her life.

In part, some of my mother's newfound ease may have been due to a pink pill, an antidepressant. Ostensibly the new medications she had to take were for her hypertension. That was the lie, the pill that was easier to swallow. Paxil was rolled into the lot, as was Aricept, various benzodiazepines, a changing assortment of antipsychotics, all of which in time lost their effectiveness or yielded peculiar side effects like the lip-smacking and foot-twirling of tardive dyskinesia. Her neurological tics were more exhausting for us to watch than for her unconsciously to do. I kept a journal of what she took and why, what her symptoms were and how she was changing as she lost bits and pieces and chunks. I often wrote that my mother seemed happier than she had ever been. I marveled over that. Was happiness in dementia true happiness?

Yet I was saddened to think that with proper medication, my mother could have been a different person. Clearly, she had suffered from major depressive disorder most of her life. She must have gotten that from her mother. She had bequeathed that to me.

At moments, I mused over what life would have been like had I been raised by a happy, depression-free mother. Imagine having a mother who was nurturing instead of worrying, a mother who would have filled my head with enthusiastic suggestions on what to wear to the dance rather than issue warnings that a single kiss from a boy would render me both pregnant and insane. Then again, if my mother and I had had a wonderfully happy relationship, I would have been wonderfully content in childhood. I would have grown up to be bubbly, well balanced, mentally stable, and pregnant many, many times from many, many kisses. Instead of becoming a fiction writer, I would have become a neurosurgeon and a concert pianist on the side, much to the surprise of my doting mother, the happy one who never would have foisted her expectations on me.

A new stage of my mother's illness began. More delusions took hold. Sometimes she became obsessed with conspiracies against her by my half sister; Lijun, she believed, was trying to steal the starring role from her in a documentary about her life. Another time she believed my husband was having an affair with a Chinese woman at Lake Tahoe. She had gone there and seen the whole sordid mess, she claimed.

This was particularly sad to me, since Lou had taken care of her as lovingly as any Chinese son. He had purchased her home, had seen to her financial needs, had served her first at every meal, and was always available to accompany her to the hospital or to search for solutions for her care. But now, at our twice-weekly dinners at her favorite restaurant, she glared at him the entire time. Day and night, she called me every twenty minutes to tell me I had to leave him. After two weeks, I figured out what I had to do to make her stop. I could not argue with delusions. I had to acquiesce to them.

When the phone rang next, I answered with a sad voice. I informed her that I had kicked Lou out of the house. (Lou, who was standing nearby, looked at me with a puzzled face.)

"So now you believe me," she said.

"You've always been right," I said. "Only you worry about me. Only you can protect me from everything bad."

Yes, my mother said.

"Everyone else, they don't care. But you do, because you are my mother. Only you are this good to me that you would worry this much. You know me better than I know myself. You know what can hurt me. You are the best mother."

"Now you believe," she whispered in a grateful voice. Then she said what every good mother would say. "Okay, go get something eat now."

"I can't," I answered. "There's nothing to eat in the house. Lou used to go to the store to get food. But now he's not here. And I can't go out at night by myself. Someone might rob me."

"But you hungry?"

"Well, only a little, but really, it's okay. I won't starve between now and morning. It's all right if I'm just hungry."

A good mother cannot bear to think her child's stomach is empty.

"You scared, all alone?" she asked.

"A little," I replied. "The house is so big now that I'm by myself. But I'll check the doors often to make sure no burglars can get in. Good thing I'll be moving to a smaller place."

"Moving? Why?"

"You know, with the divorce, Lou will get half of everything. We'll have to sell the house and cut up the money. And if I marry someone else and divorce that man, he'll get half of that half, so then I'll be left with one-quarter of what I have now. That's how it is when you divorce your husband."

My mother began to recall Lou's better qualities. He bought me groceries, he drove me around, he was strong. She advised me to forgive him. Of course, I should punish him for a short time, tonight, but then tomorrow I should take him back.

"What good advice," I told her. "Only you know how to save my marriage and my house so I won't be poor."

What had started as subterfuge on my part grew into an epiphany. I began to see how much I actually knew about my mother and myself. She was losing her mind, yes, but I was losing the defenses built up and fortified from childhood. The scars were dissolving and our hearts were becoming transparent. How could I have been so stupid not to know this all these years. It had been so simple to make my mother happy. All I had to do was say I appreciated her as my mother.

I now knew the answers to my mother's impossible questions. "When you coming home?" was a common one because I was often away on book tours. If I gave her an actual date, she would ask five minutes later, "When you coming home?"

"We're almost home," I would say over the phone, no matter how long Lou and I would be gone. "Because we've missed you so much. We love you so much we can't wait to come home and see you. You are the most important person to us in the whole world." And she would stop asking. That was all she needed to know.

I found similar ways to help her remember. I used to tell her not to eat her regular dinner at five-thirty p.m. on days we would be taking her out to a restaurant. But she would inevitably forget and, when we showed up, act surprised and annoyed. "Dinner? You don't tell me you take me to dinner." The next time we wanted to take her out, I called and said in an excited voice: "Guess what! Tonight there's a party at Fountain Court, your favorite. You know why? Because everyone who loves you will be there. You're going to be the star! We'll order all your favorite dishes—juicy prawns, and tender squid, and the fresh snow-pea greens with the little sweet sprouts you love so much. Wear your pink dress. You always look so pretty in that. You will be the prettiest girl in the entire restaurant."

And sure enough, when we arrived to pick her up, she had remembered not to eat her regular meal and she had on her pink dress. Is happiness in dementia true happiness? Yes, it is. I know for certain now.

In the last week of my mother's life, she began to talk to ghosts. "Nyah-nyah," she moaned in Shanghainese, and waved to someone she saw above her. Then she motioned to me, indicating that I should invite this ghost to come in. She spoke gibberish in a shaky voice, yet it was understandable what she meant. I could still translate: "Sit, sit. Tea. Quick, quick. Coat, coat, best coat." And I fetched the mink out of her closet and placed it where the ghost might have sat down.

My mother continued to chat excitedly to an invisible crowd of people. She grabbed my hand and pointed. "Yes, I see," I said. "So many people." At one point, I forgot about the pretense, and when a chilly fog wind blew through the open window, I took the mink coat that I had draped over the sofa and placed it over my mother's legs. She grunted and protested with spitting sounds, then pointed to the bare spot on the sofa. Oh, right—how could I forget! Nyah-nyah was there, wearing the mink coat. I put the coat back on the sofa, marveling over the contradictions of my mother's memory.

I finally thought to ask what Nyah-nyah meant.

"A Shanghainese nickname for 'Grandmother,'" my oldest

sister replied. And then I remembered a story my mother had once told me, of her being four years old, delirious and near death as she called to her grandmother to stop the pain. My mother had been horribly injured when a pot of boiling soup fell across her neck. Nyah-nyah had sat by her bedside, day and night, telling her that her funeral clothes had already been made but were very plain because she had not lived long enough to deserve anything more elaborate.

She told the little girl that everyone would soon forget her because she had lived too short a time for them to remember much. That was how Nyah-nyah, who loved my mother very much, scared her back to life. Now my mother was calling for Nyah-nyah once again. This time I think Nyah-nyah was telling my mother that her funeral clothes had already been made, and not to worry, they were fancy beyond belief.

Shortly afterward, my mother fell into a coma. Ten to twenty family members were in her rooms, at all hours. We played poker and mah jong. We ate pizza and Chinese takeout. We watched videos of her favorite movies, Rodgers and Hammerstein musicals, including one she called "Southern Pacific." I put on a CD of Chopin piano music and whispered in her ear: "That's me playing. I've been practicing harder."

For four days my mother's breathing kept us in suspense. She would take three breaths, then nothing would follow for forty-five seconds, sometimes longer. It was like watching the tidal wash in anticipation of a tidal wave. At night I lay next to her, sleepless, staring at the pulse bobbing in the cove of her throat, my own heart pounding to this steady yet uncertain rhythm. Later I put a pearl in the hollow so I could more easily see this proof of life. Though I dreaded that she would stop breathing, I was relieved that she would die of natural causes and not from suicide.

During the last hour of her life, as my mother's skin turned gray, our family murmured that we loved her very much and were sad to see her go. We whispered to her all the things we would miss: her dumplings, her advice, her humor. To myself I mourned: Who else would worry about me so much? Who else would describe in explosive detail what might happen to parts of my body if I was careless? Who would be frank enough to warn that my husband might exchange me for a younger woman unless I forced him to buy me jewels so expensive it would be impossible for him to leave both me and the gems behind?

My mother did not speak during those last four days, but with her final breath, a long release of an exhalation, she uttered a faint sound, a single sustained note. I had to bend my ear to her mouth to hear. I was the only one who heard it, but I don't think it was my imagination. It was as if our mother, this woman who had been so full of surprises until her final day, had just said, "Ah!" to signal that she had gone on to her next surprise.

After my mother died, I began to rewrite the novel I had been working on for the past five years. I wrote with the steadfastness of grief. My editor, Faith Sale, would have called that grief "finding the real heart of the story." My mentor, Molly Giles, said the bones were there, and to repair them I had to dig them out, break them into pieces, then put them back together.

And so I threw away some pages, rewrote others. I wrote

of wrong birth dates, of secret marriages, of names that were nearly forgotten. I wrote of pain that reaches from the past, how it can grab you, how it can also heal itself like a broken bone. With the help of my new ghostwriters by my side, I found in memory and imagination what I had lost in grief.

My mother (center), around age eight, Hangzhou, China, circa 1924.

· my grandmother's choice ·

In my writing room, on my desk, sits an old family photo in a plain black frame, depicting five women and a girl at a temple pavilion by a lake. When I first saw this photo as a child, I thought it was exotic and remote, of a faraway time and place, with people who had no connection to my American life. Look at their bound feet! Look at that funny lady with the plucked forehead!

The solemn little girl is, in fact, my mother. She looks to be around eight. And behind her, leaning against the rock, is my grandmother Jingmei. "She called me Baobei," my mother told me. "It means 'treasure.'"

The picture was taken in Hangzhou, in 1924 or so, my mother said, possibly spring or fall, to judge by the clothes. At first glance, it appears the women are on a pleasure outing.

But see the white bands on their skirts? The white shoes? They are in mourning for my mother's grandmother Divong, known as the "replacement wife." The women have come to this place, a Buddhist retreat, to perform yet another ceremony for her. Monks hired for the occasion have chanted the proper words. And the women and little girl have walked in circles clutching smoky sticks of incense. They have knelt and prayed, then burned a huge pile of spirit money so that Divong might ascend to a higher position in her new world.

This is also a picture of secrets and tragedies, the reasons that warnings have been passed along in our family like heirlooms. Each of these women suffered a terrible fate, my mother said. And they were not peasant women but big-city people, very modern. They went to dance halls and wore stylish clothes. They were supposed to be the lucky ones.

Look at the pretty woman with her finger on her cheek. She is my mother's second cousin Nunu Aiyi, "Precious Auntie." You cannot see this, but Nunu Aiyi's entire face was scarred from smallpox. Fortunately for her, a year or so after this picture was taken, she received marriage proposals from two families. She turned down a lawyer and married another man. Later she divorced her husband—a daring thing for a woman to do. But then, finding no means to support herself or her young daughter, Nunu Aiyi eventually accepted the lawyer's second proposal—this time, to become his number-two concubine. "Where else could she go?" my mother said. "Some people said she was lucky the lawyer still wanted her."

Now look at the small woman with the sour face. There's a reason that Uncle's Wife, Jyou Ma, has this expression. Her husband, my great-uncle, often complained aloud that his family had chosen an ugly woman for his wife. To show his displeasure, he insulted Jyou Ma's cooking. During one of their raucous dinner arguments, the table was shoved and a pot of boiling soup tipped and spilled all over his niece's neck, causing a burn that nearly killed her. My mother was the little niece, and for the rest of her life she bore that scar on her neck. Great-Uncle's family eventually arranged for a prettier woman to become his second wife. But the complaints about his first wife's cooking did not stop. When she became ill with an easily treatable disease, she refused to take any medication. She swore she would rather die than live another unnecessary day. And soon after, she died.

Dooma, "Big Mother," is the regal-looking woman with the plucked forehead who sits on a rock. The dark-jacketed woman next to her is a servant, remembered by my mother only as someone who cleaned but did not cook. Dooma was my mother's aunt, the daughter of her grandfather and his "original wife," Nu-pei. But Divong, the replacement wife, my mother's grandmother, shunned Dooma, her stepdaughter, for being "too strong," while her own daughter, my grandmother, loved Dooma. She did not care that Dooma's first daughter was born with a hunchback—a sign, some said, of Dooma's own crooked nature. She did not stop seeing Dooma after Dooma remarried, disobeying her family's orders to remain a widow forever. Later Dooma killed herself, using some mysterious means that made her die slowly over three days. "Dooma died the same way she lived," my mother said, "strong, suffering lots."

Jingmei, my own grandmother, lived only a year or two after this picture was taken. She was the widow of a poor scholar, a man who had the misfortune of dying from influenza shortly after he was appointed vice-magistrate in a small county. I only assume it was influenza, since his death in 1918 was sudden, as were the millions of other deaths during the great pandemic. Family lore, however, reports that the ghost of a man on whom he had passed a judgment for execution returned from hell and killed him.

Around the time this photo was taken, during another lakeside outing, a rich man who liked to collect pretty women spotted my widowed grandmother and had one of his wives invite her to the house for a few days to play mah jong. One night he raped her, making her an outcast. My grandmother became a concubine to the rich man, and took her young daughter to live on an island near Shanghai. She left her son behind, to save his face. After she gave birth to a baby boy, the rich man's first son, she killed herself by swallowing raw opium buried in the New Year's rice cakes. "Don't follow my footsteps," she told her young daughter, who wept at her deathbed.

At my grandmother's funeral, monks tied chains to my mother's ankles so she would not fly away with her mother's ghost. "I tried to take them off," my mother told me. "I was her treasure. I was her life." She also tried to follow her mother's footsteps. Since that time she was a small girl, she often talked of killing herself. She never stopped feeling the urge.

My mother could never talk about the shame of being a concubine's daughter, even with her closest friends. "Don't tell anyone," she said once to me. "People don't understand. A concubine was like some kind of prostitute. My mother was a good woman, high-class. She had no choice."

I told her I understood.

"How can you understand?" she blurted. "You did not live in China then. You do not know what it's like to have no position in life. I was her daughter. We had no face! We belonged to nobody! This is a shame I can never push off my back." By the end of this outburst, she was crying.

On a trip with my mother to Beijing, I learned that my uncle had found a way to push the shame off his back. He was the son my grandmother had left behind. In 1936 he joined the Communist Party—in large part, he told me, to overthrow the society that had forced his mother into concubinage. He published a story about his mother. I told him I was writing about my grandmother in a book of fiction. We agreed that my grandmother was the source of strength running through our family. My mother cried to hear this.

I look at that photo often, and it's safe to guess that my grandmother never envisioned that she would one day have a granddaughter who lives in a house she co-owns with a husband she loves, and a dog and a cat she spoils (no children by choice, not bad luck), and that this granddaughter would have her own money, be able to shop—fifty percent off, full price, doesn't matter, she never has to ask anyone's permission—because she makes her own living, doing what is important to her, which is to tell stories, many of them about her grandmother, a woman who believed death was the only way to change her life.

A relative once scolded my mother, "Why do you tell your daughter these useless stories? She can't change the past." And my mother replied, "It *can* be changed. I tell her, so she can tell everyone, tell the whole world so they know what my mother suffered. That's how it *can* be changed."

I think about what my mother said. Isn't the past what people remember—who did what, how and why? And what people remember, isn't that mostly what they've already chosen to believe? For so many years, my family believed my grandmother was a victim of society, who, sadly, took her own life, no more, no less.

In my writing room, I go back into the past, to that moment when my grandmother told my mother not to follow her footsteps. My grandmother and I are walking side by side, imagining the past differently, remembering it another way. Together we come upon a tomb of memories. We open it and release what has been buried for too long—the terrible despair, the destructive rage. We hurt, we grieve, we cry. And then we see what remains: the hopes, broken to bits but still there.

I look at the photograph of my grandmother. Together we write stories of things that were and shouldn't have been, or could have been, or might still be. We know the past can be changed. We can choose what we should believe. We can choose what we should remember. That is what frees us, this choice, frees us to hope that we can redeem these same memories for the little girl who became my mother.

·thinly disguised memoir·

Through the miracle of publishing, I have had three of my childhood fantasies fulfilled.

First of all, the six-year-old in me was astonished to find that I had been encapsulated in the humor section of *Reader's Digest*. More precisely, several excerpts from my books have been used in the "Quotable Quotes" section.

You have to realize that *Reader's Digest* was the only magazine to which my parents subscribed, and that was because it contained "Word Power." This feature elevated the value of the magazine from frivolous entertainment to valuable education. With "Word Power" as our passport, our family had access to better opportunities. We could replace weak, monosyllabic words with inflated polysyllabic ones and thus rise like helium balloons above the masses.

Another method of achieving success was to submit entries to "Life in These United States" and "Laughter, the Best Medicine." If an entry was selected, that could bring both publication *and* payment of fifty dollars—fame and fortune in one fell swoop. Here's an entry I submitted, a joke my father often told after a dinner attended by many guests:

"One day, a minister came to our house for dinner. He enjoyed the wonderful dishes my wife had spent all day cooking. He said to me, 'John, I want to thank your wife. How do I say the food is delicious?' So I told him, '*La-sa hau chr.*' He then went into the kitchen and told my wife, '*La-sa hau chr.*' And she said, 'Well, if you don't like it, just throw it in the garbage!'"

I tried to explain to *Reader's Digest* that *La-sa hau chr* meant "The garbage tastes good," but that particular bilingual joke never made it to the "Best Medicine" section.

A second childhood fantasy was fulfilled when I made it into a "Women We Love" issue of *Esquire* shortly after I was first published. I had my picture taken by a Famous Photographer. This was a great achievement to the fifteen-year-old version of myself, who still inhabits a portion of my body, which in my memory of adolescence was lumpy, distorted, perhaps even bordering on disfigured. When that issue of *Esquire* appeared on the stands, I wanted to track down all the boys who'd been at school with me at Peterson High in Sunnyvale and show them: "See? That's me. Bet you're sorry now that you never asked me to dance." Pathetic, I know.

My third and crowning fantasy-come-true was an appearance in *Playboy*. Years and years ago, I used to fret that my Maidenform held no maidenly forms. I would press my palms at chest level to inflate my pectorals isometrically. I bought creams that promised to increase the bust by at least one or two inches. Nothing worked, and like those who've bought useless Viagra-like pills nowadays, I was too mortified to file for my money-back guarantee. So imagine my surprise when I appeared in *Playboy* as a dominatrix in black leather and chains.

All right, so I am only one tiny character in a cartoon of the entire band The Rock Bottom Remainders, humorously rendered along with Stephen King, Dave Barry, and Barbara Kingsolver. But through the cartoonist's sweep of the pen, certain aspects of my persona have been generously enhanced, no surgeon's knife necessary. At last I have a figure with eye-popping cleavage good enough for *Playboy*.

None of these realized fantasies has altered my life that much. When I was much younger, I thought they would. Oh, sometimes I do get recognized. Most often this happens when I am at the pharmacy to pick up the kind of prescription you would not want to announce at a family barbecue. On one occasion, I was in the waiting room of a medical specialist's office, about to be seen for a routine but loathsome medical procedure.

"Amy Tan?" the receptionist blared. "You're here for a sigmoidoscopy? Did you have your enema yet? Here, take this, and go in that bathroom there. . . . Say, aren't you Amy Tan, the author? Sure you are! You wrote that movie, *The Happy-Go-Lucky Club*, I saw you in a magazine. Hey, everybody, say hello to Amy Tan."

This, folks, is as good as it gets. Fame and fortune. The American Dream.

The American Dream also comes with a contract to write a memoir. Many people think that this is what I have written in my novels, memoirs disguised as fiction. They tell me, "I don't blame you for divorcing your husband. I divorced mine for the same reason." They ask after my two imaginary children. They tell me they can give me a referral to a top-notch naturopath who cures multiple sclerosis. They ask if I would like to write an article for a chess magazine, since I was, according to my stories, nearly a grand champion.

Now that I've written several memoirs disguised as fiction, some readers assume I may be running out of material. After all, how many times can you write your autobiography? Some of these people offer to give me their stories. They tell me they grew up in a family that was horribly afflicted with tragedy and scandal, disease and death, tears and heartbreak. A few of these strangers have also generously suggested that we split the royalties fifty-fifty. Although it's their story, they concede that I'll be doing most of the writing. They already know who should play them in the film version.

I remember being at a book signing in Houston where a man slipped me a scrap of paper on which he had inscribed what I at first mistook to be a Dadaist poem: "Father hanged, mother murdered, uncle shot, baby son drowned, wife insane, me, almost died twice, all horrible ways. Want to write about me? Call me. Let's talk."

Now, if you were traveling alone in a strange city, would you phone this man and say, "Hey, great ideas, come on over to my hotel so we can get going on them"?

Most of the offers are sincere. I know this. Most people don't even want the fifty-fifty split. They just want me to tell their story, and they need a writer to put the words down in a way others will understand. They want people to know what they have been through. They want witnesses, because it's lonely to go through life with your heartaches. They are people who believe that they can find some sort of redemption, if only their story is told to the world, if only they can get it off their chest.

I feel terrible that I cannot help them. The problem is, I'd never be able to borrow from a stranger's life to create my stories. What's *my* reason for writing the story in the first place, if not to masochistically examine my own life's confusion, my own hopes and unanswered prayers? The metaphors, the sensory truths, the questions must be my own progeny—conceived, nurtured, and fussed over by me.

This is not to say I've been writing autobiographically, at least not in the sense that most people assume. If I write about a little girl who lives in Chinatown and plays chess, this does not mean that I did those same things.

But within that story is an emotional truth. It has to do with a mother who has helped her daughter see the world in a special way. It is a world in which the mother possesses rare magic. She can make the girl see yin when it is yang. The girl sees that her mother, who is her ally, is also her adversary. And that is an emotional memory that I *do* have, this sense of double jeopardy, realizing that my mother could both help me and hurt me, in the best and worst ways possible. So what I draw from is not a photographic memory, but an emotional one. When I place that memory of feeling within a fictive home, it becomes imagination. Anything can happen. The girl may shout back at her mother and tell her to go to hell. The mother may say, "I was wrong. I'm sorry." The possibilities are endless, but one is chosen. And as I write that possibility, it becomes a part of me. It has the power to change my memory of the way things really happened.

For me, writing from memory is more about remembering my psychological place in the world at different stages of my life. Where did I fit in my family, or why didn't I fit. It is about remembering my evolving sense of life, from thinking life was magic, to believing it was random and meaningless, to coming around to thinking it was magic all over again. My memory, then, is entirely subjective. And that, I think, is the kind of memory that is simultaneously the most unreliable *and* the most authentic element a writer can infuse into her work.

For as long as I can remember, I have been curious about how I remember. The earliest memory I have is of an event that took place under a tree. I was a year and a half old. And I know I was that age because of the season and the details of the yard and the house. I remember that I was sitting on the cool lawn on a hot day. Around me was a low fence and to my right was a white house with dark doorways that led to naps. My big brother and parents were above me. Suddenly something hit my head. My brother laughed. Although it did not hurt that much, I was startled and cried loudly to voice my displeasure, lest it happen again. After a while, I picked up what had fallen on my head. It filled my entire palm, a fuzzy golden ball.

"It was a peach," I recalled to my mother.

She thought for a while, and then said that it was not a peach but an apricot, for the parish house in Fresno was the only place we had lived that had a fruit tree in the yard. And this made sense, that it was an apricot, for an apricot would have filled my eighteen-month-old hand in the way a peach would fill my adult one.

There was another time, when I was seven, that I realized that memories were elusive, that you could not will them to stay, and that some you could not will to go away. I was old enough to understand that some things were in my memory like waking morning dreams. No matter how much I tried to hang on to them, they slipped away. And when I tried to find a way to remember them, by, say, writing about them, or drawing a picture of them, the result was not even close. And the result then became the memory that replaced the real thing.

As a child, I tried to develop a number of mnemonic devices. Whenever I felt wronged or misunderstood, I would stare at my hands, the creases in my palms. I would tell myself, I will always be the same person just as I will always have these same hands. I had knowledge that my body would continue to change, although in what ways I did not know precisely. But I stared at my hands and vowed to remember this day, these same hands, and the feeling of injustice I felt in being accused of wrongdoing when it had never been my intention at all.

Looking at my palms today, I can see those splinters from my childhood. I can feel once again the slivers slipping under my skin, hear myself promise never to forget who and what had injured me. I think of those slivers as ingredients for stories. With them, I can concoct thousands of stories, not simply a single bona fide one. The stories I write concern the various beliefs I have held and lost and found at various times of my life. And having now written several books, I realize those beliefs most often have had to do with hope: hope and expectation, hope and disappointment, loss and hope, fate and hope, death and hope, luck and hope. They sprang from the questions I had as a child: How did that happen? What's going to happen? How do I make things happen?

When I write my stories, I do not use childhood memories. I

use a child's memory. Through that child's mind, I am too inexperienced to have assumptions. So the world is still full of magic. Anything can happen. All possibilities. I have dreams. I have fantasies.

At will, I can enter that world again.

·persona errata·

Between the time I wrote my first book and today, the Internet accomplished the equivalent of the Big Bang, and the World Wide Web expanded into the Ubiquitous Uncontrollable Universe. As a result, certain errors of fact about me began to circulate and became part of my unofficial biography now often used by students, interviewers, booksellers, and public relations staffs before I come to give talks.

At first, there were only minor mistakes, for example, that I had received my master's degree and a Ph.D. from UC Berkeley, which is a fine school and one that I did attend while studying for my doctorate. But the only doctorates I have are honorary, and according to one university president who handed me a diploma, this entitles me to a free parking space in the faculty lot, though solely when I come to give a free talk. To set the record straight, I never finished my doctoral program, and my B.A. and M.A. degrees came from San Jose State University.

As the Internet became more widespread, so did the errors. They are not quite urban-legend strength, but they have definitely been magnified. I remember the day I saw announced before a live online interview that Amy Tan had won the Nobel Prize in Literature. It then occurred to me that one could actually conduct several lives of different realities, even better ones, certainly with more prestigious prizes. But as the online interview began, I typed in my greeting: "Hi, Amy Tan here, only I never did win that Nobel Prize. Wish I had. Thanks for the vote of confidence."

Most often I am aware of the mistakes when I am receiving other honors having to do with being Asian-American or a writer or Chinese or an alumna of one of the colleges I attended. Then I learn of all the other prizes I have supposedly won, among them the National Book Award, the *Los Angeles Times* Book Prize, and the Pulitzer. I was in fact nominated for the first two, so a little exaggeration there is understandable, but the Pulitzer reference is a fluke from the Web, and one that keeps replicating like a virus. It's embarrassing to start my acceptance speeches with a list of errata, which then seems to show only how truly unworthy I am to be standing on the podium or festooned stage, holding an engraved plaque or crystal bowl.

Some of the mistakes are maddening, like those in a *Los Angeles Times* piece published in 2000, which I did not read, but which a friend felt his duty to read aloud to me for my own edification; it described me as having a big smile that displayed teeth discolored by my nicotine habit. The reporter must have looked up that old *Salon* interview in which I was surreptitiously smoking on my terrace and asked the reporter to please not mention this. Whatever the source, I never realized my teeth looked that bad, and if they are indeed discolored enough to be worth mentioning, I must make it known that it is not due to cigarettes. I am proud of the fact that I gave up smoking for good in 1995, and since then I have actually brushed my teeth from time to time and have gone for routine professional teeth cleaning every six months.

Inaccuracy, I fear, has become epidemic among publications whose writers rely on the Internet for research. For there, past interviews and articles survive and even thrive, as if they were fresh off the press, perpetually part of today's news. An interview dating from 1989 said, rightly, that I had been married for fifteen years. A reporter who evidently used this interview as background in 1996 stated that I had been married for fifteen years. Other reporters, perhaps wishing to differentiate between the first set of fifteen years and the second, have referred to Lou as my "current husband."

Having a twenty-year-old photograph of me run with articles also causes me consternation. I have had PR people refuse to take me to the greenroom before an event, only to have them later rush up to me and say, "Oh, I'm so sorry. I didn't know you were *the* Amy Tan. I was looking for *someone else*." Read between the lines.

I did some sleuthing the other day to see who exactly is this Amy Tan who looks forever the same as in 1989, has been married to multiple husbands for always the same number of years, and has won all the literary prizes on earth. I found her lurking in at least one den of iniquity. This website opened with the following come-on:

> *Do you need a quality paper on Amy Tan—today, tomorrow, next week, or next month?*

> Since 1997, our experts on Amy Tan have helped students worldwide by providing the best, lowest-priced writing service on the Internet. If you've waited too long to start your paper on Amy Tan, or have more writing than you can handle, we can help. Our staff of over 200 professional writers located around the world has produced thousands of college term papers, essays, research papers, dissertations, theses, and book reports on all topics involving Amy Tan. These excellent papers are available to you instantly for only $25.99 each.

How dismal to think I can be instantly summed up for only $25.99. These papers could not possibly be correct. I've paid psychiatrists $200 for fifty minutes many times over, and I still don't understand who I am.

For years, I have felt stymied by my alternative reality. It has created a new kind of existential angst. Who was I really, if not what all these articles said I was? If the Internet and its share of misinformation went on in perpetuity, then I too would live on in immortal muddle. The real me would become lost to misstatements of fact.

Then I realized I could use the same methods by which the errata grew to quash them, all 48,291 hits. I decided to write this piece, the one right before your very eyes. It would become part of the Internet Archives Used by Reporters, and thus I would at least have recorded my rebuttal for posterity.

So herewith the facts, as put forth by the ultimate expert, Amy Tan, and you don't have to pay $25.99 to get the scoop on what in her life is only a mistake.

. . .

Erratum 1. Tan's works do not include *The Year of No Flood* (1995). That was a chapter in her novel *The Hundred Secret Senses.* At one time, Tan thought she might write a book with that title that would include the flood and then the drought that preceded the Boxer Uprising, but because she blabbed about that book so much before it was written, it ejected itself from her imagination. Apparently someone to whom she blabbed assumed she finished the novel and published it.

Erratum 2. Tan did not attend eight different colleges. It was five, she says, and that number proved excessive enough, particularly when the fund-raising season rolls around every year and she is asked to contribute to the coffers of her alma maters.

Erratum 3. Tan did not teach poetry at a university in West Virginia. She has no idea where that came from, because she has never been to West Virginia and she has never taught. But the idea is rather flattering, and she has always wished she could write poetry, let alone teach it. Along those same lines, Tan has never been a workshop leader of a writers' group, and as to those who claim to her agent and editor that she led their group, that was Molly Giles who was the leader. She has red hair. Tan has red hair only when she performs in a literary garage band called The Rock Bottom Remainders. She has never worn the red wig while leading a writers' workshop.

Erratum 4. Tan never worked in a factory alongside a certain person who was your best friend, not in this life or in any past life that she can remember. Among Tan's early jobs, she was a switchboard operator at her high school, a carhop at an A&W drive-in, and a Round Table pizza slinger.

Erratum 5. Tan has never lived in a mansion in the multimillionaired hills of Hillsborough, California. She went to a fund-raiser there once where guests were asked to shell out $25,000 to help a political candidate but she was somehow let in for free; the political candidate later lost. As to where Tan lives, that would be a more modest condominium in San Francisco, a town that has some pretty nice hills itself, and a mix of billionaires and poor, both of whom the political candidates profess to have in their camp.

Erratum 6. Tan's condominium is not the top floor of a former mansion. Her building was constructed in 1916 as apartments. Her unit is on the third and fourth floors, the fourth being a former attic. Tan, no spring chicken, having been born in 1952 (to determine approximate age, take today's year and subtract 1952), now wishes she had an elevator.

Erratum 7. Tan has never had a fight with anyone from her publishers' in a bookstore, nor did she scream and fling books around, causing store patrons to run for their lives. Tan claims that she and her publishers have always had an amicable relationship, and they fight only over bills at restaurants, and then only as an ostentatious show of politeness. Most times, Tan lets them win. They pay the bill.

Erratum 8. With the exception of arguments over restaurant bills, Tan has never had a fight with her agent, Sandy Dijkstra, and switched to a new agent. Sandy was the one who encouraged her to write fiction early on. She is like a Jewish mother, badgering Tan week after week to keep writing. Tan owes her life to her agent for giving her the life of a writer. For that reason, Tan probably also owes her lunch, but Sandy usually pays anyway.

Erratum 9. Lou DeMattei is indeed Tan's first husband. He is also her current husband. In addition, he is her only husband. They have been together since 1970, married since 1974. To discover how many total years that is, take today's year and subtract from it 1970 for togetherness or 1974 for marriage.

Erratum 10. Tan does not have two children, unless you consider, as she does, that her dogs are her children. In articles about Tan after 1997, Tan's cat, Sagwa, should be referred to not as her pet but as her late and dearly beloved kitty. Tan acknowledges that she has included children in most of her books, except the one about the cat. Predictably, these children have grown older with each subsequent book. Although they are imaginary, she is terribly fond of them. But she has never done homework with them every night, taken them to soccer practice or swim meets, cried in an emergency room when it turned out they had merely stuck beans in their ears, or gone through the cycle of being angry, then worried, then hysterical when they drove off to a forbidden place and went missing for six hours. Thus Tan cannot say with real conviction that her dogs are her children.

Erratum 11. Tan does not have yellow skin as depicted in a cartoon version of her on *The Simpsons.* It is yellow-skin depictions like these that make Tan slightly uncomfortable in being called a Writer of Color. Also, Tan did not really berate Lisa Simpson and humiliate her mercilessly in front of a TV audience. Those words were put in Tan's mouth by another cartoon character, namely Matt Groening. Other than the skin-color thing, she thinks Matt Groening is a sweetheart and a pretty nice guy. She once argued with him in public over the lunch bill, but he pushed her credit card aside and paid.

That's it for now. I will be adding to this regularly, as needed. Look for installments in 48,291 websites and growing listed by Google for "Amy Tan."

· scent ·

As a teenager, I longed for a corsage of gardenias, that symbol of prom nights and first kisses. But when I was fifteen, my brother, and then my father, were struck ill, both with brain tumors, and in lieu of going to dances, I lived in hospital waiting rooms. In less than a year, our living room was twice filled to bursting with white gardenias adorning funeral sprays. For a long time afterward, while attending some joyous occasion, such as a wedding or an anniversary party, I would be caught off guard by the oppressive sweetness of gardenias, their scent an instant reminder of unbearable grief. Recently, however, I saw a pot of gardenias in a plant store and was seduced by the milky white blooms and vibrant green leaves. I brought the gardenias home, where their lovely fragrance immediately saturated my small deck and reminded me of an earlier time, of happy expectations. Alas, unlucky gardener that I am, the blooms soon turned yellow and fell off, and I gave up watering the plant. In spite of my neglect the plant has not died. In fact, it has sprouted new leaves. And now I am watering the gardenia again. I am hoping the flowers will bloom, wondering when they will.

AMERICAN CIRCUMSTANCES AND CHINESE CHARACTER

I wanted my children to have the best combination: American circumstances and Chinese character. How could I know these two things do not mix?

I taught [my daughter] how American circumstances work. If you are born poor here, it's no lasting shame. You are first in line for a scholarship. If the roof crashes on your head, no need to cry over this bad luck. You can sue anybody, make the landlord fix it. You do not have to sit like a Buddha under a tree letting pigeons drop their dirty business on your head. You can buy an umbrella. Or go inside a Catholic church. In Amer-

ica, nobody says you have to keep the circumstances somebody else gives you.

She learned these things, but I couldn't teach her about Chinese character. How to obey parents and listen to your mother's mind. How not to show your own thoughts, to put your feelings behind your face so you can take advantage of hidden opportunities. Why easy things are not worth pursuing. How to know your own worth and polish it, never flashing it around like a cheap ring. Why Chinese thinking is best.

· The Joy Luck Club

·fish cheeks·

I fell in love with the minister's son the winter I turned fourteen. He was not Chinese, but as white as Mary in the manger. For Christmas I prayed for this blond-haired boy, Robert, and a slim new American nose.

When I found out that my parents had invited the minister's family over for Christmas Eve dinner, I cried. What would Robert think of our shabby Chinese Christmas? What would he think of our noisy Chinese relatives who lacked proper American manners? What terrible disappointment would he feel upon seeing not a roasted turkey and sweet potatoes but Chinese food?

On Christmas Eve, I saw that my mother had outdone herself in creating a strange menu. She was pulling black veins out of the backs of fleshy prawns. The kitchen was littered with appalling mounds of raw food: A slimy rock cod with bulging fish eyes that pleaded not to be thrown into a pan of hot oil. Tofu, which looked like stacked wedges of rubbery white sponges. A bowl soaking dried fungus back to life. A plate of squid, crisscrossed with knife markings so they resembled bicycle tires.

And then they arrived—the minister's family and all my relatives in a clamor of doorbells and rumpled Christmas packages. Robert grunted hello, and I pretended he was not worthy of existence.

Dinner threw me deeper into despair. My relatives licked the ends of their chopsticks and reached across the table, dipping into the dozen or so plates of food. Robert and his family waited patiently for platters to be passed to them. My relatives mur-

The Tan family—(left to right) Peter, John, me, and Daisy—in Oakland, California, the day after I was born, 1952.

mured with pleasure when my mother brought out the whole steamed fish. Robert grimaced. Then my father poked his chopsticks just below the fish eye and plucked out the soft meat. "Amy, your favorite," he said, offering me the tender fish cheek. I wanted to disappear.

At the end of the meal my father leaned back and belched loudly, thanking my mother for her fine cooking. "It's a polite Chinese custom, to show you are satisfied," he explained to our astonished guests. Robert was looking down at his plate with a reddened face. The minister managed to muster a quiet burp. I was stunned into silence for the rest of the night.

After all the guests had gone, my mother said to me, "You want be same like American girls on the outside." She handed me an early gift. It was a miniskirt in beige tweed. "But inside, you must always be Chinese. You must be proud you different. You only shame is be ashame."

And even though I didn't agree with her then, I knew that she understood how much I had suffered during the evening's dinner. It wasn't until many years later—long after I had gotten over my crush on Robert—that I was able to appreciate fully her lesson and the true purpose behind our particular menu. For Christmas Eve that year, she had chosen all my favorite foods.

· *dangerous advice* ·

My mother used to provide vivid examples of what would happen to me if I was foolish enough to ignore her advice. If I ran out into the street without looking both ways, I could be smashed by a car, flattened like a sand dab. If I ate unwashed fruit, I could end up poisoned, writhing like a snail on a bed of salt. If I kissed a boy—a boy who probably *never* brushed his teeth or washed his hands—I would wind up diseased and pregnant, as bloated as a rotten melon.

Thanks to my mother, I never eat sand dabs or snails, and I made sure I married a man who brushes *and* flosses his teeth every day. So it is strange to report that my mother did *not* warn me against skiing. Fact is, she encouraged it.

We were an urban immigrant family who lived in blue-collar California neighborhoods, then wended our way into the middle-class suburbs of Silicon Valley. Unlike my friends, I did not go to summer camp, where unlucky boys and girls had to ride rabid ponies and swim in snake-choked lakes. My summertime thrills included making lanyards in a cafeteria, seeing *The Angry Red Planet* at a bargain matinee, and going to the library once a week.

The only snowcapped mountain I had ever seen up close was the Matterhorn at Disneyland. Of course, I was not allowed to go on the Matterhorn ride.

"Why not?" I whined.

"This not fun," my mother replied. "Only dangerous."

"Everybody else is going!"

"Everybody jump off cliff, you do same?"

Smug look. "Yeah."

"Well, anyway, too many people wait in line. Wait so long, you get sunstroke."

Intentionally or not, my mother raised me to become the Great Indoors Type. In my youth I failed to develop any athletic prowess. I thought of myself as a klutz, and this self-image was reinforced over and over in PE classes. Three times a week I had to endure a cruel ritual in which girls lined up to be chosen by team captains.

"Let's see," I'd hear the captain say as she surveyed the dregs. Big sigh. "Oh well, I *guess* I can take Tan." And I'd leap up like a grateful dog at the pound, spared yet another day from being the very last to be chosen.

I was the girl who couldn't run a relay race without falling down and throwing up. I was the player who sprained her finger just looking at a volleyball. I was the bungler designated to stand in right field, where baseballs were seldom hit. The one time a girl did hit a fly out there, I was jeered for running away from the ball. Like my mother, I saw danger coming at me from all angles.

When I was sixteen, my mother decided to take me and my little brother to Europe, where she believed it was safer. I thought she'd gone crazy for sure. In August, we sailed to Holland with no Dutch language skills and no idea where we would live or go to school. After a month of wandering, we found our home for the next year: a century-old chalet in Territet-Montreux, Switzerland. It was picture-postcard perfect, set in a neighborhood of fourteenth-century houses and cobblestone pathways, with glorious views of Lake Geneva and the Alps.

My mother gave my brother and me a mandate: We were to take advantage of every opportunity presented—speaking French, going to museums, skiing . . . *Skiing?* My mother had recently seen *The Sound of Music*, and she could envision no harm in an activity that took place in a landscape that even a nun had sung praises about.

Actually, I had no choice about the skiing. It was a requirement of the school I had been enrolled in—a school attended, I should add, by wealthy kids with international lifestyles who had been skiing glaciers and drinking Bordeaux since the age of three. Several of the girls shopped in Paris on the weekends.

Your basic insecure teenager, I tried to fit in and act like my peers, as though I was bored silly by a life of plenty.

"When I was in Geneva last week," I told my new friends in a voice tinged with ennui, "I found it utterly impossible to find any ski clothes that I liked." And then I lit another cigarette.

To buy the requisite ski equipment and clothes, my mother took me to Migros, a store that was the equivalent of an American Wal-Mart. When the shop clerk asked me to raise my right arm, I didn't ask why. I extended it as fully as my five-foot-three-and-three-quarter-inch frame could muster. I was shown a pair of red 196-centimeter wood skis with cable bindings. So as not to be taken for a consumer fool, I carefully examined the proffered skis, making sure they had no chips in their paint and were suitably heavy to resist breaking.

To complete the rig, my mother selected some steel poles with leather baskets—sturdy ones, nice and heavy—as well as a pair of black Dolomite boots roomy enough for the three pairs of wool socks she had knit and insisted I wear. She also picked out a burgundy outfit that could accommodate layers of sweaters. When I emerged from the dressing room looking like a cross between an overripe eggplant and an Eskimo, she pronounced me fully equipped to go schussing.

For my first ski trip I went to Gstaad with a couple of school friends and, unbeknownst to my mother, my very first boyfriend, Franz, who was twenty-two, an excellent skier, and a deserter from the German army.

At the resort, I clamped my boots into my skis for the first time and tried to walk to the chairlift, using the herky-jerky movements of a female Frankenstein. I saw a chair swing around and grab a couple in front of me, and I was reminded of a playground carousel from my childhood, a metal contraption that resembled a giant turntable in the sand. When I was four, a boy had invited me to get on. He started to push the carousel faster and faster, until it reached the speed required to play a 45 rpm single. I hung on to the metal rung, imitating a flag in a gale wind, until centrifugal force pried off my fingers and I flew through the air screaming.

Those were my thoughts as I faced my first chairlift. When it was Franz's and my turn to get on, I politely invited the skiers behind us to go ahead. "*Mais non,*" I said in my newly acquired French. "*Après vous . . . et vous et vous . . .*" Franz picked me up and deposited me into the next chair, and up we went. He assured me that the initial run down would be easy. "Beginner slope," he said.

I know now that even the smallest of inclines looks like Instant Death to a beginner, and if I ever went back to Gstaad, I'd probably laugh to see that the run was nothing but a bunny slope, a mere pimple of a hill. But then I think: Why did it take *twenty minutes* by chairlift to reach the top?

At the top, Franz shoved me out of the chair and I slid on my backside, a tangle of skis and poles.

"Do you *really* think I can do this?" I asked as he helped me to my feet.

"*Ja*, sure," he answered. "No problem. Follow me." And then off he went, with me staring after him. Three turns later, he disappeared from view, as did the twenty skiers who went around me and plunged down the hill.

Alone at the top, I stared down the mountain. Although the temperature was below freezing, I began to sweat. At this exact moment I recalled a vision of another Swiss mountain, the Matterhorn at Disneyland. "This not fun," the mother in my mind was warning. "This *dangerous*."

Before me was a precipice of sheer ice. All the fears of a lifetime gathered in one terrifying vision. I would be squashed flat, my brains smashed like a rotten melon, rivulets of blood staining the clean white snow. And then I imagined my mother saying, "Everybody jump off cliff, you do same?" And that took me right over the edge with my knee-jerk response, "Yeah," and a half-second later the long, heavy skis were aimed straight down what I today know is the "fall line."

I quickly reached speeds that caused the scenery to blur. I pressed down on the poles to brake. That, I immediately discovered, is not a good way to stop, but it is an efficient way to snap your hands off at the wrists.

I was a runaway semi, semi-shocked, semi-delirious. I flew by the Rich and the Famous—Rod Steiger, Julie Andrews—I was skiing with the best. Only ignorance kept me from panicking completely. I thought I might be able to stay upright on my skis long enough to reach the bottom of the mountain, where I could then gradually coast to a stop. That was the plan I would have executed had not the Queen of Sweden crossed my path (I'm not making this up). She screamed, as did her retinue, and I did my first faceplant on packed snow.

Blood! There was blood on the snow. My brains must have been leaking. I don't remember which was worse: the pain or the humiliation of being asked by Jean-Claude Killy lookalikes if I was all right. I was also crossly informed by at least two people that I had nearly assassinated a beloved royal personage.

After my nose stopped bleeding, I took off my skis. Never mind that I was still some two miles from the bottom of the mountain and it might take me hours to reach it safely. If nightfall came, the rescue team could simply follow the three-foot-deep sitzmarks I was tracking down the middle of the slope.

I did not become an excellent skier that year. For forty-five minutes twice a week, I managed to use my poles to push myself across the flattest part of the parking lot until I had fulfilled my ski exercise requirements for school. Yet I was determined I would not let my newfound fear of speed defeat me. If anything, fear now fueled my defiance.

When I returned to the States, I continued to ski. Year after year I persisted, despite bad equipment, ludicrous ski outfits, and humiliating faceplants. Over the years, I've broken a pair of skis in half, been carted off a mountain in a rescue sled, and even managed, while merely standing in a lift line, to knock over a dozen skiers, like dominoes. I've learned that all this was necessary to transform myself into a person who not only seeks out terror but enjoys it tremendously.

This year, I fell down the entire length of the East Face in Squaw Valley, California, and went back up for seconds. I followed brain-altered friends whose idea of fun is skiing fast between trees in a blizzard. This year, I even took a lesson.

"Oh, going to ski again?" my mother asked one day when I told her I was heading to my cabin in Lake Tahoe.

"Yep," I said. "I'm going to try and break a couple of legs."

"Okay," she answered. "Have fun."

Who am I to ignore my mother's advice?*

* Shortly after I wrote this piece, I went helicopter skiing and tore my quadriceps, pulled my hamstring, and broke off the top of my tibia. But I'm still skiing.

·midlife confidential·

As the daughter of hardworking Christian immigrants from China, I was given little opportunity to cultivate a misspent youth.

Ours was a family that rarely went on vacations; during the first sixteen years of my life, we took only two, one when I was six, one when I was twelve, both of them brief trips to Disneyland and Knott's Berry Farm. Most of my summers were spent in Bible classes or in school cafeterias, where I wove lanyards, or planted sweet peas in milk cartons, or made maps of South America out of dried kidney beans, split peas, and lentils. Common amusements during my childhood included riding my bike around the corner, going to the library, mowing the lawn, staring at the candy counter at the corner market, feeding leaves to caterpillars that eventually died, or watching cocoons that never hatched.

I count as the most memorable moments of my life those that were laced with heart-pounding terror—times when I was so scared out of my wits I could not even scream. When I was two, for example, my mother took me to a department store where I saw one man without limbs and another with legs as long as ladders. When I was three, I stood outside an apartment window and heard the echoing screams of a girl my age whose mother was beating her nonstop in the bathroom. When I was four, I desperately clung to the rails of a hand-pushed carousel, forever it seemed, until I let go and landed facedown in the sand. When I was five, a nurse in a hospital yelled at me for wanting my doll to accompany me to the operating room. When I was six, I stared at a playmate lying in a coffin, her hands crossed flat over a Bible on her chest. When I was seven, I watched people's skin blister and foam in the movie *The Angry Red Planet*. When I was eight, I flew down a hill on a boy's bike only to realize, at the bottom, that it had no brakes. When I was nine, I caught a snake in a creek—and the scary part was *not* telling my parents that the snake had slithered between the seats of the Rambler right before we drove to the airport to pick up my grand-aunt Grace. The last experience also counted as one of the most fun car rides I ever took.

The word "fun" was not commonly used in our family, except, perhaps, in the following context: "Fun? Why you want have fun? What's so good about this? Just wasting time and money." In our family, "fun" was a bad *f*-word, and its antonym was "hard," as in hard work. Things that were hard led to worthwhile results; things that were fun did not.

Another bad *f*-word was "freedom," as in, "So you want American freedom to go wild and bring shame on your family?" Which brings me to another bad *f*-word, "friends," those purveyors of corruption and shame whose sole purpose in life was to encourage me to talk back to my mother and make her long to return to China, where there were millions of girls my age who would be only too happy to obey their parents without question. The good *f*-word, of course, was "family," as in "go to church with family," or "do homework with family," or "give your toys to your family in Taiwan."

Lest you think my parents were completely feudal in their thinking, let me clarify that they did adopt some important American precepts—for instance, the notions that "time is money" and that "a penny saved is a penny earned." As a consequence, they were also very fond of the word "free"—which should not be confused with "freedom" or the like-sounding "free," uttered in useless expressions such as "free time" or "free to do what you want." I'm referring to the sort of "free" that conveys valuable ideas such as, "You are free to go to summer school because they don't charge us any money there."

I exaggerate in saying we *never* had fun. My parents did allow certain versions of *family* fun, like walking around the campus of Stanford University, a form of entertainment that besides being free served to remind me of a destination and a reward second only to getting into heaven. Both rewards could be attained *only* if I listened carefully to my parents, meaning no boys, no pizza, and of course, no rock 'n' roll.

A few months before my fortieth birthday, I found myself suffering from a bad attitude aggravated by chronic neck pain—symptoms common among authors on book tour. In my case, I had been on the road nationally and overseas for the better half of a year. Most people think that when writers go on tour they're having loads of glamorous and exciting fun. Those people have good imaginations. As a touring author, I had lost mine.

I was spending the productive years of my life not writing but eating hot dogs at airport chuck wagons and obeying signs to "fasten seat belt while seated." I was depleting supplies of brain power trying to figure out which city I had awakened in or how to act spontaneous answering the same questions ten times a day for twenty days at a stretch.

Although happily married, I was spending more nights alone than with my husband. I had been sleepless in Seattle, Cincinnati, St. Louis, and Boca Raton. In hotel beds, I would obsess over dumb answers I had given that day, over how inarticulate I had sounded, how I was a complete disgrace to American literature. After reviling myself, I would listen through thin walls to what sounded like a woman having her tonsils removed without anesthesia, to a man who was either auditioning for the lead in *Falstaff* or suffering from explosive gastrointestinal problems. To help lull me to sleep, I would recall scientific details—such as the fact that the biggest source of room dust, accounting for something like 99.87 percent, is sloughed-off human skin. I would imagine years and years of skin particles from happy and sad strangers who had slept in this very bed now circulating in the air I breathed.

This was my mental state when I returned from my latest book tour. This was my attitude on November 6, 1991, when I heard the fax machine churning out what was sure to be a request to do yet another author appearance.

It was from Kathi Kamen Goldmark, the media escort who'd taken me to numerous book-related publicity events around the

Bay Area. As I recall, her fax said something to this effect: "Hey, Amy, a bunch of authors and I are putting together a rock-'n'-roll band to play at the ABA in Anaheim. Wanna jam with us? I think you'd have a lot of fun."

I pondered the fax. Did I look like the kind of writer who had time for a lot of fun? As to singing in public, could there be anything more similar to a public execution? Furthermore, how could I, the author of poignant mother-daughter tales, do something as ludicrous and career-damaging as play in a rock-'n'-roll band in front of thousands of readers at the American Booksellers Association convention? Amend that to a *mediocre* rock-'n'-roll band.

Two minutes later, I faxed Kathi my answer: "What should I wear?"

The very next day, I began exercising my middle-aged body into stamina strength. And soon after, Kathi and I went on a shopping spree at Betsey Johnson, the choice of every respectable fourteen-year-old. We perused the sales racks and tried on half a dozen skintight dresses. There I found it, spandex and sequins, a version of my lost youth, also known as Every Mother's Worst Nightmare.

The prospect of being a rock-'n'-roll singer presented only one small obstacle: namely, the fact that I couldn't sing. I am *not* being modest. When I was thirteen, my mother took me to a voice teacher, thinking I could learn to accompany myself Liberace style on the piano. The voice teacher had me sing progressively higher scales: "Do, re, mi, fa—*oops.*" After twenty minutes, he gave his verdict to my mother: "My dear Mrs. Tan, your daughter has no vocal skill whatsoever."

Suffice it to say, about two months before our first gig in Anaheim, I woke up one night, drenched in sweat. I called Kathi the next morning. "Kathi, Kathi," I panted, "I can't sing at ABA."

"Oh, no! A conflict came up in your schedule?"

"I mean I *can't sing.*"

Kathi's brilliant solution was twofold: I could practice singing into a live mike at a sound studio that belonged to David Phillips, a friend of hers who was reportedly a very sweet guy. Second, I could overcome stage fright by performing at a karaoke bar filled with festive patrons who, Kathi assured me, wouldn't be able to hear me above the clinking din of cocktail glasses.

At the sound studio, it took me forty minutes before anything resembling even a squeak came out of my mouth. My vocal cords were paralyzed. David, as promised, was a sweet guy—a sweet guy who played in a real band, The Potato Eaters. Plus he was cute. I had been counting on humiliating myself in front of a dweeb.

As my lips moved voicelessly next to the mike, David would cast knowing but worried looks at Kathi before gently coaxing me yet another time: "Okay, that was a good try. We'll just . . . well, try it again."

At the karaoke bar, I sang with horrible stiffness, but was comforted to find I wasn't the only egomaniac foolish enough to think I could sing publicly. The following week, I left for a vacation in Hawaii. For five hours a day, I sat on the beaches of Kona, wearing headphones and singing harmony on "Mammer Jammer" and lead on "Bye Bye, Love." To an audience of porpoises and turtles frolicking in the waves, I sang my heart out, loud and strong, bouncing my head in rhythm to the background instrumentals Ridley Pearson had recorded for the benefit of the musically disadvantaged. My husband later told me that when beachcombers came within earshot of me, they retreated with the same haste people employ for avoiding sidewalk fire-and-brimstone preachers.

When I was fourteen, I used to go to the beach on weekends, supposedly to recruit kids for Christ. That was the only way my parents would let me go. By then my hormones were raging to sin. I was no longer content to sing hymns in the church choir as my only excitement. I fantasized shrieking at the top of my lungs while running along the beach—not too quickly, of course—as lanky bad boys chased me, threatening to pick me up and toss me into the ocean. The real boys did not chase me. Nor did they accept my offers to come to a "youth fellowship shindig."

Every afternoon, while practicing the piano, I mourned that I was not a popular girl. I was not the kind who got invited to after-school garage parties where 45s were played at top volume and 7UP was laced with vodka. I hated myself for being perceived as the "good girl," unlike the "bad girls," who ratted their hair, slouched around in their fathers' white dress shirts, and stole nail polish from Kmart.

That same year, I actually discovered something good about my parents, and that is that they didn't know a thing about bad words, not the real ones at least. While they forbade my brothers and me to say "gosh," "darn," "gee," and "golly"—those being variations of "God" and "damn"—we could utter "bitch," "pissed off," "boner," and "hard-on" with impunity. My parents were blissfully ignorant as to what those words meant. My older brother, Peter, had bought a Fugs record, and when my mother asked me what this word "fug" meant, I said it stood for "happy-go-lucky," and that "Fug you" was an American way to greet someone. Well, it was, in a way.

By using my parents' naiveté to my advantage, I discovered how to be a popular girl. For one thing, I ran for freshman class secretary, which my parents interpreted as my natural Christian desire to do public service. To increase my very slim chances of winning office, I painted butcher-paper banners with the following campaign slogan: "Amy Tan Has Sec. Appeal." I already counted on my parents' not getting the pun, and indeed they didn't. But my school's vice-principal did. Just as I had figured, he made a huge stink over this inappropriate campaign slogan and ordered the banners be torn down, which then incited protests of unfair censorship from not only the freshman class but *all* the students. In short order, my name became widely known.

To clinch the election, I made a campaign speech in which I promised to raise money for school dances through the sale of kazoos, which students were not allowed to play on campus. In my speech, I passionately reasoned that there was no rule against the *possession* of kazoos. "Stop censorship," I said. "A vote for me is a vote for kazoos."

I'm happy to report that I won the election and kazoos became the ubiquitous symbol of freedom, waved at every basketball and football game. Unfortunately, my newly elected social status did not confer upon me sex appeal. Instead, I became the confidante to girls who confessed that their lips were bruised from kissing too much the night before, or to boys who wanted to know what to do when girls got mad at them for going too far.

As freshman class secretary, I also had to help organize the dances. I argued persuasively with my mother about the necessity of my going to the dances as well: "Come on! I have to be there to take care of things. What if someone doesn't pay to get in? That's like stealing. It's not like I'm going there to dance or anything."

Before going to a dance, I used masking tape to shorten my dress and asked my girlfriend Terry to lend me her tube of white lipstick. Neither measure had any effect on the boys. At the dance, I stood near the punchbowl, mortified as Terry, then Janis, then Dottie, then Cindy were asked to dance. The flick of a rotating mirrored ball beat into my brain with hypnotic force: *Nah-nah . . . nah-nah . . .*

At the end of each dance, Terry did her best to console me: "Did you see that creep who asked me to dance? The one with the great big zit at the end of his chin—I was freaked he'd drip it all over my shoulder. And then I could feel his boner pressing into my hip. God! I'd rather die a virgin. . . ."

Over time, at other parties, a few boys asked me to dance. You know the ones I'm talking about: guys who belonged to the United Nations Club, whose attempts at shaving left them with bleeding pimples, who always raised their hands in class, smug that they knew the answers. In other words, they were dorks like me, and through natural selection we, the dregs of the school, had found one another.

More often, I stood alone, unasked. Well, a girl can go to the bathroom only so many times before she has to concoct another reason why she's not dancing or otherwise thoroughly occupied. I pretended to be fascinated with the band, which was always a bad version of The Beatles, The Beach Boys, or The Lovin' Spoonful, and sometimes all three rolled into one. I fantasized that the lead singer would finally spot me and beckon me with his surly lips—"Yeah, you, the Chinese girl with the moon face. Come up here and do primitive movements with me onstage."

That would show them, all those guys who asked the other girls to dance.

And then reality would set in. That would never happen, not in a million trillion years. The lead singer? Singing to *me*? No way.

It's now May 1993, on a dark road somewhere between Northampton and Cambridge, Massachusetts. I'm in a van with Barbara Kingsolver, Ridley Pearson, Tad Bartimus, and Al Kooper. We're sprawled out over rows of bench seating. Bob Daitz, our road manager, is at the wheel. It's probably close to one in the morning, and we've just finished performing to a thousand screaming middle-agers. We should be exhausted. But instead, we're pumped full of adrenaline, steaming up the windows. Bob turns the air-conditioning on full-blast to reduce the body-odor factor.

Al slips a tape into the deck. The music is a compilation of his favorite oldies, including "Short Shorts" from his days with The Royal Teens. The song baits us: "Who wears short shorts?" Barbara, Tad, and I answer back: "We wear short shorts!" Forget napping on the way back to the hotel. Our teenage hormones are surging now.

Another song comes on and Al turns up the volume. I don't know the lyrics, but magic and miracles are floating in the air, and my voice somehow finds the harmony. A third above lead, a third below—I can switch back and forth effortlessly. Or perhaps I can't do either, but I'm so elated I *believe* I can sing with the best of them. *Ooh-wah, ooh-wah.* I could do backup for Carole King. Another song comes on. Al is singing lead and clapping. *Ooh-wah, ooh, wah.* I could do backup for Aretha Franklin. As if on cue, all of us place our feet on the ceiling of the van and begin to dance. Hot damn, I could be an Ikette. I'm dancing. I'm dancing to the moon. I'm bebopping the night away. I'm putting dirty footprints on the ceiling of a rental van. At last, finally, I'm doing primitive movements with the lead singer.

Come to think of it, on a couple of songs, I *was* the lead singer.

It was Al who suggested I sing lead on "These Boots Are Made for Walkin'." When I first saw my name written on the song list next to the title of this Nancy Sinatra classic, I was filled with the same sort of outrage I felt seeing my high school yearbook picture defaced with a mustache.

I called Kathi. "Tell Al to forget it. Of all the songs in the world, I hate that one the most. It's a joke. I wouldn't sing it in a million years."

Kathi, ever so diplomatic, broke things to me gently: "Actually, I think this could be a great song for you. You know how you always worry about whether you can really sing? Well, with 'Boots,' you don't need a great voice, just a lot of attitude."

"Attitude?"

"Yeah—you know, a bad-girl attitude. You could look cheap and sexy. You could smoke cigarettes and have guys fall all over you. Then again, you could do 'Bye Bye, Love.' That's always cute."

For my "Boots" outfit, I combed through a Frederick's of Hollywood catalogue and found a pair of zip-up patent-leather booties that would transform an ordinary pair of black business pumps into awesome, man-stomping thigh-high intimidators. At a local S&M shop, I bought a biker's cap and a leather dog leash, as well as studded cuffs, collar, and belt. Like any girl vying to be prom queen, I fretted over which of three outfits I should wear. The see-through leopard leotard? The tawdry fishnet lace? Or how about the classically simple little black bustier?

At the risk of sounding maudlin, I must confess I felt like Cinderella going to the ball. And like the birds and squirrels who dressed Disney's Cinderella in garlands of flowers and such, various well-wishers bestowed finishing touches upon me.

Lorraine Battle, the roadie who helped me do my two-minute costume change every night, thoughtfully gave me temporary tattoos, a dragon on my right biceps, a heart and dagger on my left shoulder. In Atlanta, Tabitha King handed me something in a plain brown wrapper and in big-sister fashion told me no respectable dominatrix should ever be seen without two essential fashion items: a choke chain and rubber titties with erect nipples. The manager of a lesbian bar where we played asked for my autograph shyly and, as a token of her appreciation, bequeathed a slightly frayed bullwhip that had seen a lot of action at a recent B&D ball. Each night Barbara found me cigarettes, which I smoked in dark stairwells to help put me in the proper politically incorrect mood.

And then the boys provided moral support onstage. Roy Blount, Jr., went down on bended knee and in wimplike fashion flinched as he tried to flick my Bic. When I growled, "Are you ready, boots? Start walking!" the other Remainder boys would fall supine and quake. Dave Marsh was especially sweet. As I started to stomp on him, he begged me—to no avail—not to stub out my burning cigarette on his chest; the hotel ashtray he had purloined and placed strategically was not visible to the audience. And each night the guys unselfishly volunteered to feature in the coup de grâce of my number.

"It's just not fair," Stephen King groused one night after the show. "Dave Barry got the whip jammed into his mouth *two* nights in a row! When's it going to be *my* turn?"

The roadies and ringers boosted my confidence in similar ways. I remember in particular what happened on a flight to Miami. Hoover, Mouse, and Jim were sitting in first class, while we band members had been relegated to coach. Hoover (a.k.a. Chris Rankin) must have been flirting outrageously with a flight attendant; after takeoff, she swept through the first-class curtains and handed me a Virgin Mary. "Compliments of Mr. Rankin, who is begging you please to whip him tonight," she said in honeyed tones. "If I were you, I'd whip him good, whip him till he *bleeds.*"

Recalling this outpouring of friendship brings tears to my

eyes. It also reminds me that I forgot to tell the boys where the butt of that whip had probably been before it was given to me. What a bad girl am I.

Around my fifteenth birthday, I truly became a bad girl. My forays into wickedness began with some low-grade sins. I started reading forbidden books, including *Catcher in the Rye*, which I had to buy twice because Christian family friends confiscated it from me. When a busybody caught me reading Krafft-Ebing's *Psychopathia Sexualis*, he told my mother that the contents of the book would corrupt my young mind and possibly cause me to go insane. My mother, not wanting to see me go insane, called in the minister. The minister, whose son had turned me down when I asked him to a Sadie Hawkins Day dance, came to our house to give me good counsel. He said, "If you can just be patient, if you can keep your virtue, one day, God willing"—here he swept out his arms, envisioning the heavenly promise—"hundreds of young men will be lined up around the block, waiting to ask you out!" And I thought to myself, Exactly what kind of fool does he take me for?

Cut to 1993, Washington, D.C. I am standing in my dominatrix costume, and outside the nightclub hundreds of young men are lined up to see me. All right, so there were hundreds of women as well, and they were there to see Stephen King. The point is, the minister's words came true. Oh, if only he knew how.

Soon those folks poured in to attend a preshow reception, and the band members had to go into the bar area to meet and greet the fans who had bought hundred-dollar tickets. For the reception, we Remainderettes donned wigs that Tabby King had bought us that day to give us a new look. Kathi had a long black Morticia style, Tad a Diana Ross afro. Mine was a perky blond number à la Carol Channing. And then Kathi and I put on sunglasses, exchanged laminated passes, and entered the dimly lit lounge.

We were sitting on barstools, sipping rum-and-tonics, when a woman approached Kathi and inspected her backstage pass. She gasped, her hand pressing her chest in pledge-allegiance fashion. "Amy Tan! I've loved *all* your books."

"Thanks," Kathi grunted, swishing the ice cubes in her drink. We waited for the woman's eyes to adjust to the dark and recognize her mistake, but instead, she took a seat and continued to lavish praise on me—or rather, Kathi.

"Really," she gushed, "your books are so wonderful they inspired me to write my own story."

Kathi gestured toward me. "By the way, did you meet Kathi Goldmark? She also sings with the band."

The woman gave me a perfunctory hi, then turned her full attention back to Kathi. "I have my manuscript in the car," she said. "I was wondering if maybe you could give me some advice—you know, about getting it published. If you'd like to read it now, I could go get it. . . ."

After a few minutes, I stood and said to Kathi, "I'll see you around."

Later I found out that Kathi gave her good advice: how to find a writers' group and an agent and so forth—the same suggestions I would have offered. But we both felt guilty, knowing that when the show started, the woman would instantly understand that we had fooled her, and then become angry. While changing in the dressing room, Kathi and I felt like teenagers who had let a silly prank go too far, not quite knowing how to retrieve it. I was thinking specifically about Stephen's book *Carrie* and how hurtful girls can be.

Then again, as Kathi pointed out, I had had to endure being ignored while sitting next to someone more in demand—rather like being back at the high school dance. *Not* that this social oversight on the woman's part justified what we did.

Just in case the woman we wronged is reading this, Kathi and I would like to say that we are very, very sorry. It was Tabby's fault for buying us wigs in the first place.

Right about now, I can hear my parents lecturing me: "You see? Having fun is bad. More important is family." And in a way, I discovered they were right. Because ultimately, the best part about being a Remainder was the fact that we became a family. We had family fun. . . .

Our life together included getting neck cramps while sleeping on the bus. Waking up and seeing how haggard we looked without coffee, without makeup. Teasing Dave Barry, who seemed to be perpetually sixteen years old. (I'm referring to his wrinkle-free skin, not his immature behavior.) Going to truck stops for $1.88 breakfasts, cheese-and-bacon hash browns plus grits. Propping food into Ridley's half-open mouth while he was sleeping. Taking a picture of same. Swearing on an oath of humiliating death never to reveal to anyone's spouse who among us had taken up smoking again. Opening our laptops, then not writing a single word. Mischievously telling the angst-ridden among us who had missed book deadlines how many novels, collections, essays, and movie scripts we had finished last year. Buying postcards of roadkill, and other trucker paraphernalia. Standing in line at the movies and noting how many people

On tour with The Rock Bottom Remainders in Miami, 1993.

thought Stephen King looked so much like Stephen King. Getting Tabby to name all the slang and literary words for *vagina*. Spreading rumors that Mouse had legally changed his name to Mouse. Trying on clothes with Barbara and assuring her she really did look cheap and tawdry. Listening to Bob Daitz on the phone, as he schmoozed nightclub owners into turning over a higher percentage of the take to us. Reading stories aloud from the *Weekly World News,* including the one about Chinese illegal aliens digging tunnels through the center of the earth.

Among the most memorable moments, I count those laced with pulse-surging terror. Our first day of rehearsal, for instance. Also our second day. As well as our third. Not to mention our first show. Our second show. Every show. The capper was my doing what I feared I would do all along: forget some of the lyrics to "Boots" one night, an omission that all the Remainders were kind enough to say I covered with absolute grace.

As to the most fun moments: Going to an Atlanta disco and learning Tina Turner dance steps from Bob and Lorraine. Dancing cheek to cheek with Joel Selvin during sound check in Northampton. Flinging hash browns in Dave Barry's face. Listening to everyone singing oldies at two in the morning on the bus, especially that rocker classic "Catch a Falling Star and Put It in Your Pocket." Posing vixenlike with Kathi on Al's waterbed in Nashville. Watching Tabby demonstrate transcolonic massage, her surefire method for eliminating constipation on tour.

And the special moments that bound us together as Remainders forever: Gathering around Tad when she confessed she was a bit off-key because she had to go in for scary medical tests the next day. Hearing Steve's recollections about his single mom and the fact that she knew before she died that his first novel (*Carrie*) would be published. Attending Roy's fancy college reunion in Nashville and assuring him afterward that he hadn't turned into an old fart. Receiving before each show a huge floral arrangement and personalized cartoon from Matt Groening. Closing our eyes and holding hands as Ridley's cousin Dodge, a chief of exhibitions at the National Gallery in Washington, led us to a room containing a Matisse masterpiece. Walking through the Vietnam Veterans Memorial with Tad, a former war correspondent, crying as we all sank lower into the valley of death. Listening to Dave Marsh talk about his love for his daughter Kristen. Hugging Barbara when she thought she had lost a piece of jewelry I had lent her. Hugging Tad after she called her mother in intensive care. Hugging and being hugged by everybody in moments of sadness and triumph, because hugging is something that never came naturally to me, and now it does.

When people ask me why I joined a rock-'n'-roll band, I tell them this: I wanted to have fun. I know the answer sounds superficial. But how else should I explain this irrepressible urge shaped by my childhood? Should I confess I wanted to waste my time and money? To be with friends who were purveyors of shame and corruption? To believe once again that miracles could happen?

No, this is the only logical answer: I simply wanted to have fun. And I finally learned how.

· arrival banquet ·

These are excerpts from my journal kept during a 1990 trip to China with my mother. It was our first trip there since the events at Tiananmen Square the year before.

Our plane is still on the ground in San Francisco, but there are already signs that we are in another country. A middle-aged woman sitting behind my mother clutches her meditation beads and prays aloud in Chinese that no one will take the seats next to her. The video instructions for fastening our seat belts are delivered in soothing Mandarin, albeit out of synch with the on-screen woman clicking a buckle in and out. The passengers in front of us converse loudly, discussing how to make a huge boom box fit into the tiny space under one of the seats in front of them.

"How many more hours to Shanghai?" one man shouts.

"Thirteen," comes the answer from a woman two rows away, "maybe thirteen and a half. If there are no more delays."

We are on a China Airlines flight, part of a planeload of people who will soon share dry mouth, stiff legs, and constipation. For most of the passengers on board, this is a return trip home. We, on the other hand, are among a small number of Americans going to *visit* China.

To be more precise, my mother and I are going to visit family: my two sisters, my aunt and uncle, and people connected to them by blood or marriage, which adds up to around fifty. And we are staying not in a tourist hotel, but in Auntie Elsie's apartment in Shanghai and in my uncle and aunt's apartment in Beijing. We have agreed ahead of time not to talk about politics.

Robert Foothorap, the only non-Chinese within earshot and eyesight, has come along as family friend, friendly photographer, chief baggage handler, and unbeknownst to him, American fallback position. If things become uncomfortable—my mother's biggest complaint about China is rampant filth—the "foreigner" will suddenly develop a need to stay in a hotel where he can take a hot American bath.

Eleven hours to go and my skin is already flaking off. Ma is knitting a pair of white pants for Melissa. She holds them up for me to see. The pattern is her very own, with lacelike cuffs at the bottom. In her mind's eye, her two-year-old granddaughter is the size of a six-year-old. Robert has his laptop on his tray table and is reading the instruction manual for his flight simulator, the adult version of a kiddie car wheel. And now dinner is served, a concoction of grays and browns: chunky beef atop a bed of noodles, sliced bamboo shoots and soggy snow peas decorating the sides.

"I guess this is a Western version of Oriental food," Robert says to Ma.

She peers at her meal. "This Chinese idea of American food," she corrects him. "This what I ate in China long time ago when we go to restaurant eat foreign dinner."

After recalling this, Ma decides to forgo her meal. She tells me in English that she is going to offer it to the man three seats away. I am about to stop her—explaining that no one would want to eat her leftovers—but it is too late. The man three seats away has happily accepted her offering. And now they are chatting animatedly in Chinese.

Our family in Shanghai apparently did not get our letter, the one explaining that we would be arriving at eight p.m. It is now eight-thirty Shanghai time, and they are lunging forward, two or three at once, hugging us, calling my mother "Ma" and "Grandma," and me "Auntie" and "Baby Sister." Hongchong, my brother-in-law, explains that they have been waiting at the airport since four in the afternoon, all seven of them: he and my sister, my nephew and his wife, my niece and her husband and their son.

"What a tragedy," I say in my fractured Mandarin. "You must have been anxious to pieces, waiting, wondering where we were."

"Oyo!" squeals my sister Yuhang. "Look at her, she speaks Chinese. Last time you were deaf and mute. Now you can speak!"

"Only a little," I say. Three years ago, I could manage to say "How are you?" Today I can talk about tragedies.

"Only a little?" She shakes her head in disbelief. "Hey!" she calls to the others. "Look how smart my little sister is. Now she can speak Chinese."

She hooks one arm in mine, the other in Ma's. We start to walk out of the airport. My twenty-five-year-old nephew, Xiao-dong, reaches for Ma's luggage. My mother immediately shouts back at him, "Be careful, be careful! Don't grab so fast." Xiao-dong leaps back and blinks.

"Last time, we lost a radio," Ma says. She is referring to our trip three years ago, when a Walkman disappeared somewhere between San Francisco check-in and Shanghai customs. Five minutes on Shanghai soil and Ma is already in her element. She is speaking rapid Shanghainese, dispensing advice and approval to her Chinese and American daughters, her son-in-law and grand-children. She is queen for the week, the one everybody has to obey, no talking back.

We pile our six bulging suitcases into a van, a *membao che*, or "bread truck," called so for its loaflike shape. Ten of us jam in, plus the driver, a young man who waves to us and is introduced as Xiao-dong's friend. The van is courtesy of someone's work unit—it's not clear whose. The windows are down, and as we take off, our nostrils are blasted by something that resembles the ripe stench of a pig farm on top of a toxic waste dump. As the van careens onto the road leading into Shanghai, I see that Robert finally believes some of what I have described as typical China: freestyle driving. He clutches the back of the seat ahead, alternately grinning and gritting his teeth as the van narrowly avoids a disastrous collision with a bicyclist, then a man pushing a cart, then three girls walking, then a huge truck barreling down on us in our lane. I am an optimist. If we crash, I may not have to finish the novel I'm working on.

We drive past high-rise office buildings sprouting up from farm fields of yesteryear, then come upon a residential neighborhood. Along the darkened roads we see that this part of Shanghai is still a hub of activity at nine p.m. Bicyclists flow by, their bells chiming.

"What's that? A store?" I ask Xiao-dong, pointing to an outdoor stall lit by a bare bulb.

"Hah?" He cups his hand to his ear.

"What is that?" I say, and point again. We have been writing back and forth in English, discussing his desire to immigrate to Canada, where my brother, John, lives.

Over the past year, Xiao-dong's written English, while still shaky, has improved. So has his understanding of life in a Western country—I hope. In an early letter, he had asked me to deposit $15,000 in a bank under his name and to pay for the foreign tuition at a $30,000-a-year university. He figured he could pay me back within the year, working part-time while he attended classes. I wrote back outlining a condensed course on Western economics: how much one could expect to earn with a part-time, minimum-wage salary, how much one had to set aside for taxes, medical insurance, bus fare, English classes at the YMCA, a new mattress, a new pair of Levi's, as well as contributions to rent, gas and electricity, food, and so on. I explained that I would pay for these expenses while he and his wife lived with my brother and sister-in-law in Calgary. But after the first year, he would be on his own.

"Individual freedom comes with a lot of responsibility," I wrote. "If your sister wants to immigrate later on, you will be responsible for bringing her over. We will talk about this when I come see you in China." And now I am in China.

"Is it a store?" I point again.

"Ssss-tore, ssss-tore," he says, searching for the meaning of this word. And then his face brightens with recognition. "Ah! Store!" He giggles. His wife, Jiming, looks and giggles too. It is the first time I've seen her smile. She is perhaps twenty-two, very pretty, and she has not yet said one word to me.

"*Ge-ti hu,*" he says softly. "We say *ge-ti hu,* no store. Small things, yes, can buy."

"Like a local shop?" I ask. "A neighborhood store?"

"Hah?" he says, cupping his ear again.

"What can you buy there?" I almost shout, as if he truly were hard of hearing.

He shrugs. "Auntie," he says carefully. "You don't go there."

"Why?"

"Auntie," he repeats. "You don't go there." Jiming giggles again. I understand nothing: not the English, not the meaning of the giggles, not the reason I shouldn't go there.

We pass trucks and buses with no headlights on.

"Why don't they turn on their lights?" I ask my mother. She asks Yuhang the same question.

"To save electricity," my sister answers, as though she believes this is a reasonable thing to do. I wonder whether our bus is saving electricity as well.

"What do you think?" I ask Robert. "Is this the China you expected?"

"Great," he says, his wide eyes still fixed on the road. "Just great."

And now we arrive in an area where, we are informed, model workers' apartments are located. Or is it the workers' model apartments? Dubious translations notwithstanding, this is where we find large housing complexes built by the *danwei,* or work units, supplied for a small monthly fee, probably the equivalent of a few dollars. The complexes are located on the outskirts of Shanghai in what used to be the old Chinese district.

I watch the street scene. Gone are the rabbit warrens of one-story tile-roofed constructions on twisty lanes, although we can see the remnants of some, piles of tumbled-down brick that have become roofless playhouses for children. In place of the old, modern concrete apartment buildings have sprung up. Those that are a few years old are five stories tall and have colorful laundry strewn over every balcony. The newest apartment buildings resemble luxury high-rises, with round turrets on top, similar to the rotating bars of some hotels. We are told the turrets do not actually rotate. God only knows why the architects thought this was an interesting feature to copy. We pass the skeletal beginnings of other buildings.

Our driver turns into the narrow opening in an iron fence, continuing onto what seems to be a sidewalk, until we arrive in front of one of hundreds of buildings painted a fading green.

The ten of us clamber up a dark flight of stairs littered with bicycles. And then Yuhang and Hongchong announce that we have arrived. They push a buzzer with great ceremony, and this emits a squawk that resembles the reaction of a baby being doused in cold water. *Wanh!*

Two locks click back, the door opens, the iron grate swings out, and we press forward into a fluorescent-lit apartment. Ah-mei, Auntie Elsie's servant from the old days, greets us, asking about plane delays, checking for exhaustion, directing where luggage should go. From now on, Robert and I observe, it's all Chinese or nothing. A wave of hands leads us into a sitting room. It contains a stiff-backed sofa with scratchy industrial-strength fabric, a matching armchair, four stools, a Formica table, a small green refrigerator, a telephone, and a television covered with a protective cloth.

I am led to a stool next to the table. A tumbler of tea is pressed into my hand. Excited voices buzz in my ear and I can't understand a word. I nod and smile frequently. This is what it will be like when I grow senile.

"What do I call her?" I ask my mother, gesturing to the servant. I am not old enough to call the servant by her given name.

"Call her Aiyi," my mother says. "Call her Auntie to show respect."

"Thank you, Aiyi," I say in Mandarin, holding up my tea. She laughs and shouts back a long string of Shanghainese.

Yuhang sweeps her arm out, inviting us to consider our living quarters. "What do you think? Comfortable enough?" Xiao-dong watches my face. It seems he is conscious of how his American auntie is reacting to her new surroundings.

My mother and I look around the room once again, smile and nod. "Very good," my mother says. "Clean." And I know she means it. I can tell she's relieved.

"More comfortable than staying at my house," agrees Yuhang. "Here you can be together. You have hot water. Of course, every day I will come and keep you company."

For me, anything would have been fine, as long as it was not a hotel. But this apartment exceeds my expectations. It is very clean. In fact, it is almost antiseptic, the fluorescent lighting casting a blue tinge on everything, including our faces. Robert looks slightly ill, although it may be the jet lag.

Auntie Elsie, Ma's old schoolmate who now lives in Vancouver, bought this place for her mother, who has since died. Now Elsie comes only once or twice a year. Aiyi, who has been the family servant for the past thirty years, lives here full-time as caretaker, subsisting on a salary of sixty yuan a month, about ten U.S. dollars.

The apartment is really two combined apartments, the dividing wall removed. It has a grand total of four and a half rooms, and a hallway, where we have piled our luggage.

To the left of the hallway is a kitchen, a space about six feet by nine, with built-in counters and cabinets, a sink with an overhead water heater that must be lit manually, and a propane-fueled two-burner portable cooktop. By Chinese standards, we are told, this is luxury.

Next to the kitchen is a bathroom, another luxury, because it is not shared with other apartments and it is equipped with hot water. The tub can easily fit one person if that person scrunches up with knees against chest. And the hot water must be heated ahead of time, with the overhead device in the kitchen. A tiny sink and a miniature version of a pull-chain toilet complete the amenities.

Off the hallway is a bedroom, big enough for only a small cot and a tea table. Aiyi will sleep there during our visit. Next to that—the supreme luxury—another bathroom, this one without benefit of hot water. The sight of the yellowed tub brings Ma to wonder aloud why no one teaches Chinese people to build better bathrooms. She points to the cracking tile. "Why so ugly?" Yuhang smiles and throws me a knowing expression that means, "Here we go again."

Robert's room is a living room turned into sleeping quarters.

His bed is a convertible sofa. He has a yellow-tiled balcony facing the wide street. Gray pants and white shirts are suspended from long bamboo poles that overhang the street. The laundry flaps in the wind like proletarian banners. At one end of Robert's room is a long built-in hutch, and on top of that is a picture of Auntie Elsie's mother, a dour, sparrowlike woman of some ninety-odd years when she died, and odd she was. My mother has already told me that the fierce old lady was an expert at playing one daughter off the other. She coddled Auntie Elsie, her favorite, and despised the other daughter for reasons unclear. Aiyi says she cared for the woman until she died, and she died in this very room, lying in the very bed that is now Robert's.

"Perfect," Robert says, making an A-okay sign. He seems relieved to have his own room, privacy, time away from nosy Chinese women.

The room Ma and I will share is Auntie Elsie's. It has a double bed with neatly folded quilts at the footboard. Aiyi tells us that Elsie paid extra money for the parquet floors, the built-in dresser and armoire, and the beige paint job.

We return to the sitting room. Aiyi has cooked us wonton. They are made with a vegetable that has no American name. I am told that it is wild clover, although maybe it is not actually wild, maybe it is not really clover. Whatever it is, the taste is pungent, with a lingering aroma that reminds me of garlic chives.

Aiyi is happy to see that Robert, the *nangko-ning*, or foreigner, is bent over his bowl of wontons, eating heartily. Ma remarks in English, "Yuhang happy, eating lots. She knows how to enjoy life." She tells Yuhang in Shanghainese that she has gained too much weight. Yuhang smiles and pats her cheeks. Then Ma tells me in English that Yuhang's face looks like a square, like her father's. She does not like to see reminders of her first husband in her daughter's face. Poor Yuhang. To me, she has a kind and generous face, guileless.

"Lose weight," she commands Yuhang.

Yuhang smiles, happy to be criticized like a child.

"How old are you now?" Ma asks.

Yuhang answers that she is fifty-three.

"Lose weight," Ma says. "Don't eat too much cholesterol." This last word is said in English. Yuhang nods without questioning what "cholesterol" means.

"Lose weight," I tell Robert.

"Chill out," he says.

Aiyi brings in another fresh-cooked batch of her wonderful wontons. Yuhang tells me that she and Aiyi will cook for us every day.

"Do you think you could stand to eat Chinese food morning, noon, and night?" I ask Robert. He nods. He looks like he's in Chinese heaven.

And now Ma is translating the Shanghainese conversation for Robert and me. The apartment, she explains, is a model building. It was built by the government as an example of high-standard living. We turn around and admire the room, nodding with much appreciation.

"When was it built?" Robert asks. "In the 1920s or 1930s?" He's being sincere.

"No!" my mother says. "Brand-new! Yes, can you imagine?" She throws him a secret smile.

Xiao-dong asks me in painful English, "Auntie, soon you will like to see my horse?"

"Horse?" I ask. Have conditions improved so much that my nephew can now afford to play polo in his spare time? I ask him in Mandarin, "You have a horse?" It turns out he meant "house." He adds the burr of Shanghainese to his English.

"Correct him," my mother tells me. "How he can go Canada, speak English like that?"

"Howww-sss," I say for him.

"Harrwww-sss," he says back for me.

"*Bu-shr* har!" my mother says to him. "Don't say 'har.' How. How, how, how—like *hau, hau, hau.*" Good, good, good.

"How, how, how," Xiao-dong whispers.

I know my mother is not trying to intimidate Xiao-dong. She is only doing for her grandson what no one did for her: teaching him correct English so that he does not have to suffer the same pain she has had to endure—being misunderstood at banks, misdiagnosed by doctors, ignored by her teenage children. Poor service, bad treatment, no respect—that's the penalty for not speaking English well in America.

It is now five a.m. After a half-hour struggle, I have given up. I can no longer sleep. My mother and I lie wrapped in our quilts, encased like two mummies. It is still dark, but I can see my mother's eyes are open too.

"Already awake?" I ask.

"How can I sleep?" she grumbles.

We are listening to peddlers shouting to one another on the street. Bicyclists ring their bells every few seconds. One would think it was already the middle of a busy market day.

Once we are up, we find Aiyi engaged in an efficient buzz of activity. She has heated water in the kitchen to drain into the bathroom tub. She has filled the thermos with freshly boiled water for our instant coffee. I've been told Shanghai has one of the most polluted water systems in the world: hepatitis and industrial toxins right out of the tap.

Aiyi is cleaning out the tub in preparation for our fragile American skins. When it's my turn to bathe, it takes ten minutes to fill the tub with about an inch of hot water, mixed with a little cold. It does not seem wise to wait another hour for the tub to fill. So I crouch in it, using my washcloth to swipe myself clean.

At six a.m., we are ready to go to the market to shop for our breakfast. Robert has loaded himself down with three cameras draped over his photo jacket. Ma has elected to stay in the apartment, in case Yuhang arrives. She stuffs my hand with a fifty-yuan note, telling me to make sure I pay for the groceries. Aiyi is smiling broadly, waiting for us. She clutches a plastic bag and a food saver. Just as we are about to leave, a small argument in Shanghainese erupts between Aiyi and Ma. Ma is insisting that we pay for everything. Aiyi is assuring her that she will keep track of all expenses and can wait to be reimbursed later. At least that's what it seems like they're saying, to judge from the hand gestures, the shoving of money back and forth. These fights are for the sake of politeness.

Outside we find the air is cool but not cold. The sky is bluish-gray, as if the outdoors too were lit by fluorescent bulbs. As soon as we cross the street—which is devoid of cars—we see people streaming by on bicycles and turning around to stare. We are not in a part of town that caters to tourists. It is a sure bet that no Westerners have vacationed in this part of Shanghai before. I tell Aiyi in Mandarin that the weather seems quite nice, not too cold, not too hot, although maybe it looks like rain. Thank God for my colloquial Chinese handbook and its vacuous phrases. Aiyi answers me in rapid Shanghainese. After a few more polite exchanges like this, I turn to Robert. "Aiyi speaks only Shanghainese," I inform him. "I don't speak Shanghainese. We're in trouble."

But in fact, we are not. Aiyi, like my relatives, is adept at sign language and facial expressions, as well as speech intonations that make crystal-clear what she means to tell us: "This way," "That way," and "Sure, it's okay to stop and take a photo—if it's quick."

We cut through a large apartment complex to a growing path of vendors huddled near their vegetables. Robert begins snapping pictures, motioning for permission with his eyebrows. The vendors grin. As we walk along, he continues to attract a crowd, an amiable group of people who seem perfectly at ease posing or simply carrying on with their business.

In the open market square, we stare at the array of vegetables piled high in perfect mounds. I had expected this part of Shanghai to be drab. And in a way it is. The clothing of all but the young children is a monotonous gray or blue, dyed in the same vat. But the drab clothes are the perfect accompaniment to the sharp colors of the morning market. There are clean-white turnips with purple-green tops, chartreuse-green-and-white cabbages, and tin buckets of bloody eels.

We watch a young man with dusty hair grab a wriggling black eel. The eel's mouth is wide open, its tongue moving back and forth. I cannot hide my anthropomorphic sentimentality. It looks as if the creature is crying for help. And then—*whack!*—the head is sliced off with the short knife. The eel's mouth continues to open and close, and the body writhes as the young man slowly slices it open—straight down the back, causing chills to run up mine. Robert clicks off pictures. The bucket is now a mass of eels swirling in their own bright blood. I can't help it: my lips spread out in disgust. And the young man, sensing I am a judgmental foreigner, shouts and waves Robert and me away.

When Aiyi points to the eels and asks me whether I want to eat them, I answer, "They taste good, but look ugly." She takes this as my enthusiasm to eat eels tonight. Upon trying to bargain with this free-market vendor, she discovers he has jacked his prices up. She argues with him a bit, and he grunts and motions his thumb toward me. She gives up and, grabbing my elbow, directs me toward one of the enclosed government markets where the prices are fixed.

Here the vendors sell steamed baskets of *xiao loong bao,* the dumplings Shanghai is famous for—delicately flavored rounds of meat and vegetables encased in a thin rice-flour pastry. Aiyi motions for me to stand off to the side, encouraging me to disappear the best I can with a roomful of people staring at me from my red lipstick to my cowboy-style boots.

I get the sense this place sells food only to bona fide workers. As the interloper, I'm reminded of the children's story "The Little Red Hen." "And who will help me make this bread?" the Little Red Hen asked her fellow commune animals. "Not I," said the pig. I'm the lazy capitalist pig who did no work and now wants to eat up the bread.

Aiyi stands in line, pretending she doesn't know me. At the head of the line is a lectern that towers over the customers. Behind that, a woman dispenses little pieces of paper. As much as I can gather from our limited means of discourse, Aiyi is going to buy chits for some *xiao loong bao.*

Customers sit on stools, hunched over round tables. A grandmother tosses dumplings into her grandson's mouth. Workers down huge bowls filled with dumplings; once they are finished, they stand up and push away from the table. Their places are immediately taken by other customers, one of whom pours a basketful of dumplings into an abandoned bowl and begins to eat with used chopsticks. Ma would not approve. According to her, such dirty habits are not Chinese, they are Communist—sharing everything, including germs.

At a window, women wearing round white caps take our order for dumplings, and after five minutes our number is called and we walk away with two baskets. Aiyi goes to a table, picks up a pair of chopsticks perched on a used bowl, and with them heaves the steaming dumplings into the food saver. This done, she motions for Robert and me to follow, although not too closely. There are bargains still to be found, and she won't have us interfering with her superb shopping skills.

We are outside again, only this time on the other side of the market square. Here we find long stalls covered with awnings, where we can buy all manner of assorted breakfast goodies—a fried version of *xiao loong bao,* various noodle soups cooked in broth, bean curd soup, and *da bing,* "big bread." It smells and looks wonderful, I'm instantly starved, and I want to taste everything.

It is now six-thirty a.m., and the stalls are jammed with customers. The outdoor eating tables are full, every bench space taken. More people are lined up to buy breakfast, and they turn and stare as we approach, this curious entourage of short sixty-year-old Chinese lady, younger Chinese-American woman wearing black Lycra stretch clothes, and silver-haired man wearing thousands of dollars' worth of photography equipment around his neck. Supertourist. Out here, people stare but also smile. A woman wearing pajamas stares at my boots. A young man comes up to Robert and says, "Hello."

"American," Robert says, pointing to his chest.

"Meigwo-ren," I translate. *"Jyou jin-shan."* Old Gold Mountain, the name still used in China to refer to San Francisco. The man asks me if I'm American too. I nod, then add that my mother is Shanghainese. He nods and smiles.

Aiyi goes to stand in the *da bing* line. I stand behind her, watching the activity. A man sporting what I have come to identify as the official government cook's cap rolls the *bing* out in fat doughy balls. He then smashes each of the balls down the middle in one motion, pats each out with a swirl of his palm, then slaps it against the side of a coal-fired oil drum. Using only his fingers, he peels off the *bing* that have turned golden-brown—never mind tongs or hot pads when your hands are as good as asbestos-coated from daily trials by fire. Each *bing* is tossed onto a board, brushed with a thin gloss of oil, then sprinkled with sesame seeds.

After four or five *bing* undergo this ritual, Aiyi is at the head of the line. I watch her order and pay with grime-coated slips of paper the size of stamps, the weight of tissue paper. The chits are tossed into a plastic bowl, along with other colored stamps. Together they look like confetti. I cannot figure out this system of accounting, one that could be easily upset by a puff of wind.

And now Aiyi returns to us. Success! She displays the plastic sacks filled with steaming rounds of mouthwatering *da bing*.

"Let's go home!" she says.

Aiyi will not eat breakfast with us, despite Ma's insistence. And so it's just Robert, Ma, and I around the small Formica table, neighbors from the buildings next door pointing to us. Our very first breakfast in China: the wonderful treats Aiyi bought at the market, along with rice porridge, purloined airline peanuts, and Nescafé we bought, seasoned with airline dairy creamer. As we eat, we meticulously set aside portions for Aiyi, including airline peanuts.

Immediately after breakfast, Xiao-dong arrives and we leave for the market again, this time to buy ingredients for lunch. Aiyi, Yuhang, and Ma lead the way to the vegetable stalls and the tubs of fish and eels. I walk behind with Xiao-dong. We take turns pointing to things in the market. He names them for me in Mandarin, I name them in English. I have my videocamera resting on my shoulder, filming from a distance. Robert lags behind shooting pictures, waving to us to go on without him, he'll catch up. He is doing his best not to be commandeered by four strong-willed Chinese women. We'll see how long he can last.

Back home, the morning's take is unwrapped in the kitchen. We have bought eel, small freshwater blue crabs, still alive, and all manner of vegetables. The crabs, Ma tells me, cost 165 renmenbi. There are eleven, so they cost fifteen renmenbi each, about four U.S. dollars, more than what an average Chinese worker makes in a day. Yuhang has paid for these herself, her tribute to our mother and to me, her little sister. I do not tell Yuhang that I do not like crab.

"Look here," Ma says to me. "Two tastes. This one female, this one male." For some reason my mother has selected this opportunity—in a cramped kitchen in Shanghai—to try to teach me how to cook. Perhaps this is for Yuhang's benefit as well—the cooking lessons a mother would have taught her daughter.

"Female best," she continues. She shows me how they are the ones with rounded bottoms, while the males are flat, so there is less to eat. "You eat all the juicy insides that pour out."

Aiyi and Yuhang press the legs of the crabs inward and then tie them with white string. They are immobile, alive and awaiting their steam bath.

"The crabs," Yuhang says, "have very bad tempers. Very fierce."

All at once I hear loud explosions. I can't help it, I think about guns, soldiers shooting. I head for the sitting room. "What's that?" I ask Xiao-dong in Chinese. He looks up from a Time-Life picture book about China that I brought. He acts as if he hasn't heard anything.

"That noise," I say. The explosions continue.

"Ah," he says. *"Pian pao."* He pantomimes lighting something on the ground, watching it explode. Oh, firecracker.

I feel foolish. "Did someone get married?" I ask.

He stands up, looks out the window. "It may be a wedding," he says in Mandarin. "Although probably it's to congratulate someone who has finally moved into a new home in the neighborhood."

I recall my niece's telling me that the waiting list for individual apartments is very long, one has to wait for seventeen years.

And now lunch is ready for serving. Aiyi brings the steaming crabs to the table. She sets down two bowls of dipping sauce: a dark soy sauce mixed with rice vinegar and ginger. The crabs are still bound in their ropes. Their bright blue has faded to gray. Yuhang picks a fat one for Ma, another fat one for me. Xiao-dong and Robert help themselves.

"Oyo! Lucky you, you got a female," Yuhang tells me. "Look." She taps the bottom of the crab, the rounded stomach. She snips off the strings. I feel like a child, fearful about eating the crab, unable to say no, completely at the mercy of my mother and Aiyi. Robert has no such qualms. He loves crab.

Ma demonstrates how to break open the body. *Crack!* I feel as if I were in sixth-grade science class. Behold, the internal organs. Xiao-dong is sucking on his little crab. Yuhang has broken a leg off hers and is using it as an entrenching tool. She watches as I poke at my crab. "Eat this part first," she says. I stare at an orange mass.

"What is it?" I whisper to my mother.

"Don't ask," she says. "You no wanna know. Eat." I stare at the orangy part again, certain it must be crab brains.

"Eat," commands Yuhang. "That's the best part. Eat it before it turns bad."

"How will it turn bad?" I say.

She reaches over with her crab leg and picks out the orange stuff. "Eat before it gets cold."

I had promised myself that my attitude about living in China would be "Come what may, take what comes." I pour a heavy dose of sauce and put the orange goo in my mouth. It has a creamy texture, and is slightly fishy. I don't like it, but I have not yet retched.

"Eat this." Yuhang dredges out more orange goo. "Don't waste any of it. It's too good."

I crack off a leg and dutifully begin to dig and shove and swallow, dig and shove and swallow, dig—

"Don't eat that!" I hear my mother say.

Yuhang looks over to see what I am doing to my crab. She laughs and then scolds me. "Oyo, don't eat that." She points to something that to me is indistinguishable from the orange stuff they said was so exquisite.

"Why?" I ask. "Why is this part different?"

"Anh!" she exclaims—perhaps she can't believe she has such a stupid sister. *"Da bien."* She pinches her mouth shut.

I stare at my crab. *Da bien.* Poop. I think about that American expression used to describe stupid people. Shit for brains. That's what I have in front of me. A miniature toilet bowl.

My mother takes the crab out of my hands and quickly removes the offending part. "Eat." She digs out a piece of fleshy meat, then gives the crab back to me.

I slowly start to eat again. This part does not taste so bad. I dip the meat in the vinegary sauce and eat with concentration, glad to be almost halfway through this ordeal. This part actually tastes quite good. Xiao-dong is relishing this feast. He has almost finished his crab and is poking and sucking at every possible crevice.

"Don't eat that!" I hear my mother say again.

"Don't eat what?" I ask.

She points. I don't understand what she is pointing to. "This." It is a six-sided piece, what looks like a soft piece of cartilage. "If you eat it," she explains, "it leaves the body cold."

"How does it do that?"

"Don't eat it," she says.

"But why does it leave the body cold? What does that mean?"

"Ai!" my mother says. "Don't ask why. It's enough that I tell you not to eat it."

Yuhang shakes her head. "Don't eat it." She points to another grayish mass. "And don't eat this part." To me it looks the same as the rest of the crab meat. I'm confused, a hostage forced to obey the advice and opinions of my elders.

I think about the tiny softshell crabs, of eating them, of my upcoming two weeks of life in China. The legs are bound up, movement restricted. There are exquisite tastes to be found, but the moment when one can find them is brief, transitory. If one waits too long, the flavor is lost, the taste becomes ordinary. And inside these crabs is knowledge, the kind I don't have: what is good, what is bad, and why, and why I shouldn't ask, and what will happen if I don't listen.

Welcome back to China.

·joy luck and hollywood·

This was written in response to interview questions posed by the Los Angeles Times. *I sat down one night and e-mailed my answers. A version of those was used for a story that ran on September 5, 1993.*

I was an unlikely person to get involved with filmmaking. I've never had a particular infatuation with Hollywood or tabloid stories of its stars—well, maybe I've taken a glance now and then at gossip having to do with Robert Redford. For the most part, though, I've always preferred to daydream about characters of my own making. At the same time, I didn't hold any grudges against movies as an art form. I wasn't tearing my hair out, vowing, "As God is my witness, I'll show the world how movies really should be made!" To put it simply, I was neither fan nor foe.

During the last decade, in an effort to control how I consumed my time, my appetite for television and movies dwindled to anorexic level. I spent whatever available hours I had reading or writing. Until recently, I was not in the habit of going to the movies, although, because of a nine-month book promotion schedule, I sometimes saw them as "in-flight entertainment" but on anemic screens. Occasionally, I rented videos of former box-office hits. My choices took into consideration which movies my husband might enjoy as well. In other words, no tearjerkers about reincarnated lovers and such.

But there was a period in my life, childhood, when I thought movies were the ultimate luxury. Perhaps once a month, my parents gave my brothers and me fifty cents each to see a matinee with friends—real doozies like *The Angry Red Planet*, *The Fly*, *Around the World in 80 Days*, *Flower Drum Song*, but not *The World of Suzie Wong* (too adult, according to my parents). I also saw *The Parent Trap*, *101 Dalmatians*, *Old Yeller*, *The Absent-Minded Professor*—a lot of Disney movies. I wanted to draw the cartoons that went into animated films.

Mostly I saw old movies on television, my favorite being *The Wizard of Oz*, which I watched faithfully every year on our black-and-white set, and continued to be awed by, especially when I saw it on another family's color television. I identified with Dorothy, a girl who felt she was misunderstood and went searching for a sense of home. Plus she had the greatest shoes, ruby slippers, which could take her anywhere her heart desired. But Kansas? If I had been in her shoes, I would have stayed in Oz and started a new life as a torch singer.

Shoes became an imaginative device for me as a fiction writer, especially if I was writing about a period outside my life experience. I would place myself in my character's shoes, look down at them, and start walking. When I looked up, I would see the scenery in front of me, say, China in the 1920s. I would note what was around me: To my left, a doorway, the light streaming through. To my right, a group of people staring at me critically. Up close, a coffin holding a woman, who no longer saw falseness or faults in others.

Now that I think of it, perhaps my imagination has always

worked like a movie camera, at least in terms of visual framing. Like the camera, I do five or six "setups," as I now know them to be called, those camera angles required to capture each scene from various audience perspectives. In fiction, however, I am both the audience and the character. And I never see the back of my own head.

Moreover, fiction, as opposed to film, allows me to include any characters I want; I don't need a casting agent. I can write a scene with a thousand angels dancing in the sky; I don't worry about costumes, or special effects, or choreography, or liability insurance. In fiction, I can revise ad nauseam, tossing out countless pages at a time, as well as the expensive locations that come with them. I can invent new characters, remove others. I'm not on a seventy-seven-day writing schedule. No union fines me if I make my characters work through the scenes with me after midnight or on weekends. My characters do not become upset when I tell them I've eliminated their scene. Nor do they ever change my lines and ad-lib something they think is better.

A fiction writer has the perquisites of solitude, artistic freedom, and control. She has the luxury to go into a funk for two weeks and not get anything done. Why would any writer in her right mind ever consider making a movie instead? That's like going from being a monk or a nun to serving as a camp counselor for hundreds of problem children.

I can say only that I went to Hollywood for many of the same reasons Dorothy found herself in Oz. I met a lot of remarkably nice people along the way. And they had heart and brains and courage.

Didn't Anyone Warn You?

In 1988, before *The Joy Luck Club* was published, I attended a screenwriting workshop at the Squaw Valley Community of Writers in northern California. I went partly because it was a plum to get into the program, and largely because I felt I could learn techniques about character development that would benefit my fiction.

Ten others and I attended these sessions to discover where our best stories came from—the answer being from our worst life experiences. We collaborated on an adaptation of a short story, during which I discovered how much I preferred working solo. Writing with others seemed a feat of coordination not unlike those three-legged races I used to run as a kid. How many different ways can a character enter a doorway? Ask four screenwriters.

At the workshop, we also heard war stories. One novelist-turned-screenwriter was still gnashing his teeth in regret. They had taken his literary novel, trampled it with pat formulas, padded it with shapely thighs. In the hierarchy of power and respect, they treated him as though he ranked somewhere below bacteria. They kicked him off the set. Later, he had to endure watching the movie with an audience that included his squirming literary friends, all of whom developed simultaneous coughing fits.

"Did you feel the movie ruined your novel?" someone from the workshop asked. "No," he said. "It ruined my life." Yet later I heard he was doing another screenplay. Why? What was the addiction?

The Blow-by-Blow

As well as I can remember, here is the chronology of *The Joy Luck Club*'s being made into a movie:

October 1987: Went to China for the first time.

November 1987: Sold the book proposal to Putnam.

March 1988: Met Janet Yang, an executive at MCA/Universal. Janet had read the three stories that my agent, Sandy Dijkstra, had sold to Putnam as the basis for a book. Janet and I met in an outdoor café in San Francisco's North Beach, and there she told me how much she loved the stories, how she sensed she was reading about herself. That's all she wanted to say, that she was a fan. As I recall, she felt the book would be a hard sell as a movie. But if there was interest once the book was out, she would be waiting in the wings to help.

March 1989: *The Joy Luck Club* published. After two weeks, it hit the bestseller lists, much to everyone's surprise, including mine. While I was still trying to reason that this was a temporary fluke, my literary agent started to field inquiries from movie and television producers. Sandy advised that we find a film agent, and to that end she linked me up with Sally Willcox of Creative Artists Agency, who handles a number of authors.

During the next few months, between my book promotion responsibilities, I met with a dozen or so producers and studio execs. Out of these meetings, I received five or six offers to option the book. I did not accept any of them, because I was still not sure the book should be a movie. Of course, one could get option money and the movie might never be made. But I had this little worry running through my head: What if the movie was made and it was a terrible depiction of Asian-Americans? What if the movie showed women wearing coolie hats and tight dresses slit up their thighs? What if they were given pointy, red-lacquered fingernails that they used to stab their philandering white boyfriends? (Don't laugh—Lou, my husband, saw those images on television the very day I received an option offer.)

August 1989: Met Wayne Wang. After a wonderful conversation about everything from the book to family to Asians and Asian-Americans in the arts, I knew intuitively that Wayne was the right person to direct the movie—if ever there should be a movie. I was glad to meet him, and we thought we could work together on something in the future regardless of what happened to this movie. I thought I could learn from him creatively—about stories, about the emotion of an image.

January 1990: Team formation. With Wayne, I met the screenwriter Ron Bass at the Hotel Bel-Air in Los Angeles. Ron was the only person I met who knew exactly how to turn the book into a movie. He began with a specific analysis about each of the families depicted. I had read many reviews of *Joy Luck*, but his insights about the characters as people—and not literary themes—made me feel that he knew the book better than I did.

Wayne and I mentioned the problem of so many stories, so many characters, how everyone thought it impossible to make a coherent movie out of the whole book.

"Impossible?" Ron said. "Why is it impossible? Let me tell you a few of my ideas." He pulled out a yellow pad with two pages of an outline. "First, we keep all the characters, all the stories. Second, we do what everyone in the industry tells you not to do: we use a lot of voice-over. Third, we use a wraparound that allows us to tell the stories through an ensemble, no single lead character." The book could succeed as a movie, he said, only if we broke all the rules. And for the next hour and a half, he explained in detail how the rules would be broken.

Ron also thought I should be involved in the screenwriting. I wasn't interested. I wanted to leave the book in these guys' hands and go on with my work as a fiction writer. But then he said something irresistible to a writer: "I think I could help you find the poetry of the scene." You have to realize that Ron used to be an entertainment lawyer. He knows exactly what to say to people to get them on his side.

We agreed with a handshake that we three would form a team. We would also seek creative control. Those two conditions were inviolable, and without them, I would not option the book. The way I figured it, we had about a one-in-a-million chance of getting a movie made, but if it did happen, we'd have a great time.

Spring 1990: Collaboration set up. Oliver Stone agreed to be our executive co-producer. Janet Yang, who was by then vice-president of Stone's production company, Ixtlan, had arranged a meeting with him. We met at an editing studio in Santa Monica, where he was cutting *The Doors.* He said he would help us make *The Joy Luck Club* under his deal with Carolco.

Fall 1990: Contract trouble. After six months of negotiating, we found it did not guarantee us the creative control we required, so we walked away from the Carolco deal. Meanwhile, Oliver and Janet continued to help us look for financing elsewhere. They agreed to serve as godfather and godmother, as we sought out the best resources for making the film.

January 1991: New plan of action. After the Carolco deal

fell through, Ron believed the only chance we would have for creative control was by developing the screenplay "on spec." Ron, Wayne, and I spent three days outlining the script in a narrative format that could be plugged into the grammar of a screenplay.

August–November 1991: Progress sure and steady. Ron and I completed the first draft of the screenplay.

March 1992: Met with Disney Studios chairman Jeffrey Katzenberg, and Kathryn Galan and Henry Huang of Disney and its Hollywood Pictures (Galan was then a Hollywood Pictures vice-president, Huang a Hollywood Pictures creative executive). Katzenberg had read the script, and after an informal discussion, we had a handshake deal. He gave us what we wanted—creative control—and he expressed enormous respect for Wayne as a filmmaker. We would be able to make our movie like an independent production, and we'd be supported by Hollywood Pictures, headed by Ricardo Mestres.

Later, in *Premiere* magazine, I read about the "control-freakism" that reportedly runs rampant at Disney. Naturally, I wondered what would happen in our association with Disney.

October 1992: Filming begun.

February 1993: China filming begun.

March 1993: Principal photography completed.

April 1993: Saw the first rough cut.

I Take a Meeting

I can safely say that no one I met in Hollywood resembled my imaginings of a high-powered Hollywood type, with the possible exception of Oliver Stone, who happens to look exactly like

Oliver Stone. I pictured women who wore a lot of makeup, tanned men who smoked cigars. Most of the film people I met were shockingly young and obsessively healthy, at least compared with writers I know. They sipped water, not bourbon. They didn't smoke. They wore jeans or leggings, baseball caps and running shoes. They drove Ford Broncos. Of course, I didn't realize until later: That *was* the Hollywood type.

The one Hollywoodish trait I noticed with great delight among some producers I met during the early days of book-option talk was their easy mention of Bob, Jane, Steven, and Francis, as if I too were on a first-name basis with Redford, Fonda, Spielberg, and Coppola.

Another surprise: There was never an organized agenda to meetings. People talked in broad, imprecise terms. I thought it was code for something else, shorthand for all kinds of criteria. But now that I've been in the business for a while, I realize that people leave the precision points to the lawyers.

I always felt people treated me with respect, with such enormous respect, in fact, that I felt like a fraud. Much to my surprise, given the horror stories I'd heard, no one ever discouraged me from being part of the filmmaking process. They wanted me to be involved as much as possible. I was told I would be a producer, along with Wayne, Ron, and later Patrick Markey, who came in during pre-production. But why was I a producer? The reasons: I had selected the director and the screenwriter, we had developed the script on spec, we asked for and obtained creative control. And so I often felt enormously guilty, especially during production, when I was at home writing fiction and not sitting (or freezing) on the set with everyone else.

I still find it odd to see my credits on the screen as screenwriter *and* producer. When I started this process, I didn't know what any of the terms meant: spec, development, turnaround, green-light, above the line, below the line, scale, production, post, bond company, principal photography, second unit—let alone the credits, which I used to ignore at the end of movies: first AD, gaffer, best boy, PA, and so on.

The only part of moviemaking that I dislike is the business side. And there is a lot of business. I've tried to stay away from business as much as possible; the person who handled the business details was Patrick Markey, bless his heart. I thought he had the worst job as producer—talking to people about money and contracts and the like. Yet he never tired of it and, amazingly, never lost his sense of diplomacy.

Seminar in Screenwriting

The day the bombs fell on Baghdad in 1991, Ron, Wayne, and I started to outline our screenplay. Our meetings were intense, extremely organized, filled with humor and mutual respect. We had a few minor differences in work styles. Ron liked to get up at two-thirty every morning and start writing; he ate only one meal a day, dinner. Wayne and I were more leisurely, preferring to start at eight or eight-thirty, and for some reason, gosh darn it, we needed lunch, which we often ate during our meetings. Ron worked with yellow pads and a box of a hundred sharpened pencils. I worked with a laptop and a portable printer. Wayne thought aloud.

We discussed the major elements of the movie, the emotional moments, as well as our view on the use of voice-over, subtitles, flashbacks, and other techniques. We then started to outline the entire movie, scene by scene. Ron had allocated the number of pages for each scene. Three for the opening party. Four and a half for the revelation of the letter from June's Chinese half sisters in Golden Gate Park. And so forth.

I didn't have a lot to contribute in those early days, since I barely even recognized the terms being bandied about. So I volunteered to be the chief scribe, taking notes on my laptop. Ron and Wayne worried that I was denigrating myself, and I told them I had no problems whatsoever with self-esteem. I knew when to shut up, until I had something to say, but when I got up to speed, they would definitely know it. For now, I was happy to be the screenwriting student, soaking up as much as I could. I asked a lot of questions. How does this scene make a transition into the next? What should we feel at the end of this scene?

After three days, we had sixty single-spaced pages of notes, a narrative form of the script. I volunteered to do the first draft. Ron would then revise it, and thus I would be able to learn from my mistakes. And then we would revise each other, making sure we agreed on every single word, especially in dialogue. The process of collaboration turned out to be, much to my relief, more like a relay race than a three-legged one. It fit my work style perfectly—to be engaged in intense creative discussions first, then allowed to go off and write by myself. Between drafts, Ron and I would meet with Wayne to get his take on how the script was going. It was important that the three of us be in alignment at every step. We were on the phone with one another almost daily.

Our collaboration was so thorough that by the time we saw screenings of the movie, we often could not remember who had written what. There's one line audiences seem to love, when the character Rose says to her mother, "I like being tragic, Ma—I learned it from you." Ron and I argue over who wrote that line. He says I did. I say he did.

I can't remember any major disagreements. Certainly we had "discussions," and when we didn't reach an immediate consensus, both Ron and Wayne would start pacing like stereotypical expectant dads. The project itself was always paramount, and each of us was willing to find a solution that satisfied everyone.

And so our "disagreements" went like this: Ron would say, "I'm concerned." Or Wayne would say, "I'm worried." Or I would say, "I'm confused." We would discuss the difficulty, separating out the strands of what was both important and problematic. And in this logical way, we'd get rid of problems, without sacrificing what was essential.

I would characterize Ron, the former lawyer, as our chief negotiator in most cases. If I said something like, "I'm worried about this line, it just seems wrong," he would reply, "Tell me exactly what bothers you about it." I'd start off nebulous, because I didn't know what to say specifically: "It just doesn't seem like something a Chinese mother would say." Ron would probe further: "Is it the words or the thought or the emotion?" Back and forth we would go, until we had saved the baby, thrown out the bathwater, and added a nice warm towel.

I Learn to Argue

We handled our differences this way throughout the project—screenplay development, casting, filming, editing. While we shared equal creative control, each of us took on a specific role as arbiter. In general (but not always), I was the arbiter of character questions—that is, whether a scene seemed true to the heart and soul of what I felt about the characters as I knew them. Ron's hobbyhorse was overall structure and emotional truth—namely, did the particular "beats" of the scenes lead to what we had intended? Was each emotional moment truly earned, or did it get shorthanded and appear contrived? Wayne, we realized, had to be the final arbiter on everything, because he was, after all, the director, and had to feel that everything was as he wanted to see it on screen.

Only once did I not get what I wanted. It was a late afternoon and we were all a bit punchy with fatigue and the natural high of knowing we were lines from having the script we all wanted. Ron and Wayne decided we needed a new scene, a sex scene between a young woman in the 1940s and the man she has fallen in love with. To me, the idea of a sex scene was an automatic red flag for exploitation and gratuitous thrills. Ron and Wayne asserted the importance of showing how quickly and thoroughly the character lost herself to this playboy. I countered that they wanted the requisite sex scene because they were boys. They retorted that I was nervous about seeing a sex scene with a character who emotionally represented my mother.

Our discussion degenerated from there:

"Just how do you see this sex scene happening?" I asked.

"They're at the back of the nightclub stage," Ron said.

"Onstage? In public?"

"No, no, it's after hours. And Ying Ying is leaning back as the playboy starts to kiss her tenderly, then more passionately—"

"They're *standing?*"

"Right, standing up. And then the bad man starts to brutally make love to her—"

"Standing *up?*"

"Right."

"I see. . . . Does he make love to her from the front or the rear? You see, I have to know these things, because it makes a difference whether we get a PG rating or an R."

"From the front, of course."

After Wayne added a few more details having to do with silhouettes and voice-over, he said, "All right, we agree, then—now let's write the scene."

I stood up and said: "You two want to do that scene, you write the scene. How long does it take you guys to do sex? Five minutes? Great, I'm going out now for the postcoital cigarette." And when I shut the door behind me, I could hear them howling in the room. Anyway, that was the best time I had not writing something. And now that the scene is on the screen, I'm rather fond of it.

The Asian Question

From the beginning, I had a fair amount of cynicism about the possibilities of turning a book about Asian-Americans into a movie. I knew there would be no big-name stars, no male lead, no car chase or trains being blown up. I tried to figure in my head what a movie could do to distort the story into something commercial and tailored to a mass audience. Turn it into an interracial love story? An internal dialogue ran through my head in which a high-powered producer told us, "Loved the book, loved the script. Only one thing I'd change: Make the mothers and daughters Russian."

Fortunately, nothing even close to that happened. Or at least we never met anyone who suggested such a thing. But I do think we understood the doubts about this movie without having to speak about them. How would a movie about eight non-Caucasian women play in Peoria, or particularly in Los Angeles suburbs, where focus groups were organized.

I discovered that there were a fair number of Asian-American directors on the scene. Most of them were making independent films that were shown in small art houses, if at all. They couldn't obtain the financing to do anything commercial. And we knew that if a studio sank money into a film about Asian-Americans and didn't earn it back at the box office, this might cast a pall on the future of other films about Asian-Americans. So, yes, I was aware that Hollywood might look at *The Joy Luck Club* as a proving ground.

That's a terrible burden, especially when you're just trying to create your own vision and not necessarily right past wrongs, or set the record straight on the history of China, or break down cultural barriers, or open film job markets for other Asian-Americans, or put every single stereotype to rest once and for all. If we had set out to do all those things, we would have been looking over our shoulders all the time, running scared, and would have been unable to make a movie that was personal and intimate, that had more to do with universal emotions than specific cultural concerns. Certainly, the movie's context is Chinese-American. But the subtext, or the heart of the book, involves emotions we all have.

Our abiding thought was this: If we could make a movie that seemed honest and true, a movie about real people who happened to be Chinese-American, we would have a better shot at making a movie that people would want to see, that they would be moved by, that would get them talking to their friends and so give the movie legs. It might thus bring in enough receipts to change Hollywood's mind that movies about Asian-Americans can't be successful. Maybe, just maybe, many negative assumptions about Asian-Americans on the big screen might be rethought.

I'm encouraged by the reactions to the movie among test audiences. By far, the predominant response is to the universal aspects of the movie, the heart of mother-daughter relations. This seems to leave people feeling that Asian-Americans are not so different—not so "inscrutable" or "mysterious." One blond young man in a focus group commented, "I never had sisters, but after seeing this movie, I feel I have four of them."

I know there will be people on the watch for political correctness. "Why was she married to a Caucasian?" "Why aren't there more positive male role models?" "Why isn't there more having to do with the matter of American versus Chinese culture?" I know from reactions to my fiction that there are people who believe that the raison d'être of any story with an ethnic angle is to provide an educational lesson on culture. I find that attitude restrictive, as though an Asian-American artist has license to create only something that specifically addresses a cultural hot point, and not a work about human nature that happens to depict that through Asian-Americans.

I also understand why the attitude prevails. There are very few Asian-American artists heard or seen by the mainstream. And so people naturally believe that those who have the limelight have the responsibility to address the problems.

I'm curious to see how critics review the movie. With the

book, there was a general tendency to compare my work with that of other Asian-American authors. A reviewer at *The New York Times* compared it with *Shogun, The Good Earth,* Bette Bao Lord's *Spring Moon, The Woman Warrior*—in other words, any book that had to do with Asia at large. Will our movie be compared with *Flower Drum Song, The Last Emperor, The Karate Kid, The World of Suzie Wong, M Butterfly*—purely on the basis of face and race? Would it ever be compared with other stories largely about women, say, *Terms of Endearment, Steel Magnolias, Fried Green Tomatoes*?

The Truth About Disney

Obviously, I'd be in a bad spot if I had to discuss my work with the people at Disney and I had loathed it. Happily, that wasn't the case. Disney said we had creative control, and that's what we got. Sure, they gave us notes on the rough cut. But Ricardo Mestres and Jeffrey Katzenberg seemed to go out of their way to assure us that the notes were only suggestions. We had the final say. We did take some of their suggestions, of course, but there was never any pressure that we do so. Could we tighten the pacing here? We looked at it—sure. Would the scene be better if the mother lashed out in anger at the daughter as well? Let's try it and find out.

From the beginning, they appeared very supportive and enthusiastic. We were included on marketing and distribution plans, as well as publicity and such details as the making of the trailer. By "included," I mean that people from Disney frequently called me, not just Wayne and Ron and Patrick. I was also invited to a lot of business meetings, most of which I declined to attend.

The budget was a problem. It would have been nice, certainly, to have had $20 million like most mainstream movies, instead of $10.6 million, some of which was eaten up by acts of God and the union. For one thing, California's seven-year drought decided to go on hiatus right when we started filming. It rained nearly every day. And then we went to China and nearly froze in the rain there. One scene in the script called for a family to leave their home in the midst of a drought. Sitting in a downpour, I X'ed out "drought" in the script and wrote in "flood." A lot of the cast and crew became sick, yet we had to keep shooting. We couldn't afford not to, especially after we'd lost time when peasants in some of our locations staged riots. Riots? Later I learned that's standard fare for shooting in China.

To sum up, Disney was a terrific studio to work with. The people were great in giving us support and creative control; they were watchful about money. We got a little extra in the end, though no sports cars as bonuses. After all, this is a business. And the Disney people did believe wholeheartedly in this movie, when others had doubts.

Mr. Wang, I'm Ready for My Close-Up

I had heard stories of writers who were banned from coming to the sets of movies based on their books. Security guards were on the lookout for them. Authors were supposed to sell their "properties," shake hands, disinfect when they got home, and then forget about the whole deal until the movie came out, at which time they could proclaim it an abomination.

I remembered this when I was called to attend yet another meeting, whether it was about schedules or music. I had never figured I would be *that* involved with production. Where was that famous reluctance to include the writer? Moviemaking was all-consuming. My fiction writing was suffering from frequent interruptions.

Soon we were into casting, and I was receiving tapes of auditions. I heard that among those attending tryouts were members of the real Joy Luck Club and their friends, the aunties and un-

With the cast of The Joy Luck Club *(top row); actual Joy Luck Club members (bottom row).*

cles I had known since childhood. I asked that I not be included in any final casting decisions. I didn't know anything about acting, I reasoned, and more important, I needed to be able to honestly tell those who did not make the cut that I had nothing to do with it. Can you imagine me telling one of the real Joy Luck aunties she didn't get the part? Fortunately, some of these women were cast as extras with more than a few blurred seconds of screen time next to a potted plant, which is what my husband's role was reduced to. My four-year-old niece, Melissa, received a speaking part as the daughter of Rose (Rosalind Chao). Auntie Jayne and Uncle Tuck were dinner guests at the dinner in which Waverly's boyfriend pours soy sauce over Lindo's favorite dish. Best of all, my mother and her boyfriend, a dapper eighty-six-year-old named T. C. Lee, had substantial parts as extras in the party scene shown at the beginning and the end of the movie. T.C. played to the hilt a narcoleptic guest at the crab dinner. Did nepotism have anything to do with this? Of course not. (Absolutely!)

I should mention that I too landed a part as an extra—or rather, two parts. One required me to dress in 1940s garb and wear a Betty Grable hairdo. I looked hideous and pleaded with the editor to excise the scene. My other appearance stayed in the movie. In the opening scene, Ron and I walk into a party with his two daughters, Sasha and Jennifer. Ron is talking on a cellular phone, and I'm apologizing for being late, then nagging Ron to call his lawyer back later. None of this was in the script, of course. I see how extras can get carried away with their bit parts and try to steal the scene.

After seeing take after take of one particular scene I can never watch it without developing a stomachache. In it, a character named Harold (played by Michael Paul Chan) is eating from a container of ice cream. In the filming, he ate, take after take after take. Then Wayne called for another setup. Michael Paul ate again, take after take after take. After six setups, I was sure he was going to explode.

I now have enormous respect for what actors do. And I have great respect for how Wayne treated them—always with gentleness, yet persistent in obtaining their best performance. In that ice cream–eating scene, Harold's wife, Lena (played by Lauren Tom), gets angry, then rumbles emotionally with fear and confusion. I thought each take was perfect, but Wayne would find some element of her performance—a tentativeness, or her stumbling over a word—and ask her to keep exactly that, that vulnerability. They'd do another take, and it would be even better.

Quiet on the Set

The day I first saw the sets, we drove to Richmond, where a former candy factory and warehouse had been converted into something befitting Hollywood. I walked through the doors, and there was my fully furnished imagination—interiors of houses in San Francisco and China built by Don Burt, the production designer.

How easily I had penned the details, compared with what it had apparently taken to build them. In fiction, you can throw in a few interior-decorator touches—the plastic on the furniture, the framed photo of a dead ancestor—but the production designer has to put in everything, including the fingerprints next to the light switch. I felt guilty seeing the work done on the sets, as though I hadn't written about the details with as much care and devotion.

Don came to me for props. Wayne had asked that we include as many of my family photos as possible. In this way, my father and older brother, who died long ago, were also able to be part of the movie. Wayne told me to rummage through my jewelry for a necklace we had written into the script: a green jade pendant that June's mother gives her, telling her that it's not best quality but she is.

I went to the set maybe once a week in the beginning, then almost every day during the last two weeks of principal photography in the United States. That's when Wayne anticipated he would need Ron and me to make fast changes to the script, which we did indeed have to do daily. To stay on schedule, Wayne was shooting six or seven pages of script a day—which I understood to be a lot.

In March 1993, I went to China at my own expense and attended almost all the filming there. If Wayne asked me to make script changes, I told him he had to give me a chit for breakfast.

Filming in China presented unanticipated hardships. First, there was the cold. I had been in Guilin before, when it was hot and humid. The weather there is described as "perpetual spring." Well, when I was there this time, that was spring in Minnesota. I wore seven layers of clothing and was still freezing, chilled to the bone. On one occasion, I was shaking so hard I knew I'd develop hypothermia if I didn't get out of the wind. So I went and sat in a van. Wayne and the rest of the cast and crew continued filming. I would have stayed out there if he really needed me, but I figured I shouldn't have to die just to prove I was dedicated.

Then there was the funeral we had not factored into the schedule. On the day we were to film refugees fleeing an invading Japanese army, the people living in our location were holding a funeral for a woman who reportedly lived to be a hundred before she died. It was either bad luck or bad manners—probably both—for them to allow a film crew into their village that day. The procession was long; obviously, this ceremony was going to take hours. A casket was being carried, and dancing on top was a live rooster, supposedly to chase off evil spirits like movie directors, cast, and crew. But to delay shooting even one day would cost us $70,000, money we could ill afford on our budget. Discussions were held with the family, a generous "donation" was made in honor of the dead woman, and suddenly, the gods smiled upon us. The film crew was welcomed and the villagers rejoiced at the infusion of cash. The old woman, we overheard, had brought her comrades good luck.

In our second village, we learned that the location fee, the equivalent of $5,000, had not been transferred from the middleman to the village coffers but had gone off to Hong Kong in the hands of those who had absconded with it. The village chieftain was demanding payment. What could we do? We agreed to pay the original amount: $5,000. No, said the leader, not American dollars, but renmenbi, the local money, which foreigners were forbidden to carry. We tried to argue that American dollars were just as good as renmenbi (and in fact better, $5,000 being the equivalent of 40,000 renmenbi). We even hinted that on the black market those same dollars could fetch double the usual exchange. No dice, no dollars, they said.

One villager then brought up the question of the amount itself. The people didn't want us to tell them what the shooting day was worth, they would tell us individually. This villager wanted one chicken and twenty renmenbi (about $2.50). Another villager piped up that he wanted a part in the movie and fifty renmenbi. A man argued that his pathway was being used more than others', so he should receive enough to buy more bales of hay to soak up the mud. Wayne said that he could not negotiate three hundred separate deals.

An old woman raised the hatchet that she used for chopping twigs into kindling. Then more hatchets went up, as did canes. The shouts flew, and I heard a distinctive ugly tone that signaled danger. Earlier that week we had learned that this village had seen five executions the previous year—two for rape, one for robbery, two for murder. The figure shocked us: the death penalty here was used often and swiftly. Now we considered that the number suggested also that this village was more violent than most. We observed the number of villagers staring at us with birth defects, notably a blind walleye, seen in scores of them, babies through elderly, which indicated inbreeding. I recalled someone had mentioned that this village might have taken up cannibalism during the lean years of the Cultural Revolution. That actually did happen, but whether it was this particular village was pure speculation. Nonetheless, we thought we should not test the limits of these people's endurance.

"Let's get out of here," I said to Wayne. The crew packed the essentials, for shooting scenes on the fly. As it happened, we found a waste dump, a giant pit where garbage had been tilled under. At the top was a ridge lined with trees standing against mountains. It was perfect, stark but epic. There we filmed a line of people walking into oblivion, Suyuan begging for help as she clutches her twin babies.

When we returned to the village, lo and behold, the matter had been settled. The villagers presented us with a bill itemizing each of their demands, and all this was tallied to the grand sum of a little more than 5,000 renmenbi. That was one-eighth of what we had offered in U.S. dollars. Someone tactfully pointed out the error, but whether out of pride or a deep suspicion of

American dollars, the villagers stuck to the lesser sum. Among our Chinese crew, we were able to scrounge together enough to pay them off. All were happy and filming began.

In our final village, we wound up restarting World War II. The location was a huge pasture with hills in the background that looked like gigantic ancient fish stuck tail-down into the earth. A long dirt road bisected this valley. A thousand extras were on hand, some in 1940s clothes and clinging to their most precious worldly possessions, a sack of rice, a suitcase, a pair of babies. The rest were in the uniforms of the Kuomintang, the Nationalist army, defeated by the Japanese in Kweilin (Guilin). Some walked by with bandages around their heads. Some had limbs missing and were on crutches. A burning jeep lay upturned. Watching the shoot were some locals, as well as members of the People's Army, who served as security.

Food arrived, box lunches for a thousand catered by the Sheraton Hotel in Guilin. It was pretty fancy fare by local standards, a meal that cost an average week's salary. When lunch was over, we had a few dozen boxes left, and someone from the American crew thoughtfully called out to onlookers that they were welcome to take them. Shouts immediately erupted among the extras. They wanted the leftovers: they had earned them, and they would keep them. All at once, fists were flying, people were being shoved, and the Kuomintang was fighting the People's Army. It was war all over again. Luckily, no one was seriously injured. Filming resumed with our extras looking even more tattered than before. Talk about Method acting.

Months later, one of the most curious comments I heard during a test-audience focus-group session involved the scenes shot in China. To me, these scenes are stunning—so stunning they strain credibility. A woman in the focus group said, "All the scenes were gorgeous—until we got to China. You should get rid of those matte paintings. You can tell they're fake." I turned to Wayne and poked him. "See? We didn't have to suffer in China. We could have used better matte paintings."

I Cried My Eyes Out

Moviemaking, I learned, is an emotionally draining experience. I was moved by seeing the realism of the sets, the authentic touches, and hearing the private revelations made to me by the actors, stars as well as extras, about why being in this movie meant so much to them.

During filming in the States, I began each day by popping in a videotape of the previous day's filming that had been delivered to me at home by messenger, and then I would cry my eyes out. I was amazed that the scenes I had seen enacted before me had assumed that real movie quality on film. A strange transformation had taken place, as if this reel life were more real than real life. But that's what movies are all about.

At major stages, Ron and I worked with Wayne and the editor, Maysie Hoy, as the movie was being cut. That process was fascinating but tedious, a matter of deciding over milliseconds. Our movie was running way too long, and to get it into theaters meant every one of those cuts was essential. Through meticulous editing, milliseconds could add up to minutes, and in the end it would seem as if nothing had been cut. I ended up thinking Maysie was a saint.

Around April, I saw the first rough cut. I was supposed to take notes of problem areas and such. Yet I was too mesmerized to do anything but watch it like an ordinary moviegoer. I laughed, I cried. The second time I saw it, I told Wayne: "I want you to remember this day. We're going to get a lot of different reactions to this film later. But I want us to remember that on this day, you, Ron, and I were proud of what we'd accomplished. We made our vision."

Ron insisted that I come to test previews because there, seeing how a real audience reacted, I'd get some of the biggest highs—or lows—of my life. Fortunately, it was the former. I was surprised, though, when people laughed during scenes I never considered funny. I suppose those were ironic laughs, in response to recognizing the pain of some past humiliation.

I've now seen the movie about twenty-five times, and I am not ashamed to say I've been moved to tears each time.

By the time you read this, I will have seen the movie with my mother and my half sister, who just immigrated from China. She is one of the daughters my mother had to leave behind when she came to the United States. So that will be my version of life imitating art, or sitting in front of it. I'm nervous about what my mother will think. I'm afraid she'll be overwhelmed by some of the scenes that are taken from her life, especially the one that depicts the suicide of her mother.*

I hope audiences are moved by the film, that they connect with the emotions and feel changed at the end, that they feel

* In striking contrast to the rest of the audience, my mother did not shed a tear. She told me after the movie ended that it was "pretty good. In real life, everything so much sadder. So this, already much better."

closer to other people as a result. That's what I like to get out of a book, a connection with the world.

As to reviews, I've already imagined all the bad things that can be said. That way I'll be delighted by anything good that comes out. I'm aware that the success of this movie will depend on good reviews and word of mouth. But there comes a point when you've done all you can. And then it's out of your control. Certainly I hope the movie is a success at the box office, mostly for Wayne's and Ron's sakes, as well as for the cast and crew who dedicated themselves in a manner that made me feel it was not "just another job" for them. And certainly I hope Disney thinks it was more than justified in taking a risk on this movie. By my score, however, the movie is already a success. We made the movie we wanted to make. It's not perfect, but we're happy with it. And I'll be standing in line, ready to plunk down seven dollars to see it.

In the meantime, I have a whole mess of Chinese lucky charms absolutely guaranteed to bring the gods to the theater.

I've Learned My Lessons

At various times in the making of the movie, I vowed I'd never do this again. It's too time-consuming. There are too many ups-and-downs. There's so much business, too many meetings. I've developed calluses and sangfroid about some of the inherent difficulties of filmmaking.

Yet against all my expectations, I like collaborating from time to time. I like fusing ideas into one vision. I like seeing that vision come to life with other people who know exactly what it takes to get there.

My love of fiction is unaltered. It's my first love. But yes, I'll make another film with Ron and Wayne. It will probably be of my second book, *The Kitchen God's Wife*. We've already started breaking the scenes out with page counts and narrative text. We began the day after we saw the rough cut of *The Joy Luck Club*.*

*Although we had a contract for *The Kitchen God's Wife*, I eventually decided to return to the more solitary world of fiction writing. Ron, Wayne, and I talk from time to time about doing an original screenplay. When the cards fall into place with as much luck as for our first film, I will know that it is the right and irresistible thing to do.

STRONG WINDS, STRONG INFLUENCES

I was six when my mother taught me the art of invisible strength. It was a strategy for winning arguments, respect from others, and eventually, though neither of us knew it at the time, chess games.

· The Joy Luck Club

· what she meant ·

In 1988, I received a contract to write a book titled *The Joy Luck Club.* I had completed three stories, and I had thirteen proposed stories to go, many of which were supposed to be set in China, more than a few of them during World War II.

Months before, I had hastily outlined these story ideas in a proposal that my new editor had bought. I believed I was not to deviate from this plan, and now I was worried over the parts that involved the war, a subject I was ill equipped to write about. It was time to do some serious research.

I called my mother. "Hey, Ma, what was it like during the war?"

My mother considered the question, paused to cast back to her life in China. "War? Oh, I was not affected."

I assumed by her answer that she had been tucked away in free China, that her experiences with World War II were similar to mine with Vietnam: observed from a safe distance. Ah well, some parents have interesting war stories to tell. My mother did not.

So it was not until later in our conversation that I learned what my mother really meant by her answer. She was telling me about her first marriage, to a pilot to whom she could never refer by name, only by the words "that bad man." And now, she told me, somebody had sponsored that bad man to come visit the United States as a former Kuomintang hero.

"Hnh! He was no hero!" my mother exclaimed. "He was dismissed from air force for bad morals." And she began to tell me details of their life in China—of bombs falling, of running to escape, of pilot friends who showed up for dinner one week and were dead the next.

I interrupted her. "Wait a minute, I thought you said you weren't affected by the war."

"I wasn't," insisted my mother. "I wasn't killed."

Her answer made me realize, once again, that my mother and I were at times oceans apart in our view of the world. When I was growing up, I too was "not affected." I had no idea that China had ever been involved in World War II—let alone that the war in China had started in 1937. And for the first ten years of my life, I did not know of my mother's first marriage. She kept it a secret from my brothers and me, from her closest friends. When she finally did tell me, I did not ask her any questions. In part, I did not want to think that she could have once loved a man other than my father. And when I grew older, I still did not ask her about her early life in China. Why bring up the pains of her past? Of course, the questions were still there. I wondered, I imagined, I assumed what the answers might have been.

When I set out to write my second book, I remembered that conversation with my mother, about her marriage to a man she grew to despise. I decided to write about a woman and her secret regrets, and used my American assumptions to shape the story:

that this woman's first marriage, while ending in hate, surely must have been born out of love. Why else would she have stayed in her marriage for twelve years?

That's what I started out writing. Fortunately, writing has a way of showing me how false my assumptions can be. My character rebelled against this fiction I had imposed on her. "No," she protested. "This was not love. This was hope, hope for myself." She refused to go along with the plot, and I found the story at a dead end.

And so I began again. I began by asking myself about hope. How does it change, transform, endure according to life's quirky circumstances? And what of the circumstances themselves: Do we believe they are simply a matter of fate? Or do we view them as the Chinese concept of luck, the Christian concept of God's will, the American concept of choice? And depending on what we believe, how can we find balance in our lives? What do we accept? What do we feel we can still change?

Eventually I wrote a book in which a mother poses these questions as she tells her daughter the secrets of her past. Since the story takes place during wartime, before my birth, I had to do quite a bit of research. I read scholarly texts and revisionist versions of the various roles of the Kuomintang, the Communists, the Japanese, and the Americans. I read wartime accounts published in popular periodicals—with different perspectives on these same groups. And of course, I needed a personal account of the war years to fact-check some of the mundane details of my story: How long did it take to travel from Shanghai to Yangchow? What was a typical dowry for a bride from a well-to-do family? For those answers, I went to my mother, who in response gave me more than I asked for. The question of the dowry alone led to a three-hour remembrance of things past—not simply about wedding gifts, but about family gossip and Shanghai manners, about a gangster who showed up at her wedding, about her innocence—her stupidity!—in marrying a man she hardly knew.

My mother, photographed by my father, Tientsin, China, 1945.

I know readers will wonder: How much of the story is true? With *The Joy Luck Club*, I met readers who assumed everything in my book was true, my fiction simply a matter of fast dictation and an indelible memory. My mother complained of having to deny over and over that she was one or all of the mothers in my first book. "It's all fiction," she told her friends. "None of it is true. My daughter just has a wild imagination."

While I was writing my second book, she made sure to give me some motherly advice. "This time," she said, "tell my *true* story." And with her permission—actually, her *demand*—how could I refuse? How could I resist? After all, the richest source of my fiction does come from life as I have misunderstood it—its contradictions, its unanswerable questions, its unlikely twists and turns.

So, indeed, some of the events in *The Kitchen God's Wife* are based on my mother's life: her marriage to "that bad man," the death of her children, her fortuitous encounter with my father. But with apologies to my mother, I confess that I changed her story. I invented characters who never existed in her life: Auntie Du, Helen, Jiaguo, Old Aunt and New Aunt, Peanut, Beautiful Betty, Bao-Bao Roger. I took her to places that do not exist: to a tea-growing monastery in Hangchow, to a mountaintop village called Heaven's Breath, to a scissors-making shop in Kunming, to an American dance that in real life she decided not to attend. With those imaginary details in place, I can honestly say the story is fiction, not true.

And yet it is as close to the truth as I can imagine. It is my mother's story in the most important of ways to me: her passion, her will, her hope, the innocence she never really lost. It is the reason why she told me, "I was not affected," why I can finally understand what she truly meant.

· *confessions* ·

My mother's thoughts reach back like the winter tide, exposing the wreckage of a former shore. Often she's mired in 1967, 1968, the years my older brother and my father died.

1968 was also the year she took me and my little brother—Didi—across the Atlantic to Switzerland, a place so preposterously different that she knew she had to give up grieving simply to survive. That year, she remembers, she was very, very sad. I too remember. I was sixteen then, and I recall a late-night hour when my mother and I were arguing in the chalet, that tinderbox of emotion where we lived.

She had pushed me into the small bedroom we shared, and as she slapped me about the head, I backed into a corner, by a window that looked out on the lake, the Alps, the beautiful outside world. My mother was furious because I had a boyfriend. She was shouting that he was a drug addict, a bad man who would use me for sex and throw me away like leftover garbage.

"Stop seeing him!" she ordered.

I shook my head. The more she beat me, the more implacable I became, and this in turn fueled her outrage.

"You didn't love you daddy or Peter! When they die you not even sad."

I kept my face to the window, unmoved. What does she know about sad?

She sobbed and beat her chest. "I rather kill myself before see you destroy you life!"

Suicide. How many times had she threatened that before?

"I wish you the one die! Not Peter, not Daddy."

She had just confirmed what I had always suspected. Now she flew at me with her fists.

"I rather kill you! I rather see you die!"

And then, perhaps horrified by what she had just said, she fled the room. Thank God that was over. I wished I had a cigarette to smoke. Suddenly she was back. She slammed the door shut, latched it, then locked it with a key. I saw the flash of a meat cleaver just before she pushed me to the wall and brought the blade's edge to within an inch of my throat. Her eyes were like a wild animal's, shiny, fixated on the kill. In an excited voice she said, "First, I kill you. Then Didi and me, our whole family destroy!" She smiled, her chest heaving. "Why you don't cry?" She pressed the blade closer and I could feel her breath gusting.

Was she bluffing? If she did kill me, so what? Who would care? While she rambled, a voice within me was whimpering, "This is sad, this is so sad."

For ten minutes, fifteen, longer, I straddled these two thoughts—that it didn't matter if I died, that it would be eternally sad if I did—until all at once I felt a snap, then a rush of hope into a vacuum, and I was crying, I was babbling my confession: "I want to live. I want to live."

For twenty-five years I forgot that day, and when the memory of what happened surfaced unexpectedly at a writers' workshop in which we recalled our worst moments, I was shaking, wondering to myself, Did she really mean to kill me? If I had not pleaded with her, would she have pushed down on the cleaver and ended my life?

I wanted to go to my mother and ask. Yet I couldn't, not until much later, when she became forgetful and I learned she had Alzheimer's disease. I knew that if I didn't ask her certain questions now, I would never know the real answers.

So I asked.

"Angry? Slap you?" she said, and laughed. "No, no, *no*. You always good girl, never even need to spank, not even one time."

How wonderful to hear her say what was never true, yet now would be forever so.

·pretty beyond belief·

I once asked my mother whether I was beautiful by Chinese standards. I must have been twelve at the time, and I believed that I was not attractive according to an American aesthetic based on Marilyn Monroe as the ultimate sex goddess.

I remember that my mother carefully appraised my face before concluding, "To Chinese person, you not beautiful. You plain."

I was unable to hide my hurt and disappointment.

"Why you want be beautiful?" my mother chided. "Pretty can be bad luck, not just good." She should know, she said. She had been born a natural beauty. When she was four, people told her they had never seen a girl so lovely. "Everyone spoil me, the servants, my grandmother, my aunts, because I was pretty beyond belief."

By the time she was a teenager, she had the looks of a movie starlet: a peach-shaped face, a nose that was rounded but not overly broad, tilted large eyes with double lids, a smile of small and perfect teeth. Her skin bore "no spots or dots," and she would often say to me, even into her seventies and eighties, "Feel. Still smooth and soft."

When she was nineteen, she married. She was innocent, she said, and her husband was a bad man. The day before their wedding, he was with another woman. Later he openly brought his girlfriends home to humiliate her, to prove that her beauty and her pride were worth nothing. When she ran away with the man who would become my father, her husband had her jailed. The Shanghai tabloids covered her trial for months, and all the city girls admired her front-page photos. "They cried for me," she avowed. "They don't know me, but they thought I too pretty to have such bad life."

Glam shot of me at age twelve, with my cat Fufu.

Beauty ruined her own mother as well. A rich man spotted my grandmother when she was newly widowed, strolling by a lakeside. "She was exquisite, like a fairy," my mother reported. The man forced the widow to become his concubine, thus consigning her to a life of disgrace. After she gave birth to his baby son, my grandmother killed herself by swallowing raw opium.

Although my mother chastised my adolescent beauty, she sometimes lamented my lack of it. "Too bad you got your father's feet," she would say. She wondered why I had not inherited any of the good features of her face, and pointed out that my nostrils and lips were too coarse, my skin too dark. When I was nineteen, after a car accident left my nose and mouth askew, she told me she was sorry that she could not afford the plastic surgery to fix this, as well as my misshapen left ear. By then I didn't care that I would never meet my mother's standards of beauty. I had a boyfriend who loved me.

In the last years of my mother's life, when she had developed Alzheimer's disease, she never forgot that she was a beauty. I could always make her giggle by telling her how pretty she was, how I wished I had been born with her good looks. She whispered back that some of the other women in the assisted-living residence were jealous of her for the same reason. But as she lost her ability to reason and remember, she also came to believe that my face had changed.

"You look like me," she said. I was moved to tears to hear her say this. Time and age had allowed us to come closer. Now we had the same lines formed by cautious half-smiles. We had the same loss of fat above the innocent eye, the same crimped chin holding back what we really felt. My psyche had molded itself into my mother's face.

Since my mother died, I find myself looking in the mirror more often than I did when I was twelve. How else is my face changing? If beauty is bad luck, why do I still want it? Why do I wish for reasons to be vain? Why do I long to look like my mother?

· the most hateful words ·

The most hateful words I have ever said to another human being were to my mother. I was sixteen at the time. They rose from the storm in my chest and I let them fall in a fury of hailstones: "I hate you. I wish I were dead. . . ."

I waited for her to collapse, stricken by what I had just said. She was still standing upright, her chin tilted, her lips stretched in a crazy smile. "Okay, maybe I die too," she said between huffs. "Then I no longer be your mother!" We had many similar exchanges. Sometimes she actually tried to kill herself by running into the street, holding a knife to her throat. She too had storms in her chest. And what she aimed at me was as fast and deadly as a lightning bolt.

For days after our arguments, she would not speak to me. She tormented me, acted as if she had no feelings for me whatsoever. I was lost to her. And because of that, I lost, battle after battle, all of them: the times she criticized me, humiliated me in front of others, forbade me to do this or that without even listening to one good reason why it should be the other way. I swore to myself I would never forget these injustices. I would store them, harden my heart, make myself as impenetrable as she was.

I remember this now, because I am also remembering another time, just a few years ago. I was forty-seven, had become a different person by then, had become a fiction writer, someone who uses memory and imagination. In fact, I was writing a story about a girl and her mother, when the phone rang.

It was my mother, and this surprised me. Had someone helped her make the call? For a few years now, she had been losing her mind through Alzheimer's disease. Early on, she forgot to lock her door. Then she forgot where she lived. She forgot who many people were and what they had meant to her. Lately, she could no longer remember many of her worries and sorrows.

"Amy-ah," she said, and she began to speak quickly in Chinese. "Something is wrong with my mind. I think I'm going crazy."

I caught my breath. Usually she could barely speak more than two words at a time. "Don't worry," I started to say.

"It's true," she went on. "I feel like I can't remember many things. I can't remember what I did yesterday. I can't remember what happened a long time ago, what I did to you. . . ." She spoke as a drowning person might if she had bobbed to the surface with the force of will to live, only to see how far she had already drifted, how impossibly far she was from the shore.

She spoke frantically: "I know I did something to hurt you."

"You didn't," I said. "Don't worry."

"I did terrible things. But now I can't remember what. . . . And I just want to tell you . . . I hope you can forget, just as I've forgotten."

I tried to laugh so she would not notice the cracks in my voice. "Really, don't worry."

"Okay, I just wanted you to know."

After we hung up, I cried, both happy and sad. I was again that sixteen-year-old, but the storm in my chest was gone.

My mother died six months later. By then she had bequeathed to me her most healing words, as open and eternal as a clear blue sky. Together we knew in our hearts what we should remember, what we can forget.

· my love affair with vladimir nabokov ·

After years of being asked in public, "What's your all-time favorite book?" I should have a definitive sound bite by now, you'd think. But for me, having to choose a best book conjures terrible visions of school days when I waited to be chosen as someone's friend. Because my family moved almost yearly, books became my comfort, and I wanted to embrace them all.

Certainly *Jane Eyre* fits in there with the bests. Its setting of gloom and chill matched my emotional interior. I identified with Jane's alienation, her meager hopes. Moreover, I loved her spunkiness; she was confined by circumstances, yet subtly rebellious and spiritually subversive. From *Jane Eyre*, I acquired a literary preference for gothic atmosphere and dark emotional resonance.

I also want to say the dictionary, any unabridged dictionary, is a best. I read lists of words as though they were stories. Within their nuances, I see possibilities. Like many writers, I am passionate about words. To this day, I love reading dictionaries, including lexicons of dead languages. I love the sounds and shapes of words, the way certain consonant blends can evoke related images: *glow, glisten, glimmer, glen,* along with *flabby, flap, flop, flotsam, flatter, flatulence.* I am fascinated with the origins of words, when they came into being, how they were first used. Within their histories are stories. The dictionary for me is my Scheherazade. Plus it can spell Scheherazade.

There's also *Love Medicine* by Louise Erdrich and *Annie John* by Jamaica Kincaid. I have reread both those books many times. And every time, I am inspired to think about the narrative qualities I cherish in stories. *Love Medicine* is the book that made me want to find my own voice. It influenced my early attempts at writing fiction.

Finally, we get to the clichéd litmus test of literature: I am often asked, If stranded on a desert island, what book, other than *How to Get off a Desert Island,* would you want? To provide me with endless entertainment and literary puzzles, I would choose *Lolita* by Vladimir Nabokov. I often reread passages of it for language, for "aesthetic bliss," as Nabokov called his own literary pursuit. I am infatuated with its imagery, its wit, its bonanza of allusions and arcana, as well as its parody and the prosody in perfect rhythm to its stylistic bent. The parenthetical phrase "(picnic, lightning)" is one of the most tragic, grand, and comic images in all literature. It is a miniature marvel. For me, reading *Lolita* means conducting a torrid love affair with the English language, and nearly every writer I know has been besotted with its prose.

Then there's the bonus of the annotated edition of the book, with notes by Alfred Appel, Jr., which includes a brilliant afterword by Nabokov himself. The annotations, nearly half again as long as the novel, are a brilliant reminder of the pure joy of writing, its interplay with life. French phrases, puns and poems, references to geography and lepidoptera, as well as highway routes, are scrupulously cited, often with notes from Nabokov himself. This edition is similar to DVDs, with bonus tracks and outtakes and the director's explanation of how the crash scene was faked. In it you see the absolute deliberateness with which details were chosen. There is a reason for everything, the names, for instance. Why Humbert Humbert and not Hugo or Harold or Horatio. Why Dolores, Lo, Lolita. Why Quilty. As a writer, you think, "What style! What intelligence! How lazy I have been with my own choices."

My fascination with Nabokov is also personal. In 1968, luck or fate led my mother, my little brother, and me to live in the picturesque town of Montreux, Switzerland, where Nabokov lived from 1959 until his death in 1977. Although I can't claim with certainty that I ever met him, I do recall the hotel where he lived, the Montreux Palace, a majestic structure situated by Lake Geneva, in whose mirror-still waters you could see a perfect reflection of the Alps on the opposite shore. My friends and I often walked by the hotel, bumming cigarettes off one another. And since Montreux was a smallish resort in 1968, I feel I can say, without too much exaggeration, that it is *likely* Nabokov and I might have crossed paths.

I can still picture it. There I am, in my yellow-and-pink flower-power dress, my waist-length hair streaming behind as I rush toward a secret dalliance with my boyfriend Franz, who is waiting for me in a café in the lovely Alpine hamlet of Les Avants. About fifty paces from my family's chalet is the jumping-on point for the *funiculaire,* a tram on cogwheels that ascends several hundred feet to Les Avants, which is also the hunting grounds for many a lepidopterist, including Nabokov. Seated on the slat bench in the *funiculaire* is an old man—my being sixteen makes "old" hard to judge, but I would guess he's at least sixty. He wears owlish spectacles, a tweed jacket, and sturdy brown shoes. In one hand is a butterfly net, and on his lap, a sketchbook. He gives me no glance, no word.

As the tram jerks into motion, I press the play button on my tape player, a present from my boyfriend. The soothing sound of the Stones' "Jumping Jack Flash" blasts out in harmony with the passing scenery. The old man abruptly leans forward enough to spit out one word: *"Mademoiselle."* His snakelike eyes lock on to mine and I am hypnotized with fear. I press another button and the noise stops. For the next five minutes, we are two strangers quietly cogwheeling toward the same verdant paradise but miles apart in our thoughts. In my case, I am thinking that the man across from me is a creep.

It never would have occurred to me at the time that this grumpy gramps might have been Vladimir Nabokov. At age sixteen, all I knew of Nabokov was that he, like Henry Miller and D. H. Lawrence, had written a book about sex, and his included a pervert. Since his book had been banned, that would have been qualification enough for me to make it a must read.

Alas, twenty-five years passed before I read *Lolita*. And now my admiration for Nabokov is so huge that I regret not meeting him when he and I lived in the same small town. I have searched my mind for those occasions when we might have occupied the same breathing space, that time on the *funiculaire,* for example. I shouldn't have played that awful music. I should have said something witty. Could it be that I never had the chance? After all, the scene in the *funiculaire* was just wishful thinking. I made it up.

My editor, Faith Sale, told me that by not meeting Nabokov, I also missed being scarred for life. She was a student at Cornell when Nabokov taught there, and she recalls that his words were so brutal, his manner so arrogant, he could reduce cocky students into sniveling idiots crawling on their hands and knees. He was even worse with critics and academics. He was a literary Darwinist who would have placed critics somewhere among the fungi, along with spore and mold. I've read a book devoted in large part to his retorts to reviewers, and the pages smolder when you turn them. I have the sense he was not kindhearted to most people who bumble through life, as I often do. He was, in fact, the sort who described public swimming pools brimming with people as petri dishes.

But those reports of Nabokov's meanness do not diminish my admiration for him. *Au contraire.* What author who has had her share of bad reviews would not relish the opportunity to toss into the face of a snooty critic a symbolic cream pie? I say this even though it's become my policy not to read reviews of my books, good, bad, or in between. I don't think it's wise to place your self-esteem in the hands of strangers.

Yet every now and then, some well-meaning friend will shove a nasty review under my nose, proclaiming loudly, "Even if he is with the largest, most influential newspaper in the world, I beg to differ. I don't think it's *that* dreadful." When I hear things like that, I am reduced to the emotional level of a six-year-old outcast, taunted at school for bringing Chinese food in her lunch bag. The words remain as indelible as cat piss on my bed pillow. I lie awake, thinking of ways *not* to think about them. For hours, I focus on Zenlike thoughts—right mind, right attitude, oneness with self—but as the night wears on, voodoo dolls come to mind, as does a Brazilian black-magic spell that a former roommate of mine used on an unfaithful boyfriend; the charm—swear to God—left him impotent for two years to the day. Yes, I quite approve of Nabokovian revenge.

Revenge aside, I dream of writing my own annotations one day, appended like those in Appel's edition of *Lolita*. The book included among other things the names of motels where Nabokov his wife stayed when they were on a cross-country butterfly-hunting expedition. I take a similar approach. Consider the numerous times I mention food in my writing. Contrary to what is suggested in CliffsNotes analyses, it is not my intention to write about dumplings or fish or rice cakes as symbols of abundance. They are there for simple reasons of hunger and pragmatism. The way I figure it, if I order prawns and sablefish and sesame-seed dumplings in a restaurant and the next day I write about these dishes, that food bill becomes tax-deductible as necessary research.

My husband the fairly conservative tax attorney often argues with me about my method of writing and then writing off. Red flag or not, I tell him that this method helps me decide best how to extract fictional elements from the humdrum of daily life: for example, ethnic jewelry I've bought becomes "authentic details," fascinating places I've visited become "settings," safaris and skiing lessons are "action." When difficulties arise, such as mudslides and broken legs, those are transformed into "plot," and how I handle them is called "character." I outline the formula for my husband's number-crunching edification:

> Authentic Details + Settings + Action + Plot + Character = American Novel
>
> American Novel = Work
>
> Work = Tax deductions (U.S. income only, as per American Novel itemization clause)

My husband is not as impressed as I am with Nabokov or my formulas. He disallows the deductions.

Nonetheless, Nabokov remains in my mind as a model. When I am asked what my all-time favorite book is, I remember myself as that girl sitting on a tram, an older gentleman with a butterfly net across from me. Although he appears to be in sweet reverie, I interrupt gently to tell him: "By the way, I love your books." He smiles to thank me.

It's all fiction, aesthetic bliss. And now that I've written it down, I can recall it as fond memory of truth.

LUCK, CHANCE, AND A CHARMED LIFE

And then Peanut found a fortune-teller she liked, a fat woman with a big smile who promised she knew everything—love, marriage, wealth. A sign in front of her stall bragged that she had the luckiest fortune sticks, knew all the lucky numbers, the right lucky marriage combinations, the best days for making lucky business decisions, remedies for changing bad luck into fantastic luck. Everything guaranteed.

• The Kitchen God's Wife

· *inferior decorating* ·

I am not overly superstitious. But then again, I am not one to take unnecessary chances.

Why risk displeasing the gods (or God, the Buddha, and the muses) when a subtle sprinkling of good-luck charms and a few tasteful signs of respect can make heaven smile down on earth? (Speaking of the elevated perspective of holy ones: My mother told me I should hang my inscribed Chinese banners *upside down* so that those on high can read them more easily. Nothing more annoying to deities than to have to cock their sacred heads to read a mere mortal's plea suspended hundreds of miles below.)

If you were to enter my home, you probably wouldn't see any obvious signs that I place my life in the hands of divine intervention, or, for that matter, in the hands of an interior decorator. The first impression is, I hope, one of a cozy abode: unpretentious and intelligently appointed to accommodate the fur balls of a cat. But if you stayed for tea, you might begin to notice what my husband refers to as "kitsch," or "clutter," or sometimes "Amy's junk."

These are my good-luck charms, and they come mostly in the form of dragons, fish, strategically placed mirrors, and heaven forgive me, New Age crystals. (As to the cultural deviation of the last, there's nothing mystical about their inclusion. I just happen to agree with what my niece Melissa once told me—that it warms the heart to see "Mr. Sun playing with Mrs. Glass.")

In the foyer at the top of the stairs is a rosewood chair, a bit of Chinese gothic whimsy from the 1920s. The arch of the back and the hand rests are carved with dragons, their piercing inlaid-ivory eyes guarding over its owner, me, another dragon. Next to the chair is a bamboo-and-wire birdcage. This houses only lucky turquoise and copper Chinese coins. Meanwhile, the birds (plastic and made in Taiwan), sit outside the cage and chirp warnings whenever the cage of money is disturbed. On a carved stand opposite the birdcage sits a porcelain vase big enough for me to climb into. If you were to look inside the vase, you'd see painted there a lionhead goldfish swimming about, which, along with an electronic alarm system, is excellent for chasing off devilish spirits and thieves. Above the vase is a mirror with a nineteenth-century dragon carving as its frame.

A word about mirrors: They can supposedly repel bad luck or attract good. I'm not sure about which laws of physics apply. All I know is that I once had a neighbor whose nightly hammering nearly drove my husband and me up the wall; after we aimed a curved mirror in his direction—*total silence*. In my current home, the dragon mirror is directed at a nice neighbor who has a surfeit of parking spaces in his garage. I have no garage, but I'm usually lucky enough to find a space in front of my door.

My study is where I've applied most of my decorating skills. Scattered about are chimes, banners with lucky sayings, and wooden fish—as well as a stuffed piranha for fighting off heavy-duty distractions from writing.

And the location of my study is particularly auspicious, according to Chinese principles of *feng shui* ("wind and water"). Its three bay windows overlook neighborhood rooftops and face north toward water and mountains. In terms of San Francisco real estate principles, it means I have a knockout view of the Presidio's eucalyptus forest, the Golden Gate Bridge, San Francisco Bay, Angel Island, the Marin Headlands, and Tiburon. But here's where the Chinese gods and literary muses come into conflict; the muses have decreed that I hang shades in front of the view, the better to concentrate on the computer screen, rather than on sailboats, mating pigeons, and cable TV repair people shimmying across the slanted roofs.

While I'm on the subject of computer screens, some years ago, while writing my first book, I stuck a Dymo-tape message across the top of my monitor that read: "Call Your Guardian Angel." This was my reminder to think about my sources of inspiration. One day my mother saw the reminder, sat down at my desk, and proceeded to have a "chat" with my computer, thinking that this was where her mother, whom she considered my muse, now resided in motherboard sartorial splendor. Well, just in case a hundred-year-old spirit really is my muse, I've placed three bamboo calligraphy brushes below the monitor, as well as copper clappers from Tibet.

By far my best and favorite lucky charm sits in a corner of my office. It, or rather *she*, is an exquisitely painted Chinese porcelain statue about twelve inches tall. I've grown up seeing statues in Chinese restaurants and stores. They're usually kept in miniature temples and given offerings of tea and oranges.

Shopowners tend to pick a god or goddess who corresponds to the kind of luck they wish to have flowing through their doors, say the God of Money for a constantly ringing cash register, or the God of War for aggressive business deals.

I chose an unnamed goddess while writing my then untitled second book. I didn't think it was good manners to ask her for anything as crass as good reviews and placement on bestseller lists. And anyway, if she was anything like my mother, my goddess had never even heard of *The New York Times*. In the end, I asked only that I be able to write the best book I could, and that no matter what happened to it, I would have no regrets, no sorrows. I called my statue Lady Sorrowfree and titled the last chapter after her. I titled the book *The Kitchen God's Wife*, which was how she was known, as the wronged spouse of a wandering husband. I gave her offerings of airline mini-bottles of Jack Daniel's.

Inspiration for my decorating comes from my ancestors. . . .

Do these things really work? All I know is this: I have been incredibly lucky these past few years. What I may lack in terms of sense of style, I more than make up for by giving myself a sense of luck.

And if my Chinese luck runs out, not to worry. I have the standard American charms as well: insurance and lawyers.

·room with a view, new kitchen, and ghosts·

Our San Francisco home, three heart-pounding flights up, has a few unusual touches: a widow's walk with a drop-dead view of the Golden Gate Bridge, thick walls filled with horsehair, and a remodeled attic which, until recently, was occupied by—there is no way to put this subtly—a ghost.

Mind you, this was not your run-of-the-mill phantom. Yes, we heard the usual spooky sound effects: footsteps running up and down the stairs, doors slamming, items crashing to the floor. But what made our visitations special was our spirit's taste in music. It liked the *Jeopardy!* tune, which, unfortunately, is precisely the sort of haunting melody you can't get out of your head while trying to write a novel about turn-of-the-century China.

The first time my husband and I heard it, we were sitting at our kitchen island, eating dinner. A badly whistled tune came from behind our backs: *Dah-dee-dah-dah, dah-dee-dah.* I turned to Lou. "Did you just do that?" And Lou, who does not believe in the supernatural, replied: "Uh . . . You didn't?"

The second time we heard it, we had our dental work checked. Houseguests inquired nervously about the sounds that went bump in the night. Workmen complained that the paint kept turning different colors on the walls. And once, at three in the morning, our television set turned itself on at high volume, tuned to a show featuring a preacher who shouted for us to give our souls to Jesus and our money to an 800 number. I did what any self-respecting homeowner would do. I searched the Yellow Pages and found a structural engineer who was also a psychic house-healer. One way or the other we would get to the bottom of this. And no matter what that was, this would be interesting material for a book.

For the ghostbusting occasion, I invited a few friends to serve as witnesses. Who would decline an opportunity like this, even if they did not believe in such things?

Our ghostbuster, George, turned out to be a middle-aged Chinese man with a sensible demeanor and a kind face. One would never guess he was in this peculiar line of work. He thumped on our walls, and jumped on our floorboards to test the squeak factor. "Pretty solid," he said. "Nice place you have here."

He began the spirit eviction by walking through our house. He started in the living room. "Definitely female," he said. "She once lived here. . . . I get that sense. It's quite strong. Many happy times here with her family." He walked into the kitchen. "Whoa! Things are really vibrating here. She doesn't like this room at all. Did you recently do something to change it?"

"We painted it." I gestured toward the Chinese-red walls.

George nodded. "She's saying to me, 'Look what they did to my beautiful kitchen.'"

I was a bit stung by our ghost's criticism. We moved on to the guest bedroom. "Oh, she is very fond of this room," George said. "This was her bedroom." Our poor guests. We moved upstairs to the attic, which now held a pool table. George grew very still as he let out his feelers. "She stays up here most of the time." Lou and I nodded. He pointed toward the eaves. "She hides in there." We nodded. The footsteps and loud noises had often come from that spot.

George said we needed to perform a ceremony in a quiet, darkened room. We descended to the dining room with its somber wood-paneled walls and cabinets. I drew the heavy curtains and pulled the glass pocket door closed.

A bell was rung and we all joined hands, saying "Om" with long exhalations. After seven of these, the room was warm with our nervousness. George held up a Tibetan singing bowl and ran a wooden stick around its rim, until it sang a warble that resonated through our bodies. It reminded me of the sound track of B movies in which wobbly spaceships could be seen hanging from a filament.

The prayers began: "We are sorry to tell you that you have passed from this world. This may be a shock to you, but please know another dimension awaits you. It is not good for you to remain stuck on earth any longer. We pray for you to go with God and toward those who love you. . . ."

The singing bowl kept singing. We kept waiting, not knowing where this ritual would go. Would the ghost manifest herself? Would she sizzle and melt like the Wicked Witch in *The Wizard of Oz*?

All at once, the bowl sang a fifth-note higher and smoother, and the temperature in the room dropped by ten degrees. George stopped praying. "She's left. Can you feel it?" We nodded. Lou and I paid George his fee, and he assured us we should not have any further problems, at least not with this particular spirit.

Do I actually believe in ghosts? Do I think our house was once haunted? On that score, I remain silent. So does our ghost.

· retreat to reality ·

My husband and I chanced upon a hidden meadow by the Truckee River just as the August light was fading to a glimmery alpine dusk. That was the wondrous moment when we glimpsed a pathway curving toward a storybook red cabin. By twilight, the scene had the dreamy aura of childhood imagination, the home of Hansel and Gretel, Goldilocks, the Three Bears.

The cabin's front porch was just big enough for two chairs and a romantic interlude. From there one could admire the coming of twilight, stars, a rising beacon moon. One could sit in silence, content, on an evening just like this, watching the forest blur into a gray-green scrim, feeling the air cool, hearing the mosquitoes sing, following the bats as they soared and swooped. Then, too soon, as if the meadow were an operatic stage, night's curtain descended, transforming all that beauty before us into vague memory.

We exhaled with envy for whoever lived there now. This was a retreat so simple it was grand. What Walden was for Thoreau, I imagined, Tahoe could be for Tan. Being there made me want to wax poetic. "Just two miles from Squaw," Lou said. "Not a bad place to park your ski gear."

As it turned out, the cabin was for sale. The owner had moved out six months before and the place was now rented. When a realtor took us out for a look-see, we learned that the cabin was inhabited by animals, that is, three prime specimens of *Jockus extremus,* subspecies Ski Patrol, sub-subspecies Alpine Meadows. The evidence hung in the air: stale beer and turbo-charged sweat, unwashed clothes and mildewed sleeping bags, a moldy shower stall and two very crusty toilets. On the kitchen counter lay an ode to the athletic lifestyle: Cheetos, Doritos, half-eaten burritos. I walked into a bedroom littered with four seasons' worth of sporting goods—hiking boots and river sandals, pitons and paddles, rappeling ropes and gaiters, topo maps and fanny packs, raunchy magazines, jockstraps, bras, and—count them—one, two, *three* used condoms.

One was disgusting, two was impressive, but three was definitely stretching it, so to speak. Lou and I knew what the gonzos were up to. Nice try, guys, but I'm a writer. I have imagination. I can see through the dirt, the ruse, the crude effort to keep this place as Club Ski Patrol, and I wasn't buying any of it—ha!—just the cabin. Get yourself another rental, boys.

Two months later, when the deal was done, Dave, the owner, was kind enough to drive out and give us folksy advice about the differences between living in the city and living in the wilds. "You can't just hail a cab when an avalanche blocks the road," he said. "I knew a guy, wandered out in deep snowdrifts by himself. Springtime, the snowplow turned him up like a petunia." Lou and I exchanged patient nods. This guy thought we were idiots. In truth, we were seasoned backpackers, hard-core skiers. We'd camped in snow, survived lightning storms, chased away a dozen bears at a time.

Dave went on: "See that tree? It doesn't look dead, but it is. You can tell by the lichen. You better take that soldier down before it lands on your propane tank. That tree busts your tank—blam!—there flies you and the cabin clear over to Harrah's on the South Shore."

"We don't gamble," Lou replied, and winked at me.

Dave went on: "Now here's another thing. Big problem. *Big.* Squirrels."

"Squirrels," we repeated.

"Golden-mantle squirrels," Dave affirmed. "Tiny things, look like Chip and Dale, cute as chipmunks. Let me tell you, though, they're dangerous. Hell, they're cute as scorpions. Don't ever feed 'em. They'll be crawling all over the place, drive you crazy." We duly nodded. I wondered whether living in the woods all those years had turned Dave into a curmudgeon. That's what I felt I had become living in the city—a cynic, the human extension to a telephone that was always on hold, eager to push life away from me rather than embrace it. That's why I needed to be in Tahoe. I wanted to feel grateful again to be part of the world. Gratitude led to a generosity of spirit, and that was what my soul required so I could write.

Little did I know at the time that the members of the Ski Patrol had already exacted their revenge. They hadn't just fed the squirrels. They must have fêted them with champagne brunches, barbecue picnics, and midnight buffets.

We named the first squirrel Fred. He danced around us while we did our chores, twirling and spinning gracefully like Fred Astaire. Our philosophy was "Live and let live," until, that is, Fred ran up my leg while I was applying a redwood stain to a pair of bookshelves. The creature clung to my pants and screeched as if to say, "Feed me, goddamnit!" I hollered and cursed, trying to shake him off, and Lou came racing toward me just as Fred jumped onto a paintbrush balanced on the can of stain. The brush wobbled for two seconds, then sank, squirrel and all. Fred, now Red, leapt out and left a swath of crimson on his way to a nearby tree.

Throughout the fall, squirrels hurled themselves at our screen door, their claws gripped in the mesh as they tried to bang their way in. I'd be writing, almost at that perfect point of concentration, a turning point in the story, an epiphany, when a lightning-fast blob would attach itself at the window screen, giving me the evil eye. Aside from writing and reflecting, I could bring myself oneness with nature by picking up black droppings, or by stuffing balls of steel wool (which resembled meditation pillows) into the holes the squirrels had knocked out of our knotty pine paneling.

During the winter, Lou and I made frequent trips to Tahoe to ski. After a hard day of moguls, we'd return to our snug little cabin, light the woodstove, change into our flannels, and settle in for a home-study course, "The Curious Habits of the Family *Sciuridae*." Ignorant people will tell you that squirrels fatten up on acorns through autumn, then hibernate all winter. Pure myth. In reality, they forage for food seven days a week, fifty-two weeks a year. And forget acorns. They prefer Newman's Own light-butter popcorn, bagels, bacon served in catch-and-release traps (we bought two), as well as the occasional bar of soap or antique kilim rug.

After feasting, squirrels don't sleep or even snooze. They

conduct swing-dance lessons under the eaves, accompanied by the rocking rhythms of an ultrasonic pest control unit (we bought three). They stomp into the wee hours of the night, making such thunderous noise that my mother once mistook a hundred-pound tree limb falling onto our roof for "another big squirrel."

Similar observations led Lou and me to surmise that squirrels are probably responsible for erroneous reports of poltergeist activity. The next time you see a candle or spice jar flying through the air, note whether there's a little critter teeheeing on a ledge about four feet away. Likewise, flickering lights may be caused by microsized buckteeth sawing through your wiring. Distant kin to the busy bee and beaver, squirrels are ever industrious, relentless in their quest to find every conceivable quarter-inch space between the wall and any houseguests raised on stories of rats that chewed off the noses of sleeping babies.

Spring came, and when the snow melted we hired a tree cutter to take down the dead white fir that Dave had warned us about. Fifty feet of timber fell, the earth shook, and the trunk cracked open, revealing a fleshy mass of pink the color and density of stale cotton candy. The tree cutter poked around, then gravely announced, "That there is your insulation. Squirrels turned this tree into a winter condo."

It's been years since we had our first encounter with Fred. Lou and I have made our peace with the squirrels, that is, we have learned to accommodate ourselves to their habits, just as they've adjusted to ours. We don't mind the tattered-rug look or, for that matter, the chewed-up-hiking-shoe style. It suits us. It's real Tahoe, rugged, outdoorsy, true-adventure sort of stuff. When I retreat to the cabin, I like to relate to the world in the spirit of a writer like Jack London. Wolves howling, squirrels screeching—with a little imagination, they're practically the same thing.

This year, I believe I have reached a new level of harmony. I have let go of anger, frustration, catch-and-release traps. I have come to think of the squirrels as inspiration for a book, in fact, a story like Stephen King's *The Shining* or *Misery*, or Alfred Hitchcock's movie *The Birds*—only scarier.

The story begins in a cabin by a river. The cabin is occupied by a nice, quiet writer. But she is kicked out by a bunch of randy, rowdy Ski Patrolers who buy the place. One day the writer returns with a bag of muffins, which she sprinkles around the cabin at midnight. As for the rest, you'll have to wait. I have to do more research.

The muffins are just about ready to come out of the oven.

· my hair, my face, my nails ·

I'm usually self-conscious about off-the-cuff writing, but sometimes the situations I have written about warrant the immediacy of an unedited form. This e-mail was written to friends who knew Lou and I were in Tahoe, in response to their question, "Are you all right?"

First, we're fine, back in San Francisco. The cabin, however, is another matter. We don't know how it will fare, given what we left. On Jan. 1, we saw the Truckee River was rising. Normally, the river flows about seven feet below our bridge; most winters you can ice skate under it. On Wed. the water was only inches below the bridge and roiling with logs and debris. The road to Truckee and Tahoe City was closed due to floods, and we decided that since we were warm and snug in the cabin, we should simply wait it out. But, to cover our bases, we moved the car to across the bridge. That way, if the bridge washed out, we could walk thru the snow along the river the other way to River Ranch on Alpine Meadows Road, then make our way over to the car. So we thought . . .

Much to Lou's annoyance, during dinner, I plugged into my computer and the message board to chat with folks on the weather channel. I described our situation, making sure I exaggerated the danger. "The river might rise and take out our bridge," I typed. "Do you need to be rescued?" someone typed back. "Nah," I answered.

Thursday before dawn, Lou and I heard a rumble, different from the pounding rain (which had not stopped in five days). It sounded to me as if the river had risen so high it was now flowing by our cabin. Jan, our houseguest, was fast asleep downstairs. Lou and I got up, looked out the door. "Wind," he surmised. And I said, "Then why aren't the trees blowing around?" At 8 a.m., John Leavitt, from a neighboring cabin, came by and said the whole area was devastated. The roar we heard last night was a mudslide that was only 50 feet from the back of our cabin. The slide which started higher up the mountain took down dozens of huge fir trees, boulders the size of cars, and sent this morass tumbling into the river. The river was brown with mud and swirling with hundred-foot-long trees. Our one-lane gravel road was now bisected by waterfalls and streams. Along this wrecked road were downed power lines. And closer toward the bridge was a giant mudslide that had cut a football field–sized swath down the mountain, felling trees in domino fashion, upturning the earth so that it looked as if the gods had done a bad rototilling job. Some of the logs knocked out the back end of one of the cabins. Kitchen appliances lay strewn in the mud. The propane tank had been whacked open and gas was leaking. Another cabin was pierced through its roof with the pointy end of a tree, which must have been catapulted through the air by the slide. Other cabins had mountain streams gushing through them. Fortunately, our cabin and John's were the only ones occupied, and our places were intact, although without phone, electricity, or water. Our cabin still had heat, provided by our propane tank, and, if need be, a woodburning stove.

The bridge was completely underwater; even the railings had disappeared. Leaning against the bridge was another bridge from upstream, as well as numerous logs. We had ourselves a beaver dam. And if our bridge went, then it would take all this debris and the other logs floating in the river down the white water, missing the bend, and it would land, most likely, in the bar and dining room of River Ranch.

We decided we had to get out before another slide occurred and cut its way to the river via our cabins. Lou and John went hiking across the mudslide in back of our cabin, thinking they might reach River Ranch and fetch us some help. But Lou got stuck in mud, chest-deep, which was the consistency of quicksand. And John, who is in his 60s, was tiring and didn't think he could help Lou out. The mountain started sliding again, sending down more trees and boulders. Finally, Lou and John extricated themselves and returned to the cabin, pale and exhausted, telling us that route was impassable.

Next, they went toward the bridge. Again, Lou got stuck in the deep mud, and when he pulled himself out, he headed down toward the river and spotted a couple of sheriffs across the bridge. They used a bullhorn to talk to him. Suddenly, one of them shouted, "Get the fuck out of the way," and Lou heard the unmistakable rumble of another slide. He jumped into the river, which got the sheriffs sort of excited, until he made it to shore.

So Lou and John came back and told us and Nancy, John's wife, who had joined us with their two dogs and a cat, that we were basically stuck. Our only way out was the river. There was some foolish talk about inflating our cheap summer raft and paddling across. But we all nixed that idea. Around 1 p.m., two sheriffs, dressed in wetsuits, came upon us. They had been struggling to get to us for about an hour and a half. They suggested taking us across the slide, then tying ropes to us so we could pull ourselves across the bridge. Lou said he didn't think we could make it across the slide, especially since we had four dogs and a cat with us. The sheriffs did a survey up and down the river, and via walkie-talkie, arranged a rescue using a Zodiac raft. We had to wait another hour and a half while things were set up. So Jan made the sheriffs breakfast, lunch, *and* dinner, since they hadn't eaten in two days.

At 3:00, we were ready. We'd received lessons on how to swim in the rapids should we fall in, the dogs were in bags, our computers were in backpacks.

Nancy and I were the ones chosen first to head for the river bank. We put on helmets and lifejackets, secured the dogs, and grabbed onto a rope to ease ourselves down the slippery slope. Below was the Zodiac raft with two more sheriffs in wetsuits. The river looked less turbulent and amazingly, the section right in front of our cabin had become, as the sheriffs told us, the most calm part of the entire river, the perfect place to put in. It was still raining, the dogs and cat were quiet. We took off.

The rest of our journey over was like a pleasure boating trip, smooth sailing. On the other shore, four sheriffs in wetsuits were on hand, standing in the river, ready to help us out. The minute I got on shore, a man held a TV mike to me and said, "How does it feel to be rescued?" And I missed my once in a lifetime chance to say, "My hair, my face, my nails—I must look a fright!" For those of you non–Tallulah Bankhead fans, that was her line in *Lifeboat* when she was finally rescued after a near-death experience. The reporter and cameraman did not know, of course, that I was a writer. But he did say we were his best rescue visuals for the day, what with the dogs and cat, the raging river and mountain mudslides, plus the beefy sheriffs in their wetsuits. You couldn't have scouted a better location for the evening news.

The sheriffs made three more trips to get John, Jan, Lou, and then the two sheriffs who found us. As the others stepped onto wet land, the TV reporter was there, asking the same questions. At the bridge we found our dumpster had been tossed like a cardboard box, but our cars were intact. The river water was running over the bridge and the bike path. Like tourists at Niagara, we happily posed for John as he shot photos, the devastation now behind us, literally and figuratively.

Later that evening, the TV coverage of our rescue was shown several times on CBS affiliates, and then also broadcast the next morning on NPR, or rather, they both provided coverage of "writer Amy Tan's dramatic rescue," leading Lou, who had twice defied death, to remark that had we died the headline would have read: "Amy Tan and four others killed by mudslide." This morning the phone calls came from friends who had heard that I had to leave behind my computer (I didn't), which contained my new novel (just part of it). The book editor at the *LA Times* heard that I had to be airlifted (rafted does have similar letters in it) and asked if I would write about that.

Now you know how fiction is written.

· the ghosts of my imagination ·

Who is the muse?

I've answered this question in many different ways. Sometimes I give the practical answer: The muse is really the personal process by which you synthesize your life with the work before you. It's memory added to imagination, subtracted by false starts, and multiplied by a fraction of the tons of hard work you've put into the mess.

Other times I say the muse is my mother, the woman who gave me both my DNA and certain ideas about the world. Or I pay homage to my grandmother and say that it is she who inspired me to find my voice because she had lost hers so irrevocably.

But there is another muse, one I find difficult to talk about. I cannot say who or what it is, although I can tell you what this muse feels like. This muse appears at that point in my writing when I sense a subtle shift, a nudge to move over, and everything cracks open, the writing is freed, the language is full, resources are plentiful, ideas pour forth, and, to be frank, some of these ideas surprise me. It seems as though the universe is my friend and is helping me write, its hand over mine.

For me, that spiritual-mental high would be sufficient reason for writing. And while I have experienced it with each book I've written, I have never been able to decipher its pattern so that I might repeat it as often as I would like. Whatever it is, I am grateful when it happens, fearful that it may not happen again.

To illustrate, let me take you on a journey, one that traces the beginning of a story through to its epiphany, its end. The story is *The Hundred Secret Senses,* which has a lot to do with ghosts, in part because it often seemed to me that ghostwriters were helping me write it. I say this with trepidation, knowing that some people look upon the subject of ghosts as blarney or blasphemy. The skeptic in me can scrunch up my eyebrows and find rational and mundane explanations for everything quasi-mystical that occurred during the writing of the book. But the truth is, those answers feel so utterly lifeless to me, while the way it *felt* to write leaves me with a sense of wonder, joy, and gratitude, elements I need in abundance. And so, in the spirit of Henry James, let us suspend disbelief as I tell you how my life intersected with my fiction and created this particular ghost story.

Let us begin with a sense of place. I based my fictional locale for *The Hundred Secret Senses* on a village in China that I had chanced upon while collaborating on the movie version of *The Joy Luck Club.* I had been on location in Guilin, a city renowned for its magnificent hills, caves, and waterways. One day, with the actor Russell Wong and my photographer friend Robert, I hired a driver and headed south. We had no charted destination, and took only impulse and lark as our directional guide.

And so by chance, or maybe not, we wound up in the middle of nowhere, in this instance a hamlet of pristine scenery and stone-stacked dwellings. There were no paved roads, no electricity, no plumbing other than the water that ran through gullies and irrigation ditches, and was brought into the village through hand pumps. The two hundred or so villagers spoke their own dialect, and only the children spoke Mandarin, the mandatory language taught in their school.

One woman, perhaps in her sixties, asked to have her photo taken with our Polaroid camera. While she surely must have seen herself daily in the cracked mirror nailed to the wall of her unlit room, she had never seen a picture of herself. She said as much. She peered with great anticipation while the film developed, but her smiling face fell into frowns and creases as she murmured what could only be the emotional equivalent of: "Is that what I really look like? I look so old. Look at my poor wrinkled face."

The name of the village, as I heard it from the children, was Bei Sa Po. The inhabitants seemed healthy and without evidence of the birth defects we saw in other villages, where the same walleyed facial deformities found among siblings, cousins, young aunts and uncles, along with a phlegmatic expression, suggested that close-knit families had suffered the consequences of generations of inbreeding. These children, in contrast, were bright and energetic. A group of them had built a small palace out of mud, including intricate moats, pathways, towers, and underground hiding places. Each child had his or her own troops, large, shiny black crickets, which were led forth on thin strings into battle.

Russell, Robert, and I walked through the village and climbed into the surrounding hills. From a higher point, we could see the valley with its stream and ponds, the hills reflected in them, the cluster of stone buildings, and paths that wove irregularly around natural barriers of old clumps of trees, boulders, and turns of the stream.

At the top of one hill, we found a ten-foot-high stone wall running the length of the ridge. It appeared to be some sort of medieval defense against invaders. Yet why would anyone have invaded such a tiny hamlet? Stepping through an archway, we found another valley, verdant and crisscrossed by stone hedges. We saw only two people tending the vast fields. We continued to walk, and reached another set of hills, and again a ridge lined with a high wall of rock. We stepped through another archway to see the valley on the other side.

The atmosphere changed immediately, to one of foreboding. Before us were rocky ruins and mountainsides pocked with caves. The skies seemed darker, and indeed, dark clouds had appeared, although we had not noticed them in the other two valleys. The land looked as if it had never been cultivated, with terrain as uneven as an unmade bed, and mossy boulders bursting from the earth. A collapsed hut of rocks in the center of the valley seemed to have been abandoned for hundreds of years. This was a wild place.

Russell and Robert wanted to dash down and take photos. But I begged them not to. I said I had the distinct sense that we had trespassed into a forbidden realm and that something terrible had happened in the very spot where we were standing. Words had an inhibiting effect. I emphasized the unknown consequences of trespassing. I reminded them of a news story we had read recently: A couple of tourists had been killed by bandits in a remote area of China. We turned back and twenty minutes later arrived at Bei Sa Po, just as it began to rain. When our car rumbled down the dirt road heading for Guilin, schoolchildren gathered along the side of the road and cried out to us in English: "Hello, good-bye! One-two-three, A-B-C!"

On the drive to Guilin, I was thinking that I had to use this setting in my next book. And a year or so later, when it did indeed surface as the fictional village in *The Hundred Secret Senses*, I further borrowed from the events of that day by casting the narrator as half Chinese, like the actor Russell Wong, and a photographer, like my friend Robert.

Sometime later, I was enjoying a fine meal with family at a Hakka restaurant in San Francisco, and I decided aloud that the fictional villagers should be of Hakka ethnicity so I could, of course, deduct the meal as research. But then my sister Lijun said from across the table: "Hakka people do not live in that part of China." She had lived in Guilin for ten years, and so she knew for a fact that no Hakka people lived inland. They were fishermen, not farmers. (Remember this detail: No Hakka people live inland, and certainly not in the remote mountains south of Guilin.)

I put aside this clash between fact and fiction and went heli-skiing for a week on glaciers in Canada. On the last of the seven days, and in the last hour, I did an impressive three-revolution forward cartwheel without intending to. My skis never released, but the top of my tibia did. It broke off and lodged under my kneecap, severing my nerves at the same time, so that mercifully I suffered little pain and did not even know I had sustained a serious fracture. The helicopter flew me back to the lodge in the wink of an eye, and because ninety-nine percent of all heli-skiers seem to be sports medicine physicians and other jock docs on holiday, I found myself surrounded by a retinue of the medical profession's finest.

One of these was Eric, an anesthesiologist, who routinely logged a million vertical feet of heli-skiing every year. My husband and I became friends with him; over the next three months Lou and I saw him at Squaw Valley and in southern California, and we often swapped horror stories of skiing accidents and avalanches. Eric had witnessed a mountain helicopter crash for whose victims he performed triage; four of them died. He had seen avalanches, and he described the sound, the stiff crack as the thick layer of congealed ice and snow separates from its upper half, the train rumble as the slab begins its descent, and then the crash as it achieves the speed of an ice-skating rink tilted sideways into freefall.

I had often imagined what an avalanche might be like, I told Eric. A close friend of ours, Steve, had been in one during an outing to which we had been invited but had been unable to go. Eric was like Steve in many ways. Steve was nicknamed "Jock Doc" because he was a sportsman first and a physician second. He was the ultimate risk-taker, a guy who scuba-dived among sharks and windsurfed in the crushing waves of Maui. And while he often tended to victims of horrendous accidents, curiously, he was afraid of death. One warm spring day, while cross-country skiing in an out-of-bounds area with his wife of nine months watching from above, he triggered an avalanche. A beacon for being located in case of such disaster was in his backpack. It was not turned on.

Steve had done everything right, another friend told me. He tried to swim through the avalanche, pushing himself up in the leaden ice floe with a butterfly stroke to gain his way to the top. When he was tumbled down, he managed to cup his hands in front of his face and push the snow away from his nose, doing this within the second before the snow congealed into the consistency of concrete, trapping him.

The medics who arrived at the scene knew Jock Doc personally. He was a friend, and they knew he had the aerobic fitness of a marathon runner. He had made the air pocket—this they knew because they found him with his hands clasped as if in prayer before his face. Most people, they said, would have lasted ten or fifteen minutes tops. Jock Doc, they guessed, had lasted at least forty-five.

I told Eric that all these years Steve had been gone, I could not stop wondering what he had been hoping, praying, believing during those forty-five minutes.

Eric said that he himself was afraid not so much of the pain of death's sword as of life's ledger. In his mind, the sum total of his experiences had not changed the world one iota. He was an anesthesiologist who worked for plastic surgeons, on elective-surgery cases where the money came from those who had the discretionary income to buy a better face. He was about to turn forty, and he saw himself as one more rubber raft floating in the doldrums; when he was gone, there would be another rubber raft to take his place. I asked him what it would take to prove that his life meant something—a medical discovery, charitable work, children? It's not too late, I said. You can still choose to do things differently. Eric underscored the false simplicity of my words: "It's not that simple," he said.

I thought about Eric's spiritual malaise, a common unease that plagues many from time to time, the longing to be special, the fear that one is not. I've had the sense that what I do is ultimately meaningless in the larger context of humanity and its pain and suffering. And because I often include in my writing what I feel at the moment, I decided to give my story's narrator, Olivia, the same unease. Further into the story, I wrote a scene in which an avalanche kills Olivia's imagined nemesis, a character on whom I bestowed the last name of my friend Steve. As to how I chose this character's first name, that is another story, another detour.

Summer arrived, and in July, I tottered off with my surgically repaired leg to Yaddo, a writers' retreat in upstate New York. Two weeks into my retreat, I took a weekend off to visit my editor, Faith Sale, at her country house in Cold Spring, a few counties away. Poking about her shelves, I spotted her Cornell yearbook, and decided to search for the face of Nabokov, one of my favorite writers. Faith had told me that he had taught at Cornell when she was a student. I plopped open the book on the kitchen table, where Faith sat doing the Sunday *Times* crossword puzzle. As I scanned the photos of young men and women with their 1950s hairdos, one image stopped my heart. It was that of a young woman whose steady gaze made her appear both defiant and frightened.

"My God, this one looks haunted," I said, "as if she's seen all the tragedies of the world."

"Who?" Faith asked.

I read the name aloud, and Faith gasped. "Ilse was my dearest, best friend in college." That afternoon I learned she had been brilliant and intense, both comic and serious. Ilse was born in Poland, and when she was five, her father threw her into the arms of friends before a train took the rest of the family away to Auschwitz. Ilse went to live with a Catholic family. She had to hide the fact that she spoke Yiddish as she prayed to Jesus on a cross. After the war, she was sent to the United States. Shortly after she graduated from Cornell in 1958, she checked into a hotel, signed the register claiming that she lived on a street named Tod—German for "death"—then killed herself.

I was so taken with Ilse's story that I told Faith I was going to revise the chapter I was working on. I wanted to add this back story. By coincidence, I had named my character Elza, which sounds close to Ilse. I proposed to change it to Ilse.

"Keep it," my editor said. Elza was Ilse's name in Poland, before she changed it to something she thought sounded less Jewish.

When I returned to Yaddo, everything seemed awash with references to the Holocaust. The CD music that a novelist lent me turned out to be a symphony written by a Polish Jew, who had dedicated it to the survivors of Auschwitz. One day I received a care package of dried fruit from a Jewish friend who said she was on her way to Poland to visit the village where many of her family's relatives had been slaughtered. Two nights later, I met a composer who was writing an opera about the San Francisco gay activist Harvey Milk, and he told me how the libretto was progressing. "The producers," he said, "think the librettist and I are placing too much emphasis on Harvey's upbringing as the child of Holocaust survivors."

When I returned home from Yaddo, I joined some friends for dinner at a poet's house. I learned that she also taught Holocaust literature, and that she, like my editor and Elza/Ilse, had graduated from the same university, Cornell, and in the same year.

Details like these, and many others, turned up with the persistence of a polished public-relations campaign directed by Jewish ghosts. With that kind of pressure, how could I not cast a few imaginary parts in the novel for my new imaginary friends?

I found these links between fluke and fiction to be meaningful, both a code and a carrot on a stick to make me go forward. It occurred to me that I should include tributes to other people, living and dead, as a way to thank them for being part of my life. I got so carried away that I even put in the names of my first pets, turtles named Slowpoke and Fastpoke. They died at the hands of my three-year-old little brother, who wanted to see what turtles looked like with their jackets off.

Later, while working on the Elza portion of the novel, I realized I had not yet thanked my friend Eric for his contributions, that is, his descriptions of avalanches, his discussions with me about midlife malaise. I opened the computer file that held the acknowledgments page and added his name. A week later, I received a telephone call from his brother, who told me the devastating news that on the morning of March 22, while he was heading to go skiing at Mammoth, Eric's private plane had encountered a heavy snowstorm and crashed into the side of a mountain. A few days later, as I prepared to write my contribution to his eulogy, I remembered the acknowledgments page. When had I entered Eric's name there? I opened the computer file and saw the date: March 22. That was also the birthday of Pete, a best friend and roommate of Lou's and mine, who was murdered in 1976, and the publication date of my first book, in

1989. (When I related this to my writers' group, one member said: "You know what this means, don't you? It's dangerous to be your friend!")

Lest it seem that my method of writing relies entirely on the demise of friends and pets, let me confirm that I in fact do scholarly research as well. The precise method involves pulling a scholarly text from my shelf, letting it fall open, then examining the pages that face up. I used this very technique to select a period of Chinese history in which to set my character Olivia's imagined past life. The choice came to me on a day when I was sitting gloomily at my desk. I was stuck, unable to proceed until I figured out what details to put in my fictional village, the one based on the hamlet I had stumbled upon during the filming of the movie in China. I wanted to keep the setting, but I needed a historic period and details that made sense for that region. I had to decide who these people were, what their ethnicity was, and thus, what they did, what they ate, the various minutiae and unusual but verifiable tidbits a novelist must provide for the story to come to life.

I have a number of Chinese history books on the shelf next to my desk. The one I pulled out was nice and thick, *The Search for Modern China* by Jonathan Spence. The page where my thumb inserted itself concerned the Taiping Rebellion. I read on: The Taiping Rebellion started in Thistle Mountain, just south of Guilin. Well, well, well. This was quite convenient—the same location as my fictional village.

I continued reading: The Taiping Rebellion was led by a man who believed he was the second son of God, baby brother to Jesus. Interesting—a Chinese Christian, like my father. This man,

Hong, was a Hakka who first rallied support from the Hakkas who lived in Thistle Mountain. Hakkas! Hadn't my sister told me no Hakkas lived inland? What an amazing coincidence—the very details I wanted, that corresponded with my setting.

Now that my fictional village was confidently inhabited by Hakkas, I needed to give it a suitable name. I remembered the landscape of the third valley, the one riddled with caves. I imagined the wind whistling through these caves at night, making the sound of singing ghosts. My morbid imagination, the one gleaned from a childhood of terrors, hypothesized that the caves were the gateway to death. With this image in mind, I pulled down from my shelf a pinyin–English dictionary, the sort of book used by those illiterate in Chinese, which, sadly, I am. I had to rely on my usual point-and-look method. The first entry my finger landed on was *changmian*. I read the definition: "long sleep, eternal rest, a euphemism for death." Above this was a separate entry for *chang*, which means "singing." I then looked up *mian*. This can mean either "endless" or "silky." So there, quite by coincidence, or perhaps not, I had the exact double entendre I was hoping for, *changmian*, which, depending on how you pronounce the tones, can mean "endless singing" or "death."

Much more scholarly research came my way. At one time I was having trouble locating information on limestone formations and a physics term known as the Bernoulli effect. I found myself seated next to a stranger at an impromptu dinner party one night, and I asked him what line of work he was in. He was a geology professor, he told me, and he had written about the rubble of limestone, and he happened to know how the Bernoulli effect might apply to wind erosion.

Another day, when I needed to know more about the possibility that ancient villages were situated in caves, I received a phone call inviting me to a dinner reception, to be attended by about thirty archaeologists, in honor of the foremost archaeologist in China, the man who helped excavate Peking Man. (That dinner would later inspire scenes I wrote for *The Bonesetter's Daughter*.)

On another occasion, I was writing about a puzzling image that came to mind for no apparent reason: a dark valley filled with hundreds of spires, rocks stacked on end and at oblique angles, in ways that defied the laws of gravity. The image was compelling, but I could not justify its presence. What did it mean? Why should my character come upon the scene? I wrote in circles until a friend called and suggested we go for a walk with our dogs. An hour later, I was on a length of beach I had never visited. My friend and I ducked under a pier, and when we emerged on the other side, I saw a long-haired Asian man stacking rocks, creating the same spires I had just described, dozens of them, each six or seven feet tall. Incredulous, I ran up to the builder of these rocky cairns. How is it that they don't topple over? I asked. And the man said, "I don't know. I guess with everything there's a point of balance. You just have to find it." That, I knew instantly, was the meaning of that scene, that was why the image was necessary to the story.

As with the Holocaust references, these coincidences were occurring at first once a day, then several times. The coincidences were oddly exact. How could I not notice them? It was as if in writing fiction I had opened my mind to the realm of all possibilities. Now the collective unconscious had yielded research, contacts, connections, images, and meanings. I was aware that other writers—James Merrill and William Butler Yeats of note—believed that their writings were influenced by sources that were ethereal, mystical, and spiritual in the sense that spirits were involved. Yeats believed the spirits delivered boatloads of images from the other side of the River Styx.

Then again, perhaps I noticed these "coincidences" because that is the obsessive nature of writing. It *creates* the boundaries, aligns the details into a story, a framework that guarantees that all the pieces are related to a whole. I reasoned that story-writing was a deliberate derangement of the mind. The story becomes a distorted lens, an impossibly wide perspective. And what appear to be coincidences are simply flotsam in the same stream of consciousness. This was the writerly logic I used to dismiss what was too strange to be believed as anything but the result of a skewed focus on coincidences.

And what my story still lacked was just that—focus. Thus far, I had a motley collection of anecdotes, historical research, and tributes to friends and family. As is often said in writers' workshops, the story was not yet *felt*. Mostly what I felt was pressure. I was six months past my final deadline, the one that was a year past my promised deadline, which in turn was a year past the proposed date of delivery. It was now early May, and since my book was due to come out in October, my now absolutely final deadline was July. By my estimation, I was at least a hundred pages and six months from the end, not counting revisions. In other words, what I would probably deliver to my publisher was bad news and not a book. Before I could do that, however, I received a phone call from my editor with news far worse than mine.

Faith had just been diagnosed with a rare cancer, considered untreatable, incurable, inoperable, with a prognosis of a few months, according to literature I found. In a shaky voice, my editor, my dear friend and personal food critic, jauntily remarked that she hoped to last through the summer vegetable season. To me, her words made about as much sense as if she had proclaimed that the planets had just collided. It was ridiculous, the stupidest thing I'd heard, as impossible as—well, say, my finishing my book on time.

An impetuous notion crossed my mind. I would go to New York and be with my editor, take care of her. Another part of me immediately argued against the idea. I had a book to write. She was counting on that as well. Besides, she lived in New York, and that would mean leaving my husband and home. That would require my living alone, something I had never done, in part because I have an inordinate fear of crime, having been held up at gunpoint on one occasion, nearly raped on another, and having had to identify the body of my murdered roommate. Imagine it: living in New York City, Terror Capital of the World, in an apartment by myself, lying in bed alone, dreaming of murder and mayhem, as thieves, rapists, and con men finagled with the locks on my door.

My editor was thrilled that I might come to New York for the summer. Strangeness begets strangeness, and arrangements fell into place one after another. An apartment was available. There was an airline ticket I had to use before it expired. Every time I thought about going to New York, objects I had lost would reappear. The phone would ring, and it was someone from New York. Two weeks after receiving Faith's news, I was boarding a plane to New York with a carry-on in one hand and a little dog in the other. I went for no reason I could clearly explain, then or now. I seemed to have no choice in the matter. The ghosts in my fiction and my life—my grandmother, my father, my brother, Pete, Jock Doc, Eric, Elza and her Jewish relatives, the Hakkas of Thistle Mountain—had pulled all the stops to make sure I had nothing better to do than go to New York and finish writing my novel while being with my editor. And while the ironies and coincidences had been plentiful when I was writing my novel, now they were gushing as wildly as a broken water main in the Bronx.

During the next two months in New York, my normal logic was upended, my senses were amplified. During the day, I went to the doctor's office with Faith. We went shopping for the freshest vegetables of the season. We argued over the benefits and hokeyness of alternative treatments. At night I went into a dark closet that served as my office and sat at a card table that served as my desk. With my little dog curled at my feet, I pondered the same questions I had had as a child: Why do things happen? How do things happen?

I thought about luck, fate, and destiny. Like the narrator of the book I had yet to finish, I didn't know what to believe and thus I didn't know what to hope. And during this flux of wondering and writing, I found the heart of my story. Except for one day and one night, I don't remember writing, yet I finished *The Hundred Secret Senses* in July.

It was a miracle that the book was done. I was elated. And yet some miracles didn't happen. Not yet. My friend, my editor, still had the cancer. Each day she had to cross a terrible chasm, a bottomless hole of not knowing what to hope or believe. I tried to imagine what she saw, but I did not have her perspective. My feet weren't perched on the ledge. So all I could do was remember.

I remembered those times in my life when I tried to believe that my father and brother would not die. I remembered those times when I desperately wanted to see my friends who had passed too soon. And I remembered also how I didn't want to hope too much, knowing that those hopes might turn into almost unendurable pain. In spite of what I didn't hope, the pain was still unbearable, a void so empty, so completely without meaning that it made me hope our existence did not end with the last breath and heartbeat. That same hope now made me remember all that had happened during the writing of *The Hundred Secret Senses*: how the made-up stories turned out to be true; how the research I needed dropped into my lap; how the ironies and coincidences accumulated, played off one another, forced me to wonder and consider that everything that happens is neither grand plan nor random coincidence. It is a crazy quilt of love, pieced together, torn apart, repaired again and again, and strong enough to protect us all.

Did the ghosts of friends and family come and serve as my muses? Aren't ghosts merely delusions in grief? I know now that these questions are meaningless and the answer is absolute. What are ghosts if not the hope that love continues beyond our ordinary senses? If ghosts are a delusion, then let me be deluded. Let me believe in the limitlessness of love, the beauty of contradictions, the miracle that is an ordinary part of life.

A CHOICE OF WORDS

She wanted to write a novel in the style of Jane Austen, a book of manners about the upper class, a book that had nothing to do with her own life. Years before, she had dreamed of writing stories as a way to escape. She could revise her life and become someone else. She could be somewhere else. In her imagination she could change everything, herself, her mother, her past. But the idea of revising her life also frightened her, as if by imagination alone she were condemning what she did not like about herself or others. Writing what you wished was the most dangerous form of wishful thinking.

· The Bonesetter's Daughter

· what the library means to me ·

I wrote this essay when I was eight years old, for a contest sponsored by the Citizens Committee for the Santa Rosa (California) Library. I received a transistor radio as a prize, and my essay was published in the Santa Rosa Press Democrat.

My name is Amy Tan, 8 years old, a third grader in Matanzas School. It is a brand new school and everything is so nice and pretty. I love school because the many things I learn seem to turn on a light in the little room in my mind. I can see a lot of things I have never seen before. I can read many interesting books by myself now. I love to read. My father takes me to the library every two weeks, and I check five or six books each time. These books seem to open many windows in my little room. I can see many wonderful things outside. I always look forward to go the library.

Once my father did not take me to the library for a whole month. He said, the library was closed because the building is too old. I missed it like a good friend. It seems a long long time my father took me to the library again just before Christmas. Now it is on the second floor of some stores. I wish we can have a real nice and pretty library like my school. I put 18 cents in the box and signed my name to join the Citizens of Santa Rosa Library.

At age eight (foreground), being congratulated for my essay "What the Library Means to Me," Santa Rosa, California, 1960.

· mother tongue ·

In 1989, I was invited to speak at a conference, "The State of the English Language." Upon learning that I would be on a panel with noted academicians and writers, I wrote this apologia the night before. Wendy Lesser of The Threepenny Review *later asked to publish it, and subsequently it was included in* The Best American Essays 1991.

I am not a scholar of English or literature. I cannot give you much more than personal opinions on the English language and its variations in this country or others.

I am a writer. And by that definition, I am someone who has always loved language. I am fascinated by language in daily life. I spend a great deal of my time thinking about the power of language—the way it can evoke an emotion, a visual image, a complex idea, or a simple truth. Language is the tool of my trade. And I use them all—all the Englishes I grew up with.

Recently, I was made keenly aware of the different Englishes I do use. I was giving a talk to a large group of people, the same talk I had already given to half a dozen other groups. The talk was about my writing, my life, and my book *The Joy Luck Club*, and it was going along well enough, until I remembered one major difference that made the whole talk sound wrong. My mother was in the room. And it was perhaps the first time she had heard me give a lengthy speech, using the kind of English I have never used with her. I was saying things like "the intersection of memory and imagination" and "There is an aspect of my fiction that relates to thus-and-thus"—a speech filled with carefully wrought grammatical phrases, burdened, it suddenly seemed to me, with nominalized forms, past perfect tenses, conditional phrases, forms of standard English that I had learned in school and through books, the forms of English I did not use at home with my mother.

Just last week, as I was walking down the street with her, I again found myself conscious of the English I was using, the English I do use with her. We were talking about the price of new and used furniture, and I heard myself saying this: "Not waste money that way." My husband was with us as well, and he didn't notice any switch in my English. And then I realized why. It's because over the twenty years we've been together I've often used the same kind of English with him, and sometimes he even uses it with me. It has become our language of intimacy, a different sort of English that relates to family talk, the language I grew up with.

So that you'll have some idea of what this family talk sounds like, I'll quote what my mother said during a conversation that I videotaped and then transcribed. During this conversation, she was talking about a political gangster in Shanghai who had the same last name as her family's, Du, and how in his early years the gangster wanted to be adopted by her family, who were rich by comparison. Later, the gangster became more powerful, far richer than my mother's family, and he showed up at my mother's wedding to pay his respects. Here's what she said in part:

"Du Yusong having business like fruit stand. Like off-the-street kind. He is Du like Du Zong—but not Tsung-ming Island people. The local people call *putong*. The river east side, he belong to that side local people. That man want to ask Du Zong father take him in like become own family. Du Zong father wasn't look down on him, but didn't take seriously, until that man big like become a mafia. Now important person, very hard to inviting him. Chinese way, came only to show respect, don't stay for dinner. Respect for making big celebration, he shows up. Mean gives lots of respect. Chinese custom. Chinese social life that way. If too important won't have to stay too long. He come to my wedding. I didn't see, I heard it. I gone to boy's side, they have YMCA dinner. Chinese age I was nineteen."

You should know that my mother's expressive command of English belies how much she actually understands. She reads the *Forbes* report, listens to *Wall Street Week*, converses daily with her stockbroker, reads Shirley MacLaine's books with ease—all kinds of things I can't begin to understand. Yet some of my friends tell me they understand fifty percent of what my mother says. Some say they understand eighty to ninety percent. Some say they understand none of it, as if she were speaking pure Chinese. But to me, my mother's English is perfectly clear, perfectly natural. It's my mother tongue. Her language, as I hear it, is vivid, direct, full of observation and imagery. That was the language that helped shape the way I saw things, expressed things, made sense of the world.

Lately I've been giving more thought to the kind of English

my mother speaks. Like others, I have described it to people as "broken" or "fractured" English. But I wince when I say that. It has always bothered me that I can think of no way to describe it other than "broken," as if it were damaged and needed to be fixed, as if it lacked a certain wholeness and soundness. I've heard other terms used, "limited English," for example. But they seem just as bad, as if everything is limited, including people's perceptions of the limited-English speaker.

I know this for a fact, because when I was growing up, my mother's "limited" English limited my perception of her. I was ashamed of her English. I believed that her English reflected the quality of what she had to say. That is, because she expressed them imperfectly, her thoughts were imperfect. And I had plenty of empirical evidence to support me: the fact that people in department stores, at banks, and in restaurants did not take her seriously, did not give her good service, pretended not to understand her, or even acted as if they did not hear her.

My mother has long realized the limitations of her English as well. When I was a teenager, she used to have me call people on the phone and pretend I was she. In this guise, I was forced to ask for information or even to complain and yell at people who had been rude to her. One time it was a call to her stockbroker in New York. She had cashed out her small portfolio, and it just so happened we were going to New York the next week, our first trip outside California. I had to get on the phone and say in an adolescent voice that was not very convincing, "This is Mrs. Tan."

My mother was standing in the back whispering loudly, "Why he don't send me check, already two weeks late. So mad he lie to me, losing me money."

And then I said in perfect English on the phone, "Yes, I'm getting rather concerned. You had agreed to send the check two weeks ago, but it hasn't arrived."

Then she began to talk more loudly. "What he want, I come to New York tell him front of his boss, you cheating me?" And I was trying to calm her down, make her be quiet, while telling the stockbroker, "I can't tolerate any more excuses. If I don't receive the check immediately, I am going to have to speak to your manager when I'm in New York next week." And sure enough, the following week, there we were in front of this astonished stockbroker, and I was sitting there red-faced and quiet, and my mother, the real Mrs. Tan, was shouting at his boss in her impeccable broken English.

We used a similar routine more recently, for a situation that was far less humorous. My mother had gone to the hospital for an appointment to find out about a CAT scan she had had a month earlier. She said she had spoken very good English, her best English, no mistakes. Still, she said, the hospital staff did not apologize when they informed her they had lost the CAT scan and she had come for nothing. She said they did not seem to have any sympathy when she told them she was anxious to know the exact diagnosis, since both her husband and her son had died of brain tumors. She said they would not give her any more information until the next time and she would have to make another appointment for that. So she said she would not leave until the doctor called her daughter. She wouldn't budge. And when the doctor finally called her daughter, me, who spoke in perfect English—lo and behold—we had assurances the CAT scan would be found, promises that a conference call on Monday would be held, and apologies for any suffering my mother had gone through for a most regrettable mistake.

I think my mother's English almost had an effect on limiting my possibilities in life as well. Sociologists and linguists probably will tell you that a person's developing language skills are more influenced by peers than by family. But I do think that the language spoken in the family, especially in immigrant families which are more insular, plays a large role in shaping the language of the child. And I believe that it affected my results on achievement tests, IQ tests, and the SAT. While my English skills were never judged poor, compared with math, English could not be considered my strong suit. In grade school I did moderately well, getting perhaps B's, sometimes B-pluses, in English and scoring perhaps in the sixtieth or seventieth percentile on achievement tests. But those scores were not good enough to override the opinion that my true abilities lay in math and science, because in those areas I achieved A's and scored in the ninetieth percentile or higher.

This was understandable. Math is precise; there is only one correct answer. Whereas, for me at least, the answers on English tests were always a judgment call, a matter of opinion and personal experience. Those tests were constructed around items like fill-in-the-blank sentence completion, such as "Even though Tom was _______ Mary thought he was ______." And the correct answer always seemed to be the most bland combinations, for example, "Even though Tom was shy, Mary thought he was charming," with the grammatical structure "even though" limiting the correct answer to some sort of semantic opposites, so you wouldn't get answers like "Even though Tom was foolish, Mary thought he was ridiculous." Well, according to my mother, there were very few limitations as to what Tom could have been and what Mary might have thought of him. So I never did well on tests like that.

The same was true with word analogies, pairs of words for which you were supposed to find some logical semantic relationship, for instance, "Sunset is to nightfall as _____ is to _____." And here you would be presented with a list of four possible pairs, one of which showed the same kind of relationship: *red* is to *stoplight, bus* is to *arrival, chills* is to *fever, yawn* is to *boring.* Well, I could never think that way. I knew what the tests were asking, but I could not block out of my mind the images already created by the first pair, *sunset* is to *nightfall*—and I would see a burst of colors against a darkening sky, the moon rising, the lowering of a curtain of stars. And all the other pairs of words—*red, bus, stoplight, boring*—just threw up a mass of confusing images, making it impossible for me to see that saying "A sunset precedes nightfall" was as logical as saying "A chill precedes a fever." The only way I would have gotten that answer right was to imagine an associative situation, such as my being disobedient and staying out past sunset, catching a chill at night, which turned into feverish pneumonia as punishment—which indeed did happen to me.

I have been thinking about all this lately, about my mother's English, about achievement tests. Because lately I've been asked, as a writer, why there are not more Asian-Americans represented in American literature. Why are there few Asian-Americans enrolled in creative writing programs? Why do so many Chinese students go into engineering? Well, these are broad sociological questions I can't begin to answer. But I have noticed in surveys—in fact, just last week—that Asian-American students, as a whole, do significantly better on math achievement tests than on English tests. And this makes me think that there are other Asian-American students whose English spoken in the home might also be described as "broken" or "limited." And perhaps they also have teachers who are steering them away from writing and into math and science, which is what happened to me.

Fortunately, I happen to be rebellious and enjoy the challenge of disproving assumptions made about me. I became an English major my first year in college, after being enrolled as pre-med. I started writing nonfiction as a freelancer the week after I was told by my boss at the time that writing was my worst skill and I should hone my talents toward account management.

But it wasn't until 1985 that I began to write fiction. At first I wrote what I thought to be wittily crafted sentences, sentences that would finally prove I had mastery over the English language. Here's an example from the first draft of a story that later made its way into *The Joy Luck Club*, but without this line: "That was my mental quandary in its nascent state." A terrible line, which I can barely pronounce.

Fortunately, for reasons I won't get into here, I later decided I should envision a reader for the stories I would write. And the reader I decided on was my mother, because these were stories about mothers. So with this reader in mind—and in fact she did read my early drafts—I began to write stories using all the Englishes I grew up with: the English I spoke to my mother, which for lack of a better term might be described as "simple"; the English she used with me, which for lack of a better term might be described as "broken"; my translation of her Chinese, which could certainly be described as "watered down"; and what I imagined to be her translation of her Chinese if she could speak in perfect English, her internal language, and for that I sought to preserve the essence, but neither an English nor a Chinese structure. I wanted to capture what language ability tests could never reveal: her intent, her passion, her imagery, the rhythms of her speech and the nature of her thoughts.

Apart from what any critic had to say about my writing, I knew I had succeeded where it counted when my mother finished reading my book and gave me her verdict: "So easy to read."

·the language of discretion·

Once, at a family dinner in San Francisco, my mother whispered to me: "Sau-sau [Brother's Wife] pretends too hard to be polite! Why bother? In the end, she always takes everything."

My mother acted like a *waixiao,* an expatriate, temporarily away from China since 1949, no longer patient with ritual courtesies. As if to prove her point, she reached across the table to offer my elderly aunt from Beijing the last scallop from the Happy Family seafood dish.

Sau-sau scowled. *"B'yao, zhen b'yao!"* she cried, patting her plump stomach. I don't want it, really I don't!

"Take it! Take it!" my mother scolded in Chinese.

"Full, I'm already full," Sau-sau protested weakly, eyeing the beloved scallop.

"Ai!" exclaimed my mother, exasperated. "Nobody else wants it. If you don't take it, it will only rot!"

Sau-sau sighed, acting as if she were doing my mother a big favor by taking the wretched scrap off her hands.

My mother turned to her brother, a high-ranking Communist

official who with Sau-sau was visiting her in California for the first time: "In America a Chinese person could starve to death. If you say you don't want it, they won't ask you again forever."

My uncle nodded and said he understood fully: Americans take things quickly because they have no time to be polite.

I thought about this misunderstanding again—of social contexts failing in translation—when a friend sent me an article from *The New York Times Magazine*. The article, on changes in New York's Chinatown, made passing reference to the inherent ambivalence of the Chinese language.

Chinese people are so "discreet and modest," the article stated, that there aren't even words for "yes" and "no."

That's not true, I thought, although I could see why an outsider might think that. I continued reading.

If one is Chinese, the article went on, "one compromises, one doesn't hazard a loss of face by an overemphatic response."

My throat seized. Why do people keep saying these things? As though we were like those little dolls sold in Chinatown tourist shops, heads bobbing up and down in complacent agreement to anything said!

I worry about the effect of one-dimensional statements on the unwary and guileless. When they read about this so-called vocabulary deficit, do they also conclude that Chinese people evolved into a mild-mannered lot because their language allowed them only to hobble forth with minced words?

Something enormous is always lost in translation. Something

insidious seeps into the gaps, especially when amateur linguists continue to compare, one for one, language differences and then put forth notions wide open to misinterpretation: that Chinese people have no direct linguistic means to make decisions, assert or deny, affirm or negate, just say no to drug dealers, or behave properly on the witness stand when told, "Please answer yes or no."

Yet one can argue, with the help of renowned linguists, that the Chinese are indeed up a creek without "yes" and "no." Take any number of variations on the old language-and-reality theory stated years ago by Edward Sapir: "Human beings . . . are very much at the mercy of the particular language which has become the medium of expression for their society. . . . The fact of the matter is that the 'real world' is to a large extent unconsciously built up on the language habits of the group."*

This notion was further bolstered by the famous Sapir–Whorf hypothesis, which states roughly that one's perception of the world and how one functions in it depends a great deal on the language used. As Sapir, Benjamin Whorf, and new carriers of the banner would have us believe, language shapes our thinking, channels us along certain patterns embedded in words, syntactic structures, and intonation patterns. Language has become the peg and the shelf that enable us to sort out and categorize the world. In English, we see "cats" and "dogs"; what if the language had also specified *glatz*, meaning "animals that leave fur on the sofa," and *glotz*, meaning "animals that leave fur and

***Selected Writings of Edward Sapir in Language, Culture and Personality*, ed. D. G. Mandelbaum (Berkeley and Los Angeles: University of California Press, 1949).

drool on the sofa"? How would language, the enabler, have changed our perceptions with slight vocabulary variations?

And if this were the case—if language were the master of destined thought—think of the opportunities lost from failure to evolve two little words, "yes" and "no," the simplest of opposites! Genghis Khan could have been sent back to Mongolia. Opium wars might have been averted. The Cultural Revolution could have been sidestepped.

There are still many, from serious linguists to pop psychology cultists, who view language and reality as inextricably tied, one being the consequence of the other. We have traversed the range from Sapir–Whorf to est to neurolinguistic programming, which tell us that "you are what you say."

I too have been intrigued by the theories. I can summarize, albeit badly, ages-old empirical evidence: of Eskimos and their infinite ways to say "snow," their ability to *see* differences in snowflake configurations, thanks to the richness of their vocabulary, while non-Eskimos like me founder in "snow," "more snow," and "lots more where that came from."

I too have experienced dramatic cognitive awakenings via the word. Once I added "mauve" to my vocabulary, I began to see it everywhere. When I learned how to pronounce "prix fixe," I ate French food at prices better than the easier-to-say "à la carte" choices.

But just how seriously are we supposed to take this?

Sapir said something else about language and reality. It is the part that often gets left behind in the dot-dot-dots of quotations: "No two languages are ever sufficiently similar to be considered as representing the same social reality. The worlds in which different societies live are distinct worlds, not merely the same world with different labels attached."

When I first read this, I thought, Here at last is validity for the dilemmas I felt growing up in a bicultural, bilingual family! As any child of immigrant parents knows, there's a special kind of double bind attached to knowing two languages. My parents, for example, spoke to me in both Chinese and English; I spoke back to them in English.

"Amy-ah!" they'd call to me.

"What?" I'd mumble back.

"Do not question us when we call," they'd scold in Chinese. "It is not respectful."

"What do you mean?"

"Ai! Didn't we just tell you not to question?"

To this day, I wonder which parts of my behavior were shaped by Chinese, which by English. I am tempted to think that if I am of two minds on some matter, it is due to the richness of my linguistic experiences, not to any personal tendencies toward wishy-washiness. But which mind says what?

Was it perhaps patience—developed through years of deciphering my mother's fractured English—that had me listening politely while a woman announced over the phone that I had won one of five valuable prizes? Was it respect—pounded in by the Chinese imperative to accept convoluted explanations—that had me agreeing that I might find it worthwhile to drive seventy-five miles to view a time-share resort? Could I have been at a loss for words when asked, "Wouldn't you like to win a Hawaiian cruise or perhaps a fabulous Star of India designed exclusively by Carter and Van Arpels?"

And when this same woman called back a week later, this time complaining that I had missed my appointment, obviously it was my type A language that kicked into gear and interrupted her. Certainly, my blunt denial—"Frankly I'm not interested"—was as American as apple pie. And when she said, "But it's in Morgan Hill," and I shouted back, "Read my lips. I don't care if it's Timbuktu," you can be sure I said it with the precise intonation expressing both cynicism and disgust.

It's dangerous business, this sorting out of language and behavior. Which one is English? Which is Chinese? The categories manifest themselves: passive or aggressive, tentative or assertive, indirect or direct. And I realize they are just variations of the same theme: that Chinese people are discreet and modest.

Reject them all!

If my reaction seems overly strident, it is because I cannot come across as too emphatic. I grew up listening to the same lines over and over, like so many rote expressions repeated in an English phrasebook. And I too almost came to believe them.

Yet if I consider my upbringing more carefully, I find there was nothing discreet about the Chinese language I grew up with. My parents made everything abundantly clear. Nothing wishy-washy in their demands, no compromises accepted. "Of course you will become a famous neurosurgeon," they told me. "And yes, a concert pianist on the side."

In fact, now that I remember, it seems that the more emphatic outbursts always spilled over into Chinese: "Not that way! You must wash rice so not a single grain is lost."

I do not believe that my parents—both immigrants from

mainland China—are the sole exceptions to the discreet-and-modest rule. I have only to look at the number of Chinese engineering students skewing minority ratios at Berkeley, MIT, and Yale. Certainly they were not raised by passive mothers and fathers who said, "It's up to you, my daughter. Writer, welfare recipient, masseuse, or molecular engineer—you decide."

And my American mind says, See, those engineering students weren't able to say no to their parents' demands. But then my Chinese mind remembers: Ah, but those parents all wanted their sons and daughters to be *pre-med*.

Having listened to both Chinese and English, I tend to be suspicious of any comparisons made between the two languages. Typically, one language—that of the person who is doing the comparing—is used as the standard, the benchmark for a logical form of expression. And so the other language is in danger of being judged by comparison deficient or superfluous, simplistic or unnecessarily complex, melodious or cacophonous. English speakers point out that Chinese is extremely difficult because it relies on variations in tone barely discernible to the human ear. By the same token, Chinese speakers tell me English is extremely difficult because it is inconsistent, a language of too many broken rules, of Mickey Mice and Donald Ducks.

Even more dangerous, in my view, is the temptation to compare both language and behavior *in translation*. To listen to my mother speak English, one might think she has no concept of past or future, that she doesn't see the difference between singular and plural, that she is gender blind because she refers to my husband as "she." If one were not careful, one might also generalize, from how my mother talks, that all Chinese people take a circumlocutory route to get to the point. It is, rather, my mother's idiosyncratic behavior to ramble a bit.

I worry that the dominant society may see Chinese people from a limited—and limiting—perspective. I worry that seemingly benign stereotypes may be part of the reason there are few Chinese in top management positions, in mainstream political roles. I worry about the power of language: that if one says anything enough times—in *any* language—it might come true.

Could this be why Chinese friends of my parents' generation are willing to accept the generalizations?

"Why are you complaining?" one of them said to me. "If people think we are modest and polite, let them think that. Wouldn't Americans be pleased to be thought of as polite?"

And I do believe that anyone would take the description as a compliment—at first. But after a while, it annoys, as if the only things that people heard one say were phatic remarks: I'm so pleased to meet you. I've heard many wonderful things about you. For me? You shouldn't have!

These remarks are not representative of new ideas, honest emotions, or considered thought. They are what is said from the polite distance of social contexts: greetings, farewells, wedding thank-you notes, convenient excuses, and the like.

I wonder, though. How many anthropologists, how many sociologists, how many travel journalists have documented so-called natural interactions in foreign lands, all observed with spiral notebook in hand? How many cases are there of long-lost "primitive" tribes, people who turned out to be sophisticated enough to put on the stone-age show that ethnologists had come to see?

And how many tourists fresh off the bus have wandered into Chinatown expecting the self-effacing shopkeeper to admit under duress that the goods are not worth the price asked? I have witnessed it:

"I don't know," a tourist told the shopkeeper, a Cantonese woman perhaps in her fifties. "It doesn't look genuine to me. I'll give you three dollars."

"You don't like my price, go somewhere else," answered the shopkeeper.

"You are not a nice person," cried the shocked tourist, "not a nice person at all!"

"Who say I have to be nice," snapped the shopkeeper.

So how does one say 'yes' and 'no' in Chinese?" my friends ask a bit warily.

And here I do agree in part with the *New York Times Magazine* article. There is no one word for "yes" or "no"—but not out of necessity to be discreet. If anything, I would say the Chinese equivalent of answering "yes" or "no" is dis*crete*, that is, specific to what is asked.

Ask a Chinese person if he or she has eaten, and he or she might say *chrle* (eaten already) or *meiyou* (have not).

Ask, "So you had insurance at the time of the accident?" and the response would be *dwei* (correct) or *meiyou* (did not have).

Ask, "Have you stopped beating your wife?" and the answer refers directly to the proposition being asserted or denied: stopped already, still have not, never beat, have no wife.

What could be clearer?

As for people who are still wondering how to translate the language of discretion, I offer this personal example.

My aunt and uncle were about to return to Beijing after a three-month visit to the United States. On their last night I announced I wanted to take them out to dinner.

"Are you hungry?" I asked in Chinese.

"Not hungry," my uncle said promptly—the same response he once gave me ten minutes before suffering a low-blood-sugar attack.

"Not too hungry," said my aunt. "Perhaps you're hungry?"

"A little," I admitted.

"We can eat, we can eat, then," they both consented.

"What kind of food?" I asked.

"Oh, doesn't matter. Anything will do. Nothing fancy, just some simple food is fine."

"Do you like Japanese food?" I suggested. "We haven't had that yet."

They looked at each other.

"We can eat it," said my uncle bravely, this survivor of the Long March.

"We have eaten it before," added my aunt. "Raw fish."

"Oh, you don't like it?" I said. "Don't be polite. We can go somewhere else."

"We are not being polite. We can eat it," my aunt insisted.

So I drove them to Japantown and we walked past several restaurants featuring colorful displays of plastic sushi in the windows.

"Not this one, not this one either," I continued to say, as if searching for a certain Japanese restaurant. "Here it is," I finally said, in front of a Chinese restaurant famous for its fish dishes from Shandong Province.

"Oh, Chinese food!" cried my aunt, obviously relieved.

My uncle patted my arm. "You think like a Chinese."

"It's your last night here in America," I said. "So don't be polite. Act like an American."

And that night we ate a banquet.

· *five writing tips* ·

This is an edited version of a speech given as a commencement address at Simmons College, in Boston, in 2003.

Members of the Board of Trustees, President Cheever and faculty, distinguished honorees, graduating students, and their family and loved ones who helped make today possible with their patience, hope, good faith, and low-interest loans, thank you for your kind welcome. What a delight that we meet on this glorious day at the historic and beautiful Simmons College parking lot.

Soon you, the Class of 2003, will have your degrees conferred upon you, your names called, President Cheever's hand sweeping over your anointed heads, and in elation and near-loss of consciousness from joy you will toss those mortarboards in the air. And when that moment comes, I want you to remember one of the truly great and moving moments in the history of the conferring of degrees: it is when the Scarecrow receives his honorary doctorate in thinkology from the Wizard of Oz. The Scarecrow instantly possesses his long-cherished brain. He points to his head and recites: "The sum of the square roots of any two sides of an isosceles triangle is equal to the square root of the remaining side." Well, guess what? He got it *wrong*, and everybody else did too, because they clapped and were very impressed. Oh, for years I got it wrong too, because I never really thought about what he said, that what he should have said was: "The square of the hypotenuse of a right triangle is . . ." Of course, it didn't really matter what gibberish the Scarecrow spoke, because what he was demonstrating was that he had the credentials and the confidence, and he could now BS his way through life and stay on in Oz as a politician.

But you folks won't need to rely on BS, I know that, because you are graduating from Simmons College, not Wizard School, and you not only are well educated but also possess certain principles that have been a large part of your immersion in this school's fine tradition of higher education. I am honored that you wish to give me a doctorate from Simmons, a doctorate in letters. I have been promised by President Cheever that I will have rights, privileges, and dignities that I did not previously hold, which include a free parking space in this glorious lot before me, that is, when it is not otherwise occupied for more important matters, such as ceremonies like today's. I believe that with my doctorate I will also enjoy the investiture of prodigious powers, including the ability to envision your future.

What I see in fact is a dream you will all share. Of course you may each dream it on different nights, but the dream goes like this: You are sitting in Java City, having a coffee mocha, when suddenly you realize you are late for class. The trouble is, you don't remember which class, because you haven't been to that class once since you registered for it. Mercifully, you see other students you recognize and you follow them. With great relief to you, things begin to look familiar as you make your way through the Main Campus Building, noting the same old books sewn into the walls. At last you seem to be in the right class, and you sit down toward the back, where you won't be noticed. Unfortunately, you realize, the person in the front of the room is Professor Gregory, and that means this class is the dreaded Philosophy 300, jolly times with Freddy Nietzsche. A second later, you realize as you watch Professor Gregory pass out some papers, the final exam is today. You look at your watch, five hours to go, and then read the first page of the test. It is written in Old German, in tiny type, a single question taking up the entire page, no margins. You skip to the next page. It is completely black, and you must discern the philosophical argument about your own existential identity contained within that blackness and answer it in the form of a *Jeopardy!* question. I have been a *Jeopardy!* question myself, so I know how difficult this is. The last page is a list of all the religions of the world in ancient dead languages, which you must put into the order in which Nietzsche might have despised them.

Although most of you are women, you begin to sweat profusely. But because many of you are women, you will be resourceful and wing it anyway. I've done that. Some of you, despite being women, will weep with despair, knowing the jig is up. A few of you, being men, also will cry, but you will know that it's okay to do so, because, as Simmons grads, you know this is the sign of a sensitive male. And some of you will have an incredible epiphany: "Wait a minute!" you will shout, and leap up and point to Professor Gregory, whose mouth drops open in surprise as you announce: "I don't have to take this class or this test, because I already have my degree from Simmons College!"

So there you have it: my prediction of your future, the dream you will all share. When it happens, I hope you will think of me. Having had versions of this dream so often myself, I can offer you useful advice. Frame your diploma. A scanned copy of it will suffice should you wish to hang the original on your front door, where guests are certain to see it. But frame at least one copy and hang it next to your bed. When you have this dream, open your eyes, look at your diploma, congratulate yourself, then go back to sleep.

For years and years, I had variations on this nightmare. I suppose the meaning is obvious: No matter how much we've accomplished, we still feel inadequate, unprepared. It's not surprising. Many of the greatest moments we experience are moments we cannot adequately prepare for, the birth of a child, the death of a loved one.

Nowadays I have a new version of this dream. I am no longer taking a final exam. I am about to give a speech to a lot of people who expect me to transmit the wisdom of the ages, for instance, the best way to find a literary agent. But in my dream, when I look for the prepared notes I have brought to the lectern, I see that I have grabbed by mistake the lyrics to Madonna's "Material Girl." Today, I am pleased to say, I did bring the right notes. Don't worry—it just looks like a twelve-hour speech, but that's because I printed it in twenty-four-point type, ten words to a page.

So what can I as a writer tell you today that might be useful as you leave this period of your life and enter the next? One possibility was a list of my five favorite Chinese restaurants. This would enrich your lives and your stomachs enormously.

What I ultimately decided on, instead, are five writing tips, which you may find useful in areas other than writing, perhaps even in thinking about life, how you might conduct it in a manner that is interesting and worthwhile. Here is my list:

1. Avoid clichés. They are all around us, and they are anathema to original thought. Take these, all having to do with an acceptance of fate: "That's how it was meant to be." Or "That's our lot in life." Or "History is doomed to repeat itself." Or "She was in the wrong place at the wrong time." And how about: "Some things were just meant to be," and "If it's not one thing, it's another," a cliché brilliantly parodied by Gilda Radner. And what about that great chestnut some say can be attributed to Nietzsche himself: "Shit happens."

When you are told, "It was meant to be," ask, "Who meant it? What does it really mean?" Is someone trying to make you accept an undesirable situation or one in which you have doubts? When you are told, "Shit happens," remember that plenty of other things happen as well, such as generosity, forgiveness, ambiguity, and uncertainty. When you are told, "It's simply fate," ask yourself, "What is simple about it? What are the alternatives of fate? What is fate's opposite?"

If you hear others using clichés, stop to think whether you're being lulled into inaction or the wrong action. If you hear overused expressions on the news, stop to think whether they are really meaningful. The spectrum of meaning is endless and fascinating and filled with humanity. Clichés are static, the emotion behind them long spent. If you are tempted to use them, here is a saying of my mother's: *Fang pi bu-cho, cho pi bu-fang.* Basically that translates to: "Loud farts don't stink, and the really smelly ones don't make a sound." In other words: When you're full of beans, you just blow a lot of hot air. If you want to have real impact, be deadly but silent.

Oh, also recognize the difference between a bad cliché and a good quotation. My mother's saying is a good quotation. You should use it often.

2. *Avoid generalizations.* As a fiction writer, I distrust absolute truths, homilies, bromides, sound bites, and also shorthand advice of the sort I am giving. I like specifics, the longhand version of a story in which it takes four hundred pages to answer a single question about a person's character. Literary writers, unless they are writing fairy tales, learn early never to have characters who are polar opposites, one "good," the other "evil." That's not believable. People are more than just good and evil. Intelligent readers will demand that you not reduce people to such simplistic terms, or resolve situations with "Good always conquers evil," "Might is always right," and so forth. And while such resolutions are common in murder mysteries and action stories, they are feeble in literary fiction, which is supposed to reflect subtle truths about the world. Better to be subtle rather than overbearing, subversive rather than didactic.

3. *Find your own voice.* As college graduates, you have a good start. Your own voice is one that seeks a personal truth, one that only you can obtain. That truth comes from your own experiences, your own observations, and when you find it, if it really is true and specific to you, you may be surprised that others find it to be true as well. In searching for your own voice, be aware of the difference between emulation and imitation, inspiration and intimidation.

4. Show compassion. Many beginning writers think sarcasm is a clever way to show intelligence. But more mature writers know that mean-spiritedness is wearying and limited in its one-dimensional point of view. A more successful story is one in which the narrator can treat human foibles, even serious flaws, with depth and hence compassion. Imagination brings you close to compassion. Practice imagining yourself living the life of someone whose situation differs entirely from yours—living in another country, having another religion—and the more deeply you can do so, the more you become that character as you write. You cannot help being compassionate.

5. Ask the important questions. What makes a story worthwhile is the question or questions it poses. The questions might be: What is love? What is loss? What is hope? Those three could take a lifetime to answer. My story is one answer. Your story is another.

Another question posed in literature concerns intentions. What are people's intentions, particularly as they relate to the well-being of others? What if their intentions lead to unexpected and undesirable consequences for other people? Who bears the consequences? Who should be responsible? How long do those responsibilities extend? The ultimate answers are found not just at the Supreme Court, or even among our leaders. We need personal answers, all the stories, as many as we can get. But to find them, you first must ask the questions. You need to ask yourself: What is important? What is at stake? In knowing what questions you are asking, you also know your individual voice, your own morality.

Those are the five writing tips: Avoid clichés, avoid generalizations, find your own voice, show compassion, and ask the important questions. I hope that you find them useful, if not for writing the next Great American Novel, then for thinking about your life and the world around you. What you do with your careers will be only one part of the whole of your lives. Your thoughts, your evolving answers to the important questions, are what will give you interesting lives, make you interesting people capable of changing the world.

And later in life, as more interesting answers come to you, you may look back with deep gratitude to Professor Gregory, and all those other dedicated teachers at Simmons College, who gave you nightmares but also the basis for thinking about the world and your role in it. Perhaps one day you will even think that Nietzsche was one of the most useful classes you took. You will have that dream in which you have to take the test, but you will not feel at all unprepared. You will be able to see the questions and say, "I've been thinking about the answers for a very long time, and here they are."

I wish you all interesting lives.

·required reading and other dangerous subjects·

Several years ago, I learned that I had passed a new literary milestone. I had been inducted into the Halls of Education, under the rubric "Multicultural Literature," in many schools also known as "Required Reading."

Thanks to this development, students now come up to me at book signings and proudly tell me they're doing their essays, term papers, or master's theses on me. By that I mean that they are analyzing not just my books but me, my private history and personal peccadilloes, which, with the hindsight of classroom literary investigation, prove to contain many Chinese omens that made it inevitable that I would become a writer.

When I was a student, the only writers I analyzed had long since passed on to that Great Remainder Table in the Sky. Those authors of bygone years could not protest what I said about them or their works. I could write, "What Henry James *really* meant . . ." and there was no Henry James to say, "You bloody fool, if that's what I meant, then that's what I would have said."

I, however, have the distinct pleasure of hearing, while still alive, what I really meant when I wrote *The Joy Luck Club.* One student discovered that my book is structured according to the four movements of a sonata; the proof lay in the fact that my parents had wanted me to become a concert pianist, as mentioned in my bio on the book jacket. I learned through another student who culled in-depth biographical information from an authoritative source, *People* magazine, that my book was based on my numerous bad experiences with men. I showed that essay to my husband, Lou, who has been my constant companion since 1970.

As the recipient of such academic attention, I know I'm supposed to feel honored. But what I actually feel is something more akin to shock and embarrassment. It's as though I'd eavesdropped on a party conversation and discovered that I am the subject of juicy gossip by a group of psychoanalysts—or perhaps proctologists, depending on how in-depth and obsessive the analysis has become.

On one occasion, I read a master's thesis on feminist writings that included examples from *The Joy Luck Club*. The student noted that I had used the number four something on the order of thirty-two or thirty-six times—in any case, a number divisible by four. Accordingly, she pointed out that there were four mothers, four daughters, four sections of the book, four stories per section. Furthermore, there were four sides to a mah jong table, four directions of the wind, four players. More important, she postulated, my use of the number four symbolized the four stages of psychological development, which corresponded in uncanny ways to the four stages of some type of Buddhist philosophy I had never heard of. Extending this analysis further, the student recalled that there was a character called Fourth Wife, symbolizing death, and a four-year-old girl with a feisty spirit, symbolizing regeneration. There was a four-year-old boy who drowns, and perhaps because his parents were Baptists, he symbolized rebirth through death. There was also a little girl who receives a scar on her neck at the age of four, who then loses her mother and her sense of self; she symbolized crisis.

In short, the student's literary sleuthing went on to reveal a mystical and rather byzantine puzzle, which, once explained, proved completely brilliant and precisely logical. She wrote me a letter and asked if her analysis had been correct. I was sorry I could not say yes.

The truth is, if I do include symbols in my work, they are carefully nudged out of their hiding places by others. I don't consciously place symbols in such clever fashion as some students have given me credit for. I'm not that smart. I can't plot where I will use literary devices, posting them like freeway signs that regularly announce rest stops, scenic lookouts, and the last exit before the denouement. I'm not that methodical. If I write of "an orange moon rising on a dark night," I would more likely ask myself whether the image is clichéd than whether it is a symbol of the feminine force rising in anger, as one academic suggested.

All this is by way of saying that I don't claim my use of the number four to be a brilliant symbolic device. Now that it's been pointed out to me in such astonishing ways, I consider my *overuse* of the number four to be a flaw.

I'm not suggesting that I write my stories without any consideration of the words and images I include. I choose my words carefully, with much anguish. They are, each and every one, significant to me, by virtue of their meaning, their tone, their place in the sentence, their sound and rhythm in dialogue or narrative, their specific associations with something deeply personal and often secretly ironic in my life.

I know that in one instance I used the word "four" because its open vowel sounded softer, and thus better, to me than "three" or "five." The reason that I wrote that the mah jong table has four sides was a no-brainer; I have never seen a mah jong table with more or fewer than four sides. For the same reason, I included four players at the four-sided mah jong table.

As to the ages of the children, I can say only that I was fond of the world at that age. Magic happened. When an adult explained the concept of hell to me at age four, I dug a hole in the backyard and saw naked people dancing underground; I also saw worms. My imagination and reality were nearly the same thing. I believed the stories I heard. I then saw what I believed—which is not unlike what I, as a writer, would want you to see as you read my stories. But first I have to make you believe that the stories are true. And some parts of them are, the character called Fourth Wife, for example. She is not called Fourth Wife for symbolic reasons. I wanted to pay homage to my real grandmother, who was indeed a fourth wife, who did kill herself as the result of her position in life, and who was the woman upon whom two of the stories were based.

As to the four-sided structure of the novel, I should point out that there are really only three narrators who are mothers, not four, as some reviewers and students have noted. I deliberately chose to have three at the mah jong table to create a sense of imbalance, a feeling that something or someone was missing. To me, that's what the stories are about: the search for balance in my life. Is that a symbol? I thought it was an emotion. In any case, originally I had titled the book *Wind and Water*, after the Chinese philosophy of harmony with nature. And originally there were going to be five sections to the book, three stories for each of the five elements found in harmonious nature: earth, fire, wood, water, and metal. But my agent, Sandy Dijkstra, thought that my five-part structure was too contrived, and I realized that five families made for a more difficult balancing act. Sandy liked the title of one proposed story, "The Joy Luck Club." Having grown up with the real Joy Luck Club, I thought the name sounded pedestrian. But I didn't want to argue with her about it, since I figured she wouldn't be able to sell the book to a publisher anyway, regardless of its title.

So the five elements and five sections of the book went out the window, while the proposal for a collection of fifteen stories remained. Strangely enough, my agent was able to sell the book on the basis of this proposal, and I received a contract from Putnam, stipulating that in six month's time I would deliver a work of fiction of approximately 100,000 English words. About four months into writing the remainder of the book, I realized that fifteen stories would likely be shy of the required 100,000 English words. Also, some of the words in the manuscript were not English but Chinese, and I worried that if I didn't deliver the requisite number of English words, Putnam would refuse to publish the manuscript. So seventeen stories it became.

When my editor, Faith Sale, read the seventeen stories, she made a comment that surprised me. "One of the stories doesn't fit," she said. I asked her which one.

"It's the story about Rose's former boyfriend. All the other stories have to do with a mother and a daughter."

"Really?" I said. "Mothers and daughters. That's interesting." I already told you I'm not that smart. Until that moment, it had not occurred to me that these were stories about mothers and daughters. We dropped the seventeenth story, which accounts for why there are now sixteen stories. Faith suggested we reorder the stories into a structure. I proposed that the structure be an emotional one, linked by a small fable, yet to be written, that resonated for each piece included under its rubric. In the end, I found the sixteen stories could fall into four sections.

Now that I've confessed this, you can imagine how happy but guilty I felt reading one of the first reviews of the book, which praised the clever and innovative structure of "a novel with eight voices, mysteriously interlocked like a Chinese puzzle box." Imagine how disappointed the reviewer would have been if I had told him that the structure of this so-called novel was instead the result of a more eclectic arrangement of sixteen *short stories.*

Reviewers and students have educated me not only about how I write, but about why I write. Apparently, I wish to capture the immigrant experience, to demystify Chinese culture, to show the differences between Chinese and American culture, to pave the way for other Asian-American writers—and I have a whole host of other equally noble motivations.

The truth is, I write for more self-serving reasons—that is, I write for myself. I write because I enjoy stories and make-believe. I write because if I didn't, I'd probably go crazy. Thus I write about questions that disturb me, images that mystify me, or memories that cause me anguish and pain. I write about secrets, lies, and contradictions, because within them are many kinds of truth. In other words, I write stories about life as I have misunderstood it. To be sure, it's a Chinese-American life, but that's the only one I've had so far.

Contrary to what some students, professors, reporters, and fund-raising organizations assume, I am not an expert on China, Chinese culture, mah jong, the psychology of mothers and daughters, generation gaps, immigration, illegal aliens, assimilation, acculturation, racial tension, Tiananmen Square, Most Favored Nation trade agreements, human rights, Pacific Rim economics, the purported one million missing baby girls of China, the future of Hong Kong after 1997, or, I am sorry to say, Chinese cooking. Certainly I have personal opinions on many of these topics, especially food, but by no means do my sentiments or my world of make-believe make me an expert.

And so I am alarmed when reviewers and educators assume that my very personal, specific, and fictional stories are meant to be representative, down to the smallest detail, of not just Chinese-Americans but sometimes all Asian culture. Is Jane Smiley's *A Thousand Acres* supposed to be representative of all American culture? Do all American daughters serve their tyrannical fathers the same breakfast every morning? Do all sisters betray each other? Are all conscientious objectors flaky in love relationships? Why do readers and reviewers assume that a book with Chinese-American characters can encompass all the demographics and personal histories of Chinese America?

My editor at Putnam tells me that over the years she has received hundreds of permission requests from publishers of college textbooks and multicultural anthologies, wishing to reprint my work for educational purposes. One publisher wanted to include an excerpt from *The Joy Luck Club*, a scene in which a woman invites her non-Chinese boyfriend to her parents' house for dinner. The boyfriend brings a bottle of wine as a gift and commits a number of social gaffes at the dinner table. Students were supposed to read this excerpt, then answer the following question: "If you are invited to a Chinese family's house for dinner, should you bring a bottle of wine?" My editor and I agreed to turn down that permission request.

I hear that my books and essays are now on the required-reading lists for courses in ethnic studies, Asian-American studies, Asian-American literature, Asian-American history, women's literature, feminist studies, feminist writers of color, and so forth. I am proud to be on these lists. What writer wouldn't want her work to be read? But there's a small nagging question that whispers into my ear once in a while: "What about American literature?"

I know I'm not supposed to complain, or at least not too loudly. After all, I am one of the lucky writers to be read, in classrooms, by the mainstream, and in CliffsNotes. I have had many readers tell me that they read my books because they feel the stories are about universal emotions between mothers and daughters.

But as my mother has often told me, I have an attitude. I have an attitude not just about my books but about literature in general. I have this attitude that American literature, if such a classification exists, should be more democratic than the color of your skin or whether rice or potatoes are served at your fictional dinner table. And so I ask myself and sometimes others: Who decides what is American fiction? Why is it that works of fiction by minority writers are read mainly for the study of class, gender, and race? Why is it so hard to break out of this literary ghetto?

Let me suggest one reason. At a conference a couple of years ago, an official from the California State Department of Education came up to me and said, "By the way, your books were recently approved for our state's multicultural recommended-reading list for high schools."

I smiled but perhaps did not look sufficiently impressed.

She then assured me: "Our criteria are very stringent. For a book to make it to the list, it has to pass through a gantlet of educators who must agree that it will provide a positive and meaningful portrayal of the culture it represents."

I didn't know what to say to her, because it was rather like having the surgeon general congratulate me for proving that smoking cigarettes is really a happy, wholesome habit. So instead, I simply nodded, realizing that my books were contributing to dangerous changes in how people view literature. In fact, university friends tell me that arguments are being staged now in the halls of ethnic studies departments about which books are more valuable than others—all based on those stringent criteria concerning positive and meaningful portrayals of the cultures they are supposed to represent. Factions within minority groups have arisen; the different sides throw sticks and stones at one another as they argue over what literature is supposed to represent, mean, and do. And a growing number of readers, educated readers, now choose fiction like cans of soup on a grocery shelf. If the book is labeled ethnic, it must contain specific nutritive ingredients: a descriptive narrative that provides lessons on culture, characters who serve as good role models, plots and conflicts that contain socially relevant themes and ideas, language that is wholesome in its political and ethnic correctness.

Recently I talked to just such a reader, an agent—not my agent—young and perhaps five years out of college. "I love your books, they're so educational," she told me. "What will your next book teach us? What's the lesson?" "I don't write books to teach people anything," I replied. "If readers learn something, that's their doing, not mine."

The agent said, "Really? But don't you think you have a responsibility as a minority writer to teach the world about Chinese culture?"

Her comment reminded me that if you are a minority, you may not be read in the same way that, say, Anne Tyler, John Updike, or Sue Grafton is read. In other words, your stories may not be read as literary fiction, or as American fiction, or as entertainment; they will be read more likely as sociology, politics, ideology, cultural lesson plans in a narrative form. Your fiction will probably not be allowed to reside in the larger world of imagination; it will be assigned to a territory of multicultural subject matter. I know this is happening because I have seen the student papers marked with an A for "excellent analysis of the differences between Chinese and American cultures."

It disturbs me—no, let me amend that—it terrifies me when I hear people dictating what literature must do and mean and say. And it infuriates me when people use the "authority" of their race, gender, and class to stipulate who should write what, and why. The prohibitions come in many forms: You can't write about lesbians unless you're a lesbian. You can't write about Native Americans unless you are at least twenty-five percent Native American and a registered member of your tribe. You can't write about African-American or Asian-American males unless the portrayals are positive. You can't write about Hindus unless you are a member of a lower caste. You can't write about Latinos unless you still live in the barrio.

The mandates are just as strong: If you're gay, you must write about AIDS and explicit safe sex. If you are Asian-American, you must write about modern, progressive characters, no harking back to the bad old days. If you are African-American, you must write about oppression and racism. And who are *you* to question these mandates if you're not a member of the particular minority group at issue?

I hear this type of ethnic authority invoked more often these days. It's as though a new and more insidious form of censorship has crept into the fold, winning followers by wearing the cloak of good intentions and ethnic correctness. The leaders of the cause point to the negative and tiresome stereotypes mindlessly reproduced in textbooks over the years. Why are Chinese people in American history books portrayed only as faceless railroad workers? Why should we read Hemingway when the evidence shows he was a misogynist and an anti-Semite?

The question is not whether stereotypes, misogyny, and anti-Semitism are to be condoned. It has to do with whether literature must serve as the cart and horse that hauls away human ills. Can we eliminate racism by censoring it in fiction? Did the Bolsheviks and the Chinese Red Guard improve the standards of their countries' literature by mandating what should be written and why?

Yet there are those who argue that American literature must toe some sort of political line, and if you disagree with them, it's not easy to parry with your own arguments. For one thing, anytime you talk about ethnicity, you are in danger of tripping over terminology and landing in the battleground called racism. In the unstable arena of ethnicity and race, there is no common language everyone agrees on. It's hard enough for me to determine what ethnic descriptors I use for myself. Do I refer to myself as a Chinese-American writer, an ethnic writer, a minority writer, a Third World writer, a writer of color? From person to person, and particularly writer to writer, these terms carry different emotional and political weight.

If I had to give myself any sort of label, I would have to say I am an American writer. I am Chinese by racial heritage. I am Chinese-American by family and social upbringing. But I believe that what I write is American fiction by virtue of the fact that I live in this country and my emotional sensibilities, assumptions, and obsessions are largely American. My characters may be largely Chinese-American, but I think Chinese-Americans are part of America.

As an aside, I must admit that "writer of color" is an expression I personally dislike, since, in terms of color, Chinese people have always been referred to as yellow, the color associated with cowardice, jaundice, bananas, Ping the Duck, and the middle-class Marvin Gardens in Monopoly. I'd much prefer a term such as "colorful writer," which seems to refer more to the writing itself. Or how about "writer of a different flavor"? Cuisine is probably a much closer indicator of differences in literary tastes than skin color. "Writer of color" is also an exclusionary term—you're not a member if your skin is too pale, and yet you face perhaps the same problems as a writer if you're Armenian-American or gay or lesbian or a woman. Whatever we minorities are called, as the result of common experiences, both bad and humorous, we often have an affinity with one another. We are segregated in the same ways.

Consider book reviews. More often than not, if a book is by an Asian-American writer, an Asian-American is assigned by the newspaper or magazine editor to review it. On the surface, this appears to make sense: an Asian-American reviewer may be more sensitive to the themes and meanings of the book—never mind that the reviewer is an academic in history, not a fiction writer, and possibly not even a fiction *reader*. But a reviewer who is thus qualified may dwell more on the historical relevance and accuracy of the book than on its literary merits—the language, the characters, the imagery, and the storytelling qualities that seduce the reader into believing the tale is true. The review may be favorable, but it casts the book outside the realm of literature.

And woe to you if the Asian-American reviewer champions both ethnic correctness and marginalism, and believes your fiction should *not* depict violence, sexual abuse, mixed marriages, superstitions, Chinese as Christians, or mothers who speak in broken English. "Using the mother to tell of her life in China," said one reviewer, "has deprived Tan of the full resources and muscularity of the native English-language speaker." I might have replied to that reviewer, "Exactly, and I did so because my own mother has long been deprived of telling her story, this story, because she lacked those native English-language skills."

Reviews have also done much to reinforce the idea that any book by an Asian-American writer is part of the same genre. If two or more books by Asian-American writers are published around the same time, more likely than not the book review editor will assign those books to be reviewed simultaneously by one reviewer. More likely than not the reviewer will compare the books, even if they have nothing in common except for the fact that they are written by Asian-Americans. Gus Lee's *China Boy* is compared with Gish Jen's *Typical American,* David Wong Louie's *Pangs of Love* with Fae Myenne Ng's *Bone,* and so forth. The underlying message to the reader: These books are similar, but one book is better than the other, pick only one. Some reviewers tend to reduce the books to the most obvious and general abstractions: the themes of immigration and assimilation. They overlook the specifics of narrative detail, language, and imagery that make the story and the characters unlike any that have been written before.

I was talking about this trend to a friend of mine, a reporter who writes on literary matters and wears the badge of realist. He said that we writers shouldn't complain. "Any attention is valuable. You can't demand attention. If you receive any, you should be grateful for what you get, good or bad, lumped together or not.

"The new writers," he went on, "would never get that kind of attention, unless they were grouped together for an angle. The media need an angle. Culture is the angle. A new wave in Asian-American literature is the angle. They are not going to feature the writers separately as the next Joyce Carol Oates or the next Raymond Carver. They're not going to devote column inches to talking about the beauty of their prose, the cleverness of their characterization. That's not topical. That's not interesting.

"And as to books' being compared one to another, there's a rational argument for that. Readers do the same thing. They categorize and compare. They ask themselves, 'Do I want to read a mystery or a book about China? Old China or modern China? Mothers and daughters or warlords and evil empresses?'

"Consider yourself lucky," my friend advised.

I have been lucky in this regard. Nowadays, I'm told, my books *are* usually reviewed alone, and not alongside other books by Asian-American writers. More often than not, my books are reviewed by fiction writers who may or may not be Asian-Americans. They are writers or reviewers of fiction, first and foremost. And thus they discuss the relative literary merits and faults of my books and don't focus exclusively on Chinese customs, superstitions, and positive role models. For that I am enormously grateful.

Nonetheless, I still get the occasional review that categorically lumps me with other writers purely on the basis of race or culture. Here is what a daily *New York Times* reviewer had to say about *The Kitchen God's Wife*:

> It competes unsuccessfully with novels like Malcolm Bosse's [*The*] *Warlord*, Gary Jenning's *Journeyer*, and the works of James Clavell, Maxine Hong Kingston in *The Woman Warrior* and *China Men*, Bette Bao Lord in *Legacies: A Chinese Mosaic*, and Nien Cheng in *Life and Death in Shanghai*, [which] have covered similar territory in greater depth.

I mentioned this to Bette Bao Lord, and we both found ourselves asking out loud: "What's been covered before? China? Suffering? Mothers? Death? Hope? Love? Pain?" I wasn't disagreeing with the reviewer's conclusion—those other books he cited might have been better—but what, exactly, was the basis of the comparison? And why was *The Warlord* on the list? After this review, I made it a policy not to read reviews of my books.

I'd had unfavorable reviews before, but this one struck me as—dare I say the word?—racist. The point is, minority writers tend to be perceived as different from their white colleagues. Our responsibilities are supposedly more specific.

No wonder, then, that I am frequently asked questions about "the responsibility of the writer." The assumption is that the writer—any writer—by virtue of being published, has a responsibility to the reader. According to this ethic, the writer's musing, his or her imagination and delight in the world of make-believe, must be tamed and shaped by a higher consciousness of how the work will be interpreted—or rather, *mis*interpreted—by its readers. God forbid that a reader in some remote Texas hamlet believe that all Chinese men today have concubines, or that all Chinese mothers speak in broken English, or that all Chinese kids are chess grand masters.

A professor of literature who teaches in southern California told me he uses my books in his class, but he makes it a point to lambaste those passages that depict China as backward or unattractive. He objected to any descriptions that had to do with spitting, filth, poverty, or superstitions. Was China free of these elements, I asked him. And he said no, the descriptions were true, but still he believed it was "the obligation of the writer of ethnic literature to create positive, progressive images."

I secretly shuddered and thought, Oh well, that's southern California for you. A short time later, I met a student from UC Berkeley, a school I attended. The student was standing in line during a book signing. When his turn came, he swaggered up to me, took two steps back, and said in a loud voice: "Don't you think you have the responsibility to write about Chinese men as positive role models?"

I told him, "I think you have the responsibility as a reader to think for yourself."

Mary Gaitskill, author of *Bad Behavior* and *Two Girls, Fat and Thin*, commented on this matter of writers and their responsibilities. This is from her contributor's notes to a story, "The Girl on the Plane," which appeared in the 1993 edition of *The Best American Short Stories*:

> In my opinion, most of us have not been taught how to be responsible for our thoughts and feelings. I see this strongly in the widespread tendency to read books and stories as if they exist to confirm how we are supposed to be, think, and feel. I'm not talking about wacky political correctness, I'm talking mainstream. . . . Ladies and gentlemen, please. Stop asking, "What am I supposed to feel?" Why would an adult look to me or any other writer to tell him or her what to feel? You're not *supposed* to feel anything. You feel what you feel. Where you go with it is your responsibility. If a writer chooses to aggressively let you know what he or she feels, where you go with it is still your responsibility.

I can only suppose that if writers were responsible for people's thoughts and for creating positive role models, we would then be in the business of writing propaganda, not art as fiction. Fiction makes you think; propaganda tells you how to think.

Yet some minority writers believe that's what fiction by minority writers should do: tell people what to think. These writers believe, for example, that if you're Asian-American, you should write about contemporary Asian-Americans—none of that old-China stuff—and that your work should be exclusively for Asian-Americans and not a mainstream audience. If your work is inaccessible to white readers, that is proof it is authentic. If it is read by white people, that is proof the work is a fake, a sellout, and hence the writer is to be treated as a traitor, publicly branded and condemned. While the numbers within this faction are small, their influence in academia and the media is substantial. They shout for attention and they receive it.

A couple of years ago, at a conference on Asian-Americans and the arts that I attended, a literature professor spoke passionately into the microphone about the importance, the necessity, of "Asian-Americans' maintaining our marginalism." She rallied the crowd to believe it was the responsibility of Asian-American writers and artists to remain apart from the mainstream. She believed in a Marxist model of thinking for minorities, that the dominant class was the enemy and minorities should work separately from them as part of the struggle. "There is strength in marginalism," she shouted, and most of the audience applauded wildly.

To me, that kind of thinking is frightening, a form of literary fascism. It is antithetical to why I write, which is to express myself freely in whatever direction or form I wish. I can't imagine being a writer and having others dictate to me what I should write, why I should write, and whom I should write for. And this is the real reason I consider myself an American writer: I have the freedom to write whatever I want. I claim that freedom.

I've been trying to understand why these factions exist in the first place. I suspect that they have their origins in bitterness, anger, and frustration in being excluded. I've experienced those same feelings in my life, growing up Chinese-American in a white community. As a teenager, I suspected the real reason I was never asked to dance had to do with my being Chinese rather than, say, my nerdiness. As a cynical college student, I realized my forefathers never ate turkey, never dropped down chimneys dressed in red costumes. In my twenties, I joined various Pacific Asian groups and became an activist for multicultural training programs for special educators.

If not for a few circumstances that led me to where I am today, would I have become one of those activists for ethnically correct literature? If I hadn't found my voice in a published book, would I too have shouted from a lectern that there is strength in marginalism? If I had written book after book, starting in the 1970s, and none of them had been published or reviewed, would I also have been tempted to feel there was a conspiracy in the publishing industry? Would I have believed that those Asian-Americans who did get published and reviewed had sold their souls and were serving up a literary version of chop suey for American palates?

As I think about those questions, I remember being an English major in 1970 (at a time, by the way, when there were fewer than 450,000 Chinese-Americans in all the United States, including Hawaii). In the American literature classes I took, I read Hemingway, Faulkner, Fitzgerald, Dreiser, Sinclair Lewis, and so forth—no American writers who were women or minorities. It didn't bother me—or rather, I didn't question that it could be any other way. During those years that I was an English major, the only female novelist I read was Virginia Woolf; I had originally thought there was another, Evelyn Waugh, who, I later discovered, was very British and a man. The only minority writers I read were in a summer school class I took called "Black Literature," where I read Richard Wright, James Baldwin, and Ralph Ellison—but again no books by women. I didn't even imagine there was such a thing as a book by an Asian-American woman; Maxine Hong Kingston's *The Woman Warrior* didn't come out until 1976.

Back in my college days, the early seventies, the teachers and students were also politicizing fiction. When I read *An American Tragedy, The Grapes of Wrath, Babbitt, Tender Is the Night,* I was required to look at character flaws as symbols of social ills. I became adept at writing weekly papers, alluding to the trickier symbols and more subtle themes that I knew would please my professors. I could tell by the tone of their lectures which books they admired, and which ones we had to read so that, should we one day become literary critics, we would know how to heap scorn properly. I would wade through each semester's stack of required reading, pen and paper at hand, ready to catch symbols and social themes with much the same focus as that of a gardener searching for weeds, snails, and leaf rot. When I completed my literature requirements, I stopped reading fiction, because what I had once loved I no longer enjoyed.

I didn't start reading fiction again regularly until 1985. I don't think it was coincidence that most of what I read was by women writers, among them: Flannery O'Connor, Isabel Allende, Louise Erdrich, Eudora Welty, Laurie Colwin, Alice Adams, Amy Hempel, Alice Walker, Lorrie Moore, Anne Tyler, Alice Munro, Harriet Doerr, and Molly Giles. I was not gender-exclusive: I also read works by Gabriel García Márquez, Raymond Carver, David Leavitt, Richard Ford, and Tobias Wolff. But mostly I read fiction by women, because I had so rarely read novels by women in my adult years, and I found I enjoyed their sensibilities, their voices, and what they had to say about the world. I was feeling again the thrill I had felt as a child choosing my own books, falling in love with characters, reading stories because I couldn't stop myself. Now I kept reading, day and night, until I couldn't stop myself from *writing*.

When my first book was published, in 1989, I was at the advanced age of thirty-seven. Interviewers asked me why I had waited so long to write fiction. I could answer only, "It never occurred to me that I could." By that, I didn't mean I lacked the desire. In part I didn't think I could because I didn't have the talent or necessary disposition to think of tricky symbols and plant them in carefully tilled rows of sentences. I didn't think I could because I wasn't an expert on white whales or white males. The idea of my becoming a published fiction writer was as ludicrous as, say, my wearing a dominatrix costume while singing rock 'n' roll onstage at the Hollywood Palladium with Bruce Springsteen, which, by the way, I recently did. Suffice it to say, the way that I used to read literature did not encourage me to become a writer. If anything, it discouraged me.

This short history of my educational background is to show by example that minorities and women were largely ignored in the literature curriculum until a couple of decades ago. I understand the reasons professors and students campaigned for the inclusion of ethnic studies programs. With the creation of these separate programs, at last we had stories of Asian-Americans written by Asian-Americans, taught by Asian-Americans, and read by Asian-American students. At last we had a history that went beyond the railroads and laundries of the Gold Rush days. And because so little was available, we found our sources for material overlapping. We looked to story to provide history. In any case, to have our story included in the curriculum, we had to create a separate department, separate and equal as we could make it.

Unfortunately, in some educational arenas this notion of separatism remains the primary focus. As writers, we're asked, "Are you one of them or one of us?"—meaning we can't be both. We're asked, "Are you writing American literature or Asian-American literature?"—meaning one is not the other. We're asked, "Are you writing for Asian-Americans or for the mainstream?"—meaning one necessarily excludes the other. And those of us, including Bharati Mukherjee, Maxine Hong Kingston, and me, who say we are American writers have been censured by the separatists, reviled on podiums, and denounced with expletives in the student press.

In the past, I've tried to ignore the potshots. A *Washington Post* reporter once asked me what I thought of so-and-so calling me "a running-dog whore sucking on the tit of the imperialist white pigs."

"Well," I said as dispassionately as possible. "You can't please everyone, can you?" Readers are free to interpret what they will or won't out of a book, and they are free to appreciate or not appreciate what they've interpreted. In any case, reacting to critics makes a writer look defensive, petulant, and like an all-around bad sport.

But lately I've started thinking that I shouldn't take such a laissez-faire attitude. I've come to think I must say something, not so much to defend myself and my work, but to support American literature and what it has the possibility of becoming in the twenty-first century, a truly American literature, democratic in its inclusion of many colorful voices, men and women, gay and straight, of all ethnicities and races.

Until recently, I didn't think it was important for writers to express their private intentions in order for their work to be appreciated. My domain is fiction, and I believed the analysis of my intentions was the domain of literature classes. But I realize that the study of literature does have its effect on how books are being read, and thus on what might be read, published, and written in the future. For that reason, I believe writers today must talk about their intentions, if for nothing else, to serve as an antidote to what others define as what our intentions should be.

So why do I write?

Because I once thought I couldn't, and I now know I can. Because I have qualities in my nature shaped by my past—a secret legacy of suicide, forced marriages, and abandoned children in China; an eclectic upbringing that included no fewer than fifteen residences, ranging from tough neighborhoods in

Oakland, California, to the snobbish environs of Montreux, Switzerland; a distorted view of life shaped by two conflicting religions, the death of my father and brother in a year's time, and the murder of my best friend. Those elements and others in my life have combined to make me feel that writing provides the sort of freedom and danger, satisfaction and discomfort, truth and contradiction that I can't find anywhere else in life.

I write stories because I have questions about life, not answers. I believe life is mysterious and not dissectable. I think human nature is best described in even a long-winded story and not in a psychoanalytical diagnosis. I write because often I can't express myself any other way, and I think I'll implode if I don't find the words. I can't paraphrase or give succinct morals about love and hope, pain and loss. I have to use a mental longhand, ponder and work it out in the form of a story that is revised again and again, twenty times, a hundred times, until it feels true.

I write for very much the same reasons that I read: to startle my mind, to churn my heart, to tingle my spine, to knock the blinders off my eyes and allow me to see beyond the pale. Fiction is an intimate companion and confidant for life.

I write because I have been in love with words since I was a child. I hoarded words from the thesaurus and the dictionary as though they were magic stones, toys, treasures. I loved metaphors and used them before I knew what the word meant. I thought of metaphors as secret passageways that took me to hidden rooms in my heart, and my memory as the dreamy part of myself that lived in another world. I played with my memory of both real and imaginary life the way girls play with their Barbies and boys with their penises. I dressed it up, changed it a dozen times, manipulated it, tugged at it, wondered if it would enlarge and pulsate until others noticed it too. I thought of it as a weapon, a secret, a sin, an incorrigible vice.

I write because it is the ultimate freedom of expression. And for that reason it is also as scary as skiing down a glacier, as thrilling as singing in a rock-'n'-roll band, as dangerous as falling on your face doing both.

Writing to me is an act of faith, a hope that I will discover what I mean by truth. But I don't know what that will be until I finish. I can't determine it ahead of time. And more often than not, I can't summarize what it is I've discovered. It's simply a feeling. The feeling is the entire story. To paraphrase the feeling or to analyze the story reduces the feeling for me.

I also think of reading as an act of faith, a hope I will discover something remarkable about ordinary life, about myself. And if the writer and the reader discover the same thing, if they have that connection, the act of faith has resulted in an act of magic. To me, that's the mystery and the wonder of both life and fiction—the connection between two unique individuals who discover in the end that they are more the same than they are different.

And if that doesn't happen, it's nobody's fault. There are still plenty of other books on the shelf to choose from.

· angst and the second book ·

I am glad that I shall never again have to write a Second Book.

About two weeks after I turned in the manuscript for *The Joy Luck Club* to Putnam, a friend showed me a book, whose title I've mercifully forgotten, which listed hundreds of major novelists throughout the centuries, with career summaries glimpsed through bar graphs. The graphs, similar to records of annual rainfall amounts, represented the relative critical success of each of the authors' books, a statistical epitaph of sorts. For some, a flood of sudden success—then unrelenting drought, book after book after book.

"Isn't it interesting," my friend noted, "how many writers went on to write lousy second books?"

I never considered that the critics might have been wrong. Instead, I stayed up half the night reading that book, and by morning I had decided that whatever those writers had lacked—confidence, stamina, vision, sharp red pencils—I would stock in extra portions. Each of my books, I determined, would outdo its predecessor, increasing in scope, depth, precision of language, intelligence of form, and thus critical acceptance and perhaps even readership.

Of course, that's what I determined *before* I was published, before *The Joy Luck Club* ever hit the bestseller list, before I attended my first literary luncheon, where a woman asked me with absolute sincerity, "How does it feel to have written your best book first?"

Shortly after the book was published, I was in New York having lunch with my editor, Faith Sale, as well as a friend of hers, another writer, the author of four books. The friend asked me if I had started the Second Book.

"I have some ideas," I said vaguely. I was loath to admit in front of Faith that I had not the slightest idea what I would do next. "I just haven't decided which one to go with," I added. "All I know is that it won't be Son of Joy Luck."

"Well, don't sweat over it too much," the other writer said. "The Second Book's doomed no matter what you do. Just get it over with, let the critics bury it, then move on to your third book and don't look back." I saw the bar graphs of my literary career falling over like tombstones.

I was to hear this same doom and gloom, or permutations of it, from many writers. Actually, I cannot recall *any* writer—with or without splashy debut—who said the Second Book came easily. The Second Book is bound to be trashed, one said, especially if the first was an unexpected success. The Second Book is always a disappointment, said another, because now everyone has preformed expectations. Critics will say it is too much like the first. Readers will complain that it is too different.

"It's as though you're always competing against yourself,"

said one writer friend, whose first book met with unanimous praise, quickly propelling him upward to literary heights. The Second Book was compared with the first and received mixed reviews. The third and fourth earned renewed praise, but the first always managed to creep into reviews as the standard. "You begin to hate the first book," he said. "It's like the kid brother sticking his tongue out, going, 'Nah-nah-nah.'"

"The critics are always worse when the first book was really, really big," confided another writer. "With the first, they put you on this great big pedestal. But by the time the Second Book comes around, you realize you're not sitting on a pedestal at all. It's one of those collapsible chairs above a tank of water at the county fair."

"It's like that Mister Rogers song," said another writer friend, "the one that says, You'll never go down, never go down, never go down the drain. My daughter heard that song. And after that, she started screaming in the bathtub, scared out of her mind she was going to be sucked down the drain. And then the next day I went to speak at a literary luncheon and overheard some people whispering, 'Can she do it again? Can she really do it again?' They put the fear in me. They were saying, 'Honey, you *can* go down the drain.'"

Only one person—a reporter on the literary scene—told me not to worry. "The Second Book is *nothing*," he said. "Everyone expects it to be weaker than an impressive first book. The real problem comes after the third book. Then the reviews begin: 'Her first novel was terrific, but now, after two weak efforts in a row, it's becoming increasingly likely that its virtues were only an aberration.'"

I've noticed that first books are often praised for their freshness, their lack of self-consciousness. In my case, "lack of consciousness" may have had something to do with it. And here I am referring not to what I know or don't know about the craft of writing but to what I didn't know about publishing. While I was writing my first book, I still believed that "PW" referred only to the accounting firm of Price Waterhouse, and not the trade magazine *Publishers Weekly* as well. I did not know the importance of a "boxed review." I had never heard "blurb" used as a verb. When I was told my book was being sold to the "clubs," I thought that meant as in Med or Rotary. I guessed that first serial rights were a writer's adjunct to the First Amendment. I am serious. Ask my editor.

And then the reviews started to come in. They surprised me, every one of them. I read reviews that praised me as having skills that I never knew I had—related to my unusual use of structure and the simplicity of my prose. And I read the critical ones as well, which pointed out faults that I also never knew I had—related to my unusual use of structure and the simplicity of my prose. And then I read one, which I cannot quote exactly, since I threw it away, that said something to this effect: "It will be hard, if not impossible, for Amy Tan to follow her own act." Shortly after that, I broke out with hives.

I should explain that I have never been a particularly nervous person or someone prone to psychosomatic illnesses. But while writing the Second Book, I developed literal symptoms of the imagined weight of my task. Each morning, when I was not on the road doing promotion for my first book, I would dutifully sit at my desk, turn on my computer, and stare at the blank screen.

And sure enough, my imagination would take off unbidden, unrestrained. And I would imagine hundreds, thousands of people looking over my shoulder, offering helpful suggestions:

"Don't make it too commercial."

"Don't disappoint the readers you've already won over."

"Make sure it doesn't look like a sequel."

"But what about Updike? What about stories that multiply like Rabbit's?"

"Seriously, what are the themes that will shape your oeuvre?"

"What's an oeuvre?"

"Forget oeuvre. Don't even think about themes."

"Just don't make it exotic. That's too obvious."

"Just make sure the men are portrayed in positive roles this time."

"No, no, if you think about political correctness, you're dead."

"Think about sources of inspiration."

"*Don't* think about the advance."

"*Don't* think about how much every single word on this page is worth."

"Don't think."

With all these imaginary people weighing me down, I developed a pain in my neck, which later radiated to my jaw, resulting in constant gnashing, then two cracked teeth, and a huge dental bill. The pain then migrated down my back, making it difficult for me to sit up straight during the long hours necessary for writing a Second Book. And while I was struggling to sit in my chair, with hot packs wrapped around my waist, I did not write fiction: I wrote speeches—thirty, forty, fifty of them, all about the old book, a book that was rapidly becoming the source of my irritations.

And when I was not writing speeches, I was giving them. And when I was not giving speeches, I was answering telephone calls or responding to letters asking me to appear at a fund-raiser, to give a talk at a university, to blurb the book of a first-time novelist, to donate money to a worthy cause, to judge a writing contest, to teach at a creative-writing workshop, to serve on a panel on the Asian-American experience, to write an introduction to someone's book, and so on and so forth. For a while, I averaged a dozen requests a day. For a while, I tried to answer them all. I said yes to many. But I also said no to many: No to being a judge for the Miss Universe contest. No to posing for a Gap ad. Thanks but no thanks to the five or six people who offered to let me write their complete life stories, fifty-fifty on the royalties since I was already a proven author. And when I found that I still had no time to write, that fully nine months out of the past year had been spent on the road and in strange hotel rooms, that I had no more than three consecutive days at any given time to write fiction, I started to say no to all of the requests. I wrote long, guilt-ridden letters of apology. And when I had written about a book's worth of apologies, I moved and changed my phone number.

In between my bouts of back pain, jet lag, and guilt, I did start writing my Second Book, or rather, my second *books*. For example, I wrote eighty-eight pages of a book about the daughter of a scholar in China who accidentally kills a magistrate with a potion touted to be the elixir of immortality. I wrote fifty-six pages of a book about a Chinese girl orphaned during the San Francisco earthquake of 1906. I wrote ninety-five pages about a girl who lives in northeast China during the 1930s with her missionary parents. I wrote forty-five pages about using English to revive the dead Manchu language and the world it described on the plains of Mongolia. I wrote thirty pages about a woman disguised as a man who becomes a sidewalk scribe to the illiterate workers of San Francisco's Chinatown at the turn of the twentieth century.

By my rough estimation, the outtakes must now number close to a thousand pages. Yet I don't look on those pages as failed stories. I see them as my own personal version of cautionary tales—what can happen if I *do* watch out, what can go wrong if I write as the author everyone thought I had become and not as the writer I truly was. What I found myself writing was a Second Book based on what I thought various people wanted—something fairy tale–like, or exotic, or cerebral, or cultural, or historical, or poetic, or simple, or complex. Simultaneously, I found myself writing the imagined review that the book was clichéd, sentimental, contrived, didactic, pedantic, predictable, and—worst of all, for the literary writer—a saga, perfect for a miniseries.

Perhaps these stories would have, or should have, died of their own accord before they could have reached their own happy or unhappy ending. But some of the stories could have been saved, the weedy bits trimmed away, as with any writing, until the true seed could be found, then taken as the core of the real book. It could have been a single image, part of a character, an imagined sound.

But those books were not meant to become anything more than a lesson to me on what it takes to write fiction: persistence imposed by a limited focus. The focus of a pool player, who sees none of the posturing of the opponent, only the trajectory of the object ball to its pocket. The focus required of a priest, a nun, a convict serving a life's sentence.

What I am talking about is idealistic, of course—to think that any writer could really ignore praise, criticism, phone calls, dinner invitations, let alone a spot on the rug, a spice rack in need of alphabetical organization. All these things demand attention.

So what I did was more mundane. I let the answering machine take my calls. I put on earphones and listened to the same music day in and day out to obliterate my censoring voice. And I wrote with persistence, telling myself that no matter how bad the story was, I should simply go on like a rat in a maze, turning the corner when I arrived there. And so I started to write another story, about a woman who was cleaning a house, the messy house I thought I should be cleaning. After thirty pages, the house was tidy, and I had found a character I liked. I abandoned all the pages about the tidy house. I kept the character and took her along with me to another house. I wrote and then rewrote six times another thirty pages, and found a question in her heart. I abandoned the pages and kept the question and put that in my heart. I wrote and rewrote one hundred fifty pages and then found myself at a crisis point. The woman had turned sour on me. Her story sounded like one long complaint. I felt sick for about a week. I couldn't write. I felt like the rat who had taken the wrong turn at the beginning and had scrambled all this way only to reach a dead end. It appeared that my strategy simply to plow ahead was ill fated.

Who knows where inspiration comes from? Perhaps it arises

from desperation. Perhaps it comes from the flukes of the universe, the kindness of muses. Whatever the case, one day I found myself asking, "But *why* is she telling this story?" And she answered back: "Of course I'm crabby! I'm talking, talking, talking, no one to talk to. Who's listening?" And I realized: A story should be a gift. She needs to *give* her story to someone. And with that answer, I was no longer bumping my nose against a dead-end maze. I leapt over the wall and on the other side mustered enough emotional force to pull me through to the end.

So what I have written finally is a story told by a mother to her daughter, now called *The Kitchen God's Wife*. I know there are those who will say, "Oh, a mother-daughter story, just like *The Joy Luck Club*." I happen to think the new book is quite different from the old. But yes, there is a mother, there is a daughter. That's what found me, even as I tried to run away from it.

I wish I could say that was the end of writing my Second Book, that I found my inspiration, and the rest was clickety-clack on the keyboard. But no, that happens only in fiction. In real life, I had hundreds of moments of self-doubt. I deleted hundreds of pages from my computer's memory. And one incident made me laugh out loud. When I was still some two hundred pages from finishing the book, a friend called with my first "review." It turned out that a woman in a book club in Columbus, Ohio, had stood up at the end of a discussion on *The Joy Luck Club* and announced with great authority: "Well, I just read Amy Tan's second book, and believe me, it's not *nearly* as good as the first!"

I still wonder what book the woman in Ohio read. Was this indeed proof of the apocryphal tale of publishing that puts fear in every writer's heart—that you're doomed to fail before you even start? No matter, because I would be the first to agree with the woman in Columbus. My second book was awful. After all, even I couldn't bear to finish it—that tale about the elixir of immortality. And the third book—about the orphan girl who becomes a con artist—that wasn't very good either. Thumbs down also on my fourth, fifth, sixth, and seventh books. But the eighth book—eight is always a lucky number—the eighth book is *The Kitchen God's Wife*. And regardless of what others may think, it is my favorite.

How could it not be? I had to fight for every single character, every image, every word. And the story is, in fact, about a woman who does the same thing: she fights to believe in herself. She does battle with myths and superstitions and assumptions—then casts off the fates that accompany them. She doesn't measure herself by other people's opinions. "What use?" she says. "Then you are always falling, falling, falling, never strong enough to stand up by yourself and go your own way." She is no innocent. She sees her fears, but she no longer lets them chase her.

And sometimes, in secret, she lets her imagination run wild with hope. She would not mind, not really, if someone came up to her at a literary luncheon and said, "How does it feel to have written your best book second?"

· the best stories ·

This was written as an introduction to The Best American Short Stories 1999.

Forty years ago, not long before I turned seven, my father started reading to me from a volume of three hundred sixty-five stories with an equal number of pages.

The stories were supposed to be read in sequence, a tale a day, beginning with a sledding caper on a snowy January 1. They concerned ongoing events in the lives of children who lived in lovely two-story homes on a block lined with trees whose changing leaves reflected the changing seasons. Each of the children had a father and a mother, as well as two sets of grandparents, and these older folk conveyed simple truths while taking out cookies from a hot oven or fish from a cold stream. Each day, the children had small adventures with baby animals, balloons, or bicycles. They enjoyed nice surprises, got into small troubles, and had fun problems that they could solve. They made thingamajigs out of mud and stone and paint, which wound up being the prettiest ashtrays Mommy and Daddy had ever received. Within each of those three hundred sixty-five stories, the children learned a valuable lifelong lesson, which they promised never to forget.

By the middle of the book, I had learned to read well enough to finish a book in one day. And being impatient to know what happened to the children the rest of the year, I polished off the remaining stories in one sitting. On the last day of the year, the children went sledding again, completing the happy circle. Thus I discovered that between January 1 and December 31, those children had not changed much.

I was glad, for that was the year I accumulated many worries, which I numbered on my fingers. One was for the new home we had moved to, the fifth of more than a dozen we would occupy during my childhood. Two was for the dead rat crushed in a trap that my father had showed me, believing this would assure me that it was no longer lurking in my bedroom. Three was for my playmate Rachel, whom I saw lying in a coffin while my mother whispered, "This what happen you don't listen to mother." Four was for the operation I had had on my tonsils, which made me think I had not listened to my mother. Five was for the ghost of my playmate, who wanted me to come live with her. Six was for my mother's telling me that when she was a child her mother had died, and the same sad fate might befall me if I didn't appreciate her more. Eventually, I ran out of fingers.

That year, I believed that if I could make sense of my worries, I could make them stop. And when I couldn't, I would walk to the library. I went there often. I would choose my own books. And I would read and read, a story a day.

That girl from forty years ago has served as your guest editor for *The Best American Short Stories 1999*. I felt I should tell you about my earliest literary influences, because I'm aware that if you scan the table of contents you might suspect that I have been reactionary in my choices. You may wonder whether they are a vote against homogeneity, a vote for diversity in preordered proportions.

This collection holds no such political agenda. The stories I have chosen are simply those I loved most among those given to me for consideration. This is not to say my literary judgment is without personal bias. I am a particular sort of reader, shaped by all kinds of influences—one of them being those bedtime stories of long ago, for I still do most of my reading in bed.

I also now realize that I dearly loved those stories. In fact, I regret that I finished them so quickly that my father no longer had to read them aloud to me each night. For what I loved most was listening to his voice. And what I love most in these twenty-one stories is the same thing. It is the voice of the storyteller.

At the beginning of 1998, the year the stories collected here first appeared in magazines, I found myself in an airport lounge in Seoul, waiting for a connecting flight to Beijing. For reading material, I had brought with me *The Best American Short Stories 1992*, the volume guest edited by Robert Stone. I remember settling in with a cup of ginseng tea, then glancing up and seeing, with a shock of recognition, a woman who seemed like a younger version of me. She was Asian, I would guess even Chinese-American, and she was with a husband who looked quite similar to mine in height and build and coloring. But what was more striking than these superficial similarities was what she held in her hands: the same teal-blue volume of *The Best American Short Stories 1992*.

Did she notice me as well? She gave no indication that she did. Meanwhile, I had an urge to run up to her and ask all kinds of questions: Was she a writer? What story was she reading? Why had she picked this book to bring on a long flight to Asia?

I remembered those times my mother used to embarrass me as a child, going up to strangers in public places just because they happened to look Chinese. So I stayed put, reading from my book, then wondering how she could *not* notice me, our similarity. After all, it wasn't as though we were reading the same blockbuster novel of the year. It wasn't a travel book on Asia. It wasn't even the most recent volume of *The Best American Short Stories.* So what was it about our lives, our tastes, our choices that had brought us to this literary meeting point in Seoul?

Shortly after I returned home, I was asked to serve as guest editor of this volume. And from October 1998 until February 1999, I read stories, manna from heaven, or wherever it is that the series editor, Katrina Kenison, makes her home. After I had made my selections and sat down to write this introduction, I thought about that woman at the airport. I wondered whether she would one day read these stories and find compatibility with my choices. Or would she pose the hard-nosed literary question: "Huh?"

That is the response I sometimes have after seeing certain movies or plays that others have raved about. In fact, my husband and I have friends we have long associated with a particular film, *Babette's Feast.* We recalled their saying it was subtle and unpretentious, artless in the way pure art should be. So we went to see it. Huh? We found it tedious, interminable. Like laboratory mice shocked once, and hence once too often, we learned to ignore any future recommendations for movies from these friends. We did so for about the next ten years. And only recently did we realize we had mistaken this couple for another, who absolutely adore slow-paced Scandinavian films about depression at the dinner table.

Nonetheless, *Babette's Feast* had me thinking the other day that the same avoidance principle might apply to people who take on the role of literary arbiter for others—reviewers, critics, panels for prizes, and yes, even guest editors. Such people may have an eye for literary conventions and contrivances, allusions and innovations on the art. But what are their tastes based on? What are their biases? Is part of their aesthetic sense the common prejudice in the arts that anything popular is by definition devoid of value? Do they tend to choose work that most resembles theirs? Perhaps those critics who publicly declare, "This is good, and that is not," ought to present a list of more than just the titles of their most recently published works.

I, for one, would like a résumé of habits, a précis of personality. What movies would they watch twice? Do they make clever and snide remarks, but mostly about people who are doing better than they? When recounting conversations, do they imitate other people's voices? When sharing a meal with friends, do they offer to pick up the whole tab, split the bill evenly, or apportion it according to what they ordered and how little wine they drank? When a friend of theirs has suffered a terrible loss, do they immediately call, or wait until things have settled down a bit? What are their most frequent complaints in life? What do they tend to exaggerate? What do they downplay? Do they think little dogs are adorable, or appetizers for big dogs? And of course, I would want to know what books they love and what books they loathe and why.

In other words, if you ran into these people at a party, would you *even like* them? I am being only half facetious. I do think the answers say something about people's sensibility to life and human nature, and hence their sensibility to stories beyond the surface of craft. The stories we love to read may very well have to do with our emotional obsessions, the circuitry between our brain and our heart, the questions we thought about as children that we still think about, whether they are about the endurance of love, the fears that unite us, the acceptance of irreversible decay, or the ties that bind that turn out to be illusory. In that context, I also think that if *Babette's Feast* is your favorite film, then you might not like the stories I have picked.

Anyway, for the woman at the airport, for our friends whose taste in movies was wrongly maligned, and for anyone now taking a flier on my judgment, I will reveal what kinds of tastes I developed in reading between forty years ago and this year.

A worrisome child, I developed an osmotic imagination, and I loved fairy tales for their richness in the grotesque. I read them all—Hans Christian Andersen, the Brothers Grimm, Aesop, whatever was on the library shelf—a book a day, many of them devoured at bedtime, which, my mother said, was how I ruined my eyes and why I had to wear glasses at a young age.

Because my father was a part-time Baptist minister, I also read Bible stories, which I thought were quite similar to fairy tales, for they too contained gory images, gut-clenching danger, magical places, and a sense that things are never as they first appear. By the end of these stories, much had always changed.

Kingdoms and seas rose and fell. Humble creatures turned into handsome princes or prophets. Seas parted, a few loaves became food for thousands. And bearded giants lost their heads.

I loved those stories because, along with the horrific, they contained limitless and amazing ways in which people, places, and circumstances changed. They gave me a sense of instability and distrust, but also wonder, that mirrored my own life. I remember one Halloween, being lost on a dark street, then finally seeing my mother, her red swing coat. I flew toward her, hugged the back of her coat, crying for joy because I was no longer lost, only to see a stranger's startled face looking down at me. As a child, I thought it was a terrifying magic that had transformed my mother into a woman with blond hair. My mother changed quickly in other ways as well. One moment she could be hovering, smothering in her protectiveness. The next, she might toss furniture upside down in a rage. She had a need to cling to and then reject everyone she loved, a quirk in her personality that began with her traumatic childhood. But I would not understand this for perhaps another thirty years. I was simply afraid of the ways she could change, of being caught unawares.

At least with a fairy tale, I could immerse my imagination like my big toe in a tub of hot water and retract it if the story didn't agree with me at the moment. Part of the thrill, however, was seeing what I could take, guessing what might happen, delighting if I was surprised, decrying the injustice if I was unfairly fooled. Kind creatures turned into genies. People who died or fell down holes or went lost could be transformed into happier beings, or they wound up in lands that nobody else knew existed. In stories, you could hide or escape.

Since my father was a minister and my mother a believer in

bad fate, I used to wonder why these things happened. Was it a lesson, a curse, or a trick? Was it a reward for goodness, a punishment for evil? Was it by luck or accident? Or did things happen for reasons we could never know—or would *not want* to know? I was a child who rode a whirligig of questions and flew out in all directions.

Whatever the case, I was addicted to stories about the morbid: the beheadings, the stonings, the man who was three days dead and stank when he came back to life. These were people with fates worse than mine. So far, at least. But just in case, I wanted to prepare for dangers that might await me.

Around this same time, I discovered a book at home that was useful to me in this regard. It was a medical textbook my mother was studying so she could become a licensed vocational nurse. The textbook concerned medical anomalies, and on its pages were descriptions and photographs of people with acromegaly, elephantiasis, hirsutism, leprosy, superfluous or missing appendages, deformities that vied with *Ripley's Believe It or Not* for instilling open-jawed disbelief.

I tried to imagine the lives of those people, how they felt, their thoughts as they stared back at me through the photographs. I imagined them before they had their disease. I imagined them cured. I imagined my taking them to school, all the kids screaming in terror, while I alone remained calm, a true friend. I imagined them changing into genies, princes, and immortals. I imagined I might become just like them, plagued and miserable, but soon to be transformed into someone else. These people were my imaginary playmates. Their consciousness, I believed, was mine. And those notions were among the first stories I made up for myself.

Like many children, I read to be scared witless, to be less lonely, to believe in other possibilities. But we all become different readers in how we respond to books, why we need them, what we take from them. We become different in the questions that arise as we read, in the answers that we find, in the degree of satisfaction or unease we feel with those answers. We differ in what we consider about the real world and the imaginary one. We differ in what we think we can know—or would want to know—and how we continue to pursue that knowledge.

In the hands of a different reader, the same story can be a different story.

I believe that now, although in college I allowed myself to believe otherwise. Back then I had reached a point where I believed good taste was an opinion held by others, namely the designated experts. I was an English major, and my sophomore year I wrote a paper on Hemingway's *The Sun Also Rises.* Although I thought it was well written, I did not like it much, the cynicism, the fact that by the end the characters had not changed much—which was the point, but one I did not find all that interesting. I said so in my paper, and the following week my professor chose to read it aloud in class. He said it was remarkably different from papers he had read in all his years of teaching. I blushed, thinking this was high praise. And then he started to read my sentences in a tone that became increasingly less benign. Soon his face was livid, as he gasped between each of my paragraphs: "Who is *this* writer to criticize Hemingway, the greatest American writer of our century? *This* writer is an idiot! This novel deserves a better reader!" If this writer had had the means, she would have killed herself on the spot.

The next year, in another English class at another college, the same novel was assigned. This time I wrote a paper that noted the brilliant characterization, how despite the panorama of events and the opportunities afforded the characters, nothing much changed in their lives, and how this so convincingly captured the realism of ennui. The book represented the pervasive American sense of a lost generation whose lives, singly or together, held no hope or direction. My paper received high praise.

By the time I graduated, I was sick of reading literary fiction. My osmotic imagination had changed into one with filters, lint traps. I thought that literary tastes were established norms that depended on knowing what others more expert than I thought was best.

For the next twelve years, I read an occasional novel. But I did not return to my habit of reading a story a day until 1985. By then I had become a successful but unhappy person, with work that was lucrative but meaningless. I was in one of those situations that cause people to join a religious cult or spend a lot of money on psychotherapy, or take up the less drastic and more economical practice of writing fiction.

Since I was a beginning writer, I believed that the short form was the easier one to tackle. It was the IRS approach to writing: Use the short form if you have less to account for and the standard amount to withhold. From a remainder table at my local bookstore, I picked up *The Best American Short Stories 1983*, the volume coedited by Anne Tyler. I was just starting to write short stories. I had been raised by a mother with impossibly high standards. This was the book for me, the best. With suggestions from my more literary-minded friends, I read short story collections, and the ones I targeted first were by women. Of course, I read fiction by men as well, even Hemingway, which I reread with new appreciation, but mostly for his clean prose style. I was especially interested in fiction by women, because almost all the literary works I had read as an English major were by men, the one exception being Virginia Woolf. I discovered that stories by women included more stories *about* women, and I was startled to read, for the first time perhaps since *Jane Eyre,* so many books with a sensibility sympathetic with mine. Many of their voices were intimate, involving questions, ambiguities, and contradictions common among us, yet they were thoughts and emotions I had not seen expressed in other stories I had read.

Being a new writer, I was also intrigued with the craft, the art of the short story. I joined a writers' workshop. That is where, I think, I ceased being a typical reader. I started looking at the parts and not just the whole of the story, which is a terrible habit, in a way. It's like being Dr. Frankenstein, seeing how life was created out of previously inanimate parts. The Dr. Frankenstein in me would sometimes act as cosmetic surgeon, determining where the excess fat of the story was, how a little lift here, a tuck there could improve the result. But what did I really know? What seemed "essential" to me was "garrulous" to another writer.

As a beginning writer, I was still trying to figure out what qualified as a proper short story versus a prose poem, an anecdote, a character piece, a novella. I actually thought there were agreed-upon answers to questions like these: What is voice? What is story? Does voice determine story, or vice versa? How should characters develop? What are the elements of a good ending? What are the virtues of short stories in general?

Along with these big abstract questions, I had pragmatic

worries over craft: Why do so many writers these days use the present tense? Is it *supposed* to sound like dispassionate stage directions? What are the pros and cons of using first person, third person, or for that matter, second person? Should the narrative follow a chronological sequence? Or is it more admired (that is, more intelligent-looking) to jump around, fracture things a bit to resemble more realistically the way our poor memories work?

Then there was this: What is the existential meaning of the big white space between paragraphs? What is being said by *not* being said?

I actually believed that someone else's answers to those questions would help me become a better writer. I remember thinking that if someone could help me deconstruct the stories, and figure out what works, I could then take these principles, tried and true and judged the best, to methodically write my own stories.

So I read piles and piles of short stories in those early years of learning to write. I confess that with some stories I would arrive at the end with that same sense of epistemological wonder: "Huh?" In other words, I just didn't get it. And this led me to believe that my former professor was right: I was missing some finer aesthetic sense. Perhaps I was too much of a realist and did not understand abstractions and fragments. Or perhaps the problem was that I was a romanticist, certainly not a postmodernist, or whatever it was or was not that also made me unable to appreciate, say, a dollop of paint on a white canvas in a modern art museum. Maybe I didn't get the stories because I was trying too hard to understand them. I was trying to analyze them rather than just read them, experience them for all the many ways art can appeal.

Of course, I did understand some stories right away, too

soon, too handily, with a fanfare of French horns and a boink on the head. They were weighted with epiphany, beginnings and endings that resonated too neatly, or were boldfaced with the import of hindsight.

And with other stories, I noticed a trend: as in those bedtime stories of my childhood, nothing much changed between the first page and the last. The stories concerned ordinary people doing ordinary things with just a bit of inner unease, and featured an omniscient narrator who provided the precise details that proved their lives were moving at glacial speed. These were Chekhovian tales, except that they took place in more ordinary places and were about more mundane moments. Or perhaps they weren't Chekhovian after all, since a Chekhov ending always included some observed detail that made the whole story transcendent. Whereas these stories petered out, as if they had run out of energy—like life itself, or *The Sun Also Rises*, with its realism of ennui. Maybe that was the effect the writers were going for. Either that, or I just didn't get them.

Nevertheless, ennui was the arty way I ended one of the first short stories I wrote. I sent it off for admission to my first writers' workshop at the Squaw Valley Community of Writers. When my manuscript came up for critique, Elizabeth Tallent, my assigned leader, asked me in front of eleven other writers why my story ended with a bank of fog rolling over the coastal mountains as the narrator is headed for the airport. Naturally, I could not say to a *New Yorker* writer that the deadline for submission had been upon me, and I had run out of time and ideas, as well as interest. So I said the fog was a metaphor for confusion, which it was, mine.

I experienced more fog in my reading and writing. By continuing to read and write, though, I gradually changed. But it was not through deconstruction. It was through an awareness that each writer has a distinct consciousness, attentiveness, inventiveness, and relationship to the world, both real and fictional. I discovered that the short story is a distillation of all that. The way the individual writer chooses to experience, edit, and express that is a matter of taste. And what I liked to read was not necessarily what I wanted to write. My reasons for writing had to do with what wasn't yet there.

I became a much better reader and, I think, as a consequence, a better short story writer, or so I thought. In 1988, I completed my first book of fiction, *The Joy Luck Club,* which I wrote as a collection of short stories. When the galleys went out for early comments, however, most reviewers called it a novel.

Last October, I was having an awful time writing my fourth book when the first batch of forty stories for this volume, photocopies of tear sheets, arrived in the mail for my consideration. Naturally, I worried that my bad writing might affect my reading. Conversely, I worried that reading excellent stories would depress me and further undermine my writing. I worried that my fluctuating estrogen levels would impair the consistency of my judgment. I worried that I would overlook a masterpiece and that everyone, including my former professor, would rage: "Who is *this* writer to ignore our country's greatest writer?" I am still the worrier I was as a child. I still try to sort out my worries, categorize them, organize them, find possible solutions to contain them or make them go away. And they still sit in my brain like a blood clot waiting to dissipate or explode.

To begin, I set up a process so I would be as fair as possible. With one hundred twenty stories to read over four months, that worked out to a story a day, quite doable and also the correct way to go about this, I thought. If I read too many stories at once, I might be comparing them, and for the wrong reasons. So I decided to read one story each evening, while sitting in bed. To ensure that I was not susceptible to distractions, such as the ringing phone or my dogs barking at ghosts, I would wear headphones and listen to an environmental tape of rainfall. On the series editor's recommendation, I would read the stories blind, that is, with the names of the writers and magazines blacked out. This way, I would keep an open mind. I would not be swayed by whether the writer was male or female, new or well established, or of a racial background that one could check on a marketing survey. Not that I would have such specious biases, but why worry that they might creep up unconsciously?

After a week, I worried about other biases. That by listening to rain, I was apt to choose stories set in stormy weather and overlook those with more sun-baked settings. That on days when my mind was cluttered with crisis, I would judge the stories I read as either better or worse than they really were. That with some stories I was annoyed from the start because they had been printed in six-point type with clever graphics that made them impossible to read without squinting and cursing. (Don't the art directors of America realize that a huge percentage of magazine readers are baby boomers, newly presbyopic, and not pleased to be reminded of the fact?)

At times I also found myself trying to scratch beneath the surface and guess who the writer might be. I was a kid before Christmas, shaking the gifts to see if I could tell what was inside. I believed that certain writers' voices were as distinctive as fingerprints, and I thought I had detected six of them (I was wrong in half the cases). If I couldn't guess the names, at least I could figure out the gender. But when I looked back at a pile of stories I had read, and tried to discern what traits might be marked male or female, I saw that my hunches were in most cases based only on whether the narrator was a man or a woman (and half the time this proved to be a flawed way to guess).

So I broke nearly all the rules, or tried to. My proposed schedule to read a story a day? That lasted one day. Sometimes I could not stop from reading five or six. It was like eating a box of truffles. Sometimes, caught up in my own work, I went days without reading a single story. But one rule I did abide by, and it was one I did not set out to follow initially. I read each story from start to finish without interruption, so that I could sense its rhythm. For me, the rhythm is set in the first sentence; it continues in the pacing of the rest of the story, the way it breathes and exhales at the end. The rhythm is like a meditation. Its essence would be lost if I were to read a story in isolated chunks. The short story is more akin to a poem in how it should be read: the effect depends on my breathing along with it in one continuous stream.

I kept this principle while reading in bed, on a plane, in doctors' waiting rooms, on long car rides—in all those places where people might take time to read a short story in a magazine. If I fell asleep in bed before finishing a story, the next morning I started that story again from the beginning. If the nurse said the doctor was ready to see me before I was ready, I started the story again after my appointment. And in January, like fifty million other Americans suffering from holiday bloat, I joined a gym and took these stories along. This, I discovered, is where much of America's magazine reading takes place in concentrated blocks of time. If I did not finish a story within the twenty-five minutes I was programmed to be on the undulating machine, I kept pumping and sweating until I read the last word. Between reading the first story and the last, I discovered also that good fiction can change you in quite beneficial ways. I lost five pounds.

I also found that reading short stories helped my writing. It sprang me out of the doldrums, and I regained the fervor and compulsion toward writing that I had when I started reading massive amounts of fiction back in 1985. By reading so many stories, so many voices, I unleashed what had propelled me to write fiction in the first place: the need to find my own voice and tell my own story. As with conversation, one story begets another.

But what a curious experience to read so many stories in a concentrated period of time, grabbing them in no particular order, for randomness in fiction can generate its own cosmic connections. A story about a dying parent would be followed by another about a dying parent, one about a difficult mother by another about a difficult mother. Pizza Huts and Domino's popped up in clusters like mushrooms after rain, as did references to the color cranberry and barking dogs, tourists in India and people falling under ice, reunions after sexual indiscretions, and alcohol-addled sons; and there were many, many thoughts before dying. Bound together, they might be a codex on the collective unconscious. Or is that just a result of the kind of person I am? I do tend to connect the dots and find patterns, yet the patterns could be meaningless. In any case, in reading them together, I was conscious that certain stories had similar images and situations and that some appealed to me much more than others.

In many of the hundred twenty stories, I found elements of fairy tales, the grotesque. Here is where an actual bias does come in. I was delighted to find them, stunned that so many of the stories had these qualities—not so much in structure, but in imagery: underground worlds, a woman's stumbling upon a much darker version of Snow White and the Seven Dwarves, a secret place that no one else knows exists, ghosts in the attic, tractors that talk. I saw a similar fairy-tale quality in how characters formed: the narrator discovers that others are not who they appear to be. The change occurs not through the wave of a wand, but through death or danger or despair.

There was one other worry I had as a reader. I looked at the stories I had placed in my pile of favorites. Many had an exotic flavor. Either the narrators were ethnic or the settings were outside America. I could imagine readers smugly nodding and saying, "Well, of course *she* would pick *those*, um-hm." I then looked at the larger pile of those I had decided to eliminate, and within those were also a good many with exotic settings and ethnic narrators. I noticed that there were a fair number of stories in both piles about hunters and cowboys and gritty-teethed people living in remote parts of North America. So what was it about me that would account for that? I guess I am the kind of reader who has less fondness for the ordinary. Maybe I'm still that kid who wants to see things I've never seen before. I like being startled by images I never could have imagined myself.

By their nature, these were stories with distinctive voices,

voices with interesting things to say. I imagine that contributed to why certain magazine editors had chosen them. Having read the hundred twenty, I know how quickly stories can blur into sameness and fall away from memory. The splendid ones are left standing. But in the end, only the vivid remain. Different does not always equal vivid, but the converse is certainly true.

For those hoping that I might make some observations on the demographics of this collection and its significance to literary trends or diversity in American culture or the year 1998, I am sorry to disappoint. I don't think most writers of literary fiction deliberately set out to write stories that are topical or representational. Great stories resist generalizations and categories. For me even to try to guess at how the subconscious of twenty-one writers followed certain patterns would be presumptuous, and I would likely be wrong. And think how embarrassing it would be if I ran into any of these writers at a party.

I will leave it to the writers themselves to tell you what their intentions might have been, if they so choose to reveal them.

Why do *I* think these stories are the best? What do they say about my tastes? Will they find harmony with yours, with those of the woman in Seoul, with those of my friends with the movie recommendations?

I chose stories that have strong storytelling qualities. By this, I mean they have a narrative thread, pulled taut by interesting complications, and this leads to some thought or emotion or clear-eyed perception. In these stories, when I reached the last page, I felt a *change*; I did not say, "Huh?" Yet the stories did not present their endings with the clang of gongs. There is nothing preening or preachy about them. Rather, by the end, they quietly but perceptibly lifted themselves and me out of our skins. I'm not saying that each story was uplifting like a birthday balloon let go. The weightlessness was sometimes more akin to a bed of static, a sudden loss of gravity, a tiny aphid's being tumbled upward by wind. Sometimes this did not occur until the last few paragraphs—sometimes not until the last sentence. But always, by the end, I found myself suspended just a moment longer by a sense of wonder over the story's ability to make me feel what I felt. Every story in this collection did that for me.

I am also an ardent admirer of prose style. That does not, however, mean that I always want it to be as fancy as Humbert Humbert's, though *Lolita* is a favorite of mine for language. Whether seemingly simple or fancy, the prose I like is such that everything is there for a reason—every word, every image, every bit of dialogue is needed; it adds, builds, and its dexterity is also transparent. And yet it has a generosity, there's no skimpiness. That's the craft part for me. While the prose may seem offhand and effortless, it is imbued with a particular sensibility and intelligence and purpose. That higher sense permeates the story, and only when you leave the story do you realize how palpable it still is. The stories here gave me that sensation, each in its own way.

What I look for most in a story, what I crave, and what I found in these twenty-one, is a distinctive voice that tells a story only that voice can tell. The voice is not merely the language, the prose style, the imagery. It is that ineffable combination of things that creates a triangulated relationship among narrator, reader, and fictional world. It may have an intimacy or a distance, a trustworthiness or an edginess. The voice is this hour's guide to eternity and will immerse me in a unique consciousness that observes some nuances of human nature and overlooks others. It is the keeper of forgiveness and condemnation. It will order perception and juxtapose events and rearrange time, then deliver me back to my own consciousness slightly askew.

By the end of the story, what I've witnessed and experienced as reader is so interesting, so intense, so transcendent that if someone were to ask me what the story was about, I would not be able to distill it into an easy answer. It would be a sacrilege for me to say it is about, say, survival or hope or the endlessness of love. For the whole story is what the story is about, and there is no shorthanding it. I can only say please read it yourself.

If this collection holds a common thread with regard to my tastes, it is what I think the best of fiction is by its nature and its virtues. It can enlarge us by helping us notice small details in life. It can remind us to distrust absolute truths, to dismiss clichés, to both desire and fear stillness, to see the world freshly from closer up or farther away, with a sense of mystery or acceptance, discontent or hope, all the while remembering that there are so many possibilities, and that this was only one.

The best stories do change us. They help us live interesting lives.

HOPE

Now help me light three sticks of incense. The smoke will take our wishes to heaven. Of course, it's only superstition, just for fun. But see how fast the smoke rises—oh, even faster when we laugh, lifting our hopes, higher and higher.

· The Kitchen God's Wife

· what i would remember ·

When I was in my twenties, at a time when my mother and I were not getting along that well, she asked me, "If I die, what you remember?"

Here we go, I thought, the old Chinese-torture routine. I answered something like this: "Come on, you're not going to die."

She persisted. "What you remember?"

I struggled to come up with an answer. "You know, all *kinds* of things. Like, well, you know, you're my mother."

And then my mother said, in a both sad and angry voice: "I think you know little percent of me."

Those words came back to me when, one day in 1985, I received a phone call telling me my mother was probably dead. At the time, I was in Hawaii on vacation and had left no phone number where I could be reached. So it was not until my friend Gretchen, who was with my husband and me in Hawaii, had checked her answering machine back home that I learned that four days had already passed since my mother had suffered an apparent heart attack. She was now in intensive care.

As I went to a phone booth to call the hospital, I was sure it was too late. She was dead. I tried to imagine her alive, and all I could do was picture her saying those words: "What you remember?" Now I asked myself, What should I remember? What had I lost? What had been my mother's greatest hopes and fears? What was important to her? I had a surge of remorse and guilt, realizing she had been right all along: I knew little percent of her. What a sad fact.

With shaky hands, I dialed the number. As I waited to be connected from the switchboard to the nursing station in intensive care, I made a vow to God and whoever was listening, "If my mother lives, I will get to know her. I will ask her about her past, and this time I'll actually listen to what she has to say. Why, I'll even take her to China, and yes, I'll write stories about her. . . ." Soon a nurse would tell me in quiet tones that I would have to speak to a doctor, and the doctor would say, "I'm sorry, but I have some very bad news. . . ."

All at once, I heard my mother's voice. "Amy-ah?"

"Oh . . . Mom? Are you okay?"

"Yes, fine, fine. Where you?"

"Hawaii."

"Hawai-hee? When you go Hawai-hee?"

"Listen. I thought you had a heart attack. I thought—"

My mother cut me off with a huff. "Heart attack. No, no, no, no. I go to fish market, and the fishmonger he try cheating me. Make me so mad. All sudden got a pain in my chest, hurt me so bad, so I drive to Kaiser Hospital. They put me here, ICC, do all kinds test, but turn out I have angina, cause by stress! So you see, that fishmonger, he wrong. Stress me out."

I let out an audible sigh.

Then she asked, "You worry? That's why call? Yes? Ha, *ha!* You worry for *me!*" She was enormously pleased. So there I was, in a phone booth at a shopping center in Hawaii, crying and laughing at the same time. After I hung up, I heard a voice saying, "Hey, don't forget now. You *promised* . . ."

So I did take her to China. I endured three weeks of being with her twenty-four hours a day. Three weeks of her giving me her expert advice, criticizing my clothes, my eating habits, the bad bargains I made at the market. I hated it and I loved it. And when I returned home, I began to write stories about her life.

At the beginning of *The Joy Luck Club,* I imagined a young woman whose mother has just died. They are now separated by death, seemingly without a reconciliation. There was never any one great fight that divided them, just life itself over the years, petty misunderstandings, and the desire of the mother to give her daughter advice and the daughter's desire to find her own way. So what would this daughter remember?

In the end, the daughter learns something, realizes something, something obvious that has been there all along, and she is ready to take her mother's place at the mah jong table, on the east, where things begin.

On the dedication page of *The Joy Luck Club,* I wrote:

To my mother
and the memory of her mother

You asked me once
what I would remember.
This, and much more.

· to complain is american ·

This is taken from an informal panel at Renaissance Weekend, an annual gathering of creators and thinkers from all walks of life, in which I was asked to address the topic "What's Bugging Me Lately?"

I find it disconcerting to be asked to gripe in public. It goes against the tenets of how I was raised. "You shouldn't make a big stink over nothing," my mother would say. "Just like farting."

Yet I grew up thinking my mother was the biggest complainer I knew. Bad service in restaurants? She would let the whole world know, pointing to the greasy bowl or the sticky chopsticks. "Hey, see this?" she would say loud enough for all the hungry customers to hear: "You expect me to eat with this dirty thing?"

Perhaps it is because of my upbringing that I would rather foment trouble quietly. Besides, I have little to complain about personally. Life has been good to me, more than good, remarkable in fact, beyond anything I could have ever imagined, and I have a wild imagination.

But being a writer, I also remind myself that talking about the unspeakable is part and parcel of my work. I *can* complain. I *should* complain. Writers do and often should bring up subjects that are uncomfortable. As an Asian-American writer, or "writer of color," as some would say, I am expected to lash out on a range of social issues. And as an American writer, which is how I think of myself—no hyphenated term—I have the right to express myself on any subject and in any direction I wish. I believe that what makes me an American writer more than anything else is my taking for granted this unalienable right called freedom of speech.

And so, as an American writer, I have refused, even early in my career when I was still unknown, to have a story of mine printed because the people at the magazine wanted to change one word. One measly word, they said. The word was "shit," what a character says to his wife. If the editor had said to me, "We're a family magazine. Can we just have the man look glumly at his wife?" I might have replied, "Sure." But this magazine editor wanted to replace "shit" with "Christ." I ask you, Which is more offensive to say in such a context? Why should I let this editor's interpretations of morals govern mine?

This may seem petty to you, one word, but I hold it as not just my right but my responsibility as an American writer to reject arbitrary censorship. In a case like that, trivial as it may seem, I stand against editorial tinkering that reflects the larger question of who defines "good taste." As a writer, I think a great deal about intentions and consequences, about personal responsibility, credit, and blame. These come with everything I write. But they also come up when I am asked a question like this: "What should we do about human rights in China?"

I am not an expert on the rule of law and its absence in China. But it just so happens that I think about this subject quite a bit, in part because the media often ask me, but even more because I have family in China—a sister who lives in Shanghai, her husband and children, as well as numerous cousins, an aunt, and my mother's brother, my dear old uncle, who was the Vice-Secretary of Trade Unions, a man who survived the Long March and now enjoys the Long Yarn. When I visit, he loves to tell me about the brave martyrs, some of them his friends, who helped with the revolution. Being a retired official of high standing, my uncle has a car and a driver, and he has escorted me around town in this lap of luxury so that I can conveniently see the sights. Once, when I was to attend a dinner at the residence of the American ambassador and his wife, my uncle tersely told me it was "not convenient" for him to take me, nor was it convenient for the U.S. embassy's car to come any closer than one block from where he lived. This happened at the time the embassy had given refuge to the dissident Fang Lizhi. You might say that my uncle and I do not always see eye to eye on things.

The last time I was in Beijing, I was there with my husband on behalf of an American group raising money for Chinese orphanages. Lou and I were to attend a dinner for four hundred fifty people—foreign diplomats, executives of overseas divisions of large corporations, and the cream of the philanthropic Beijing international society. The event, the first of its kind there, was sold out, and the donated money would go toward bedding, clothing, and corrective surgeries that would not only increase children's chances of being adopted but also help them survive in a country where central heating is not common, and where the government allotment for each orphan amounts to a few dollars a month. These poor conditions have less to do with governmental neglect than with the realities of keeping 1.2 billion people fed.

Lou and I had pledged a sum of money that would enable many children to have surgeries to repair cleft palates, clubfeet, and other birth defects. We had an opportunity to meet some of the children who needed the help. We held them and never felt closer to knowing that our money was going to a very worthy cause.

At the event, to take place in a hotel ballroom, I was supposed to tell a few jokes before dinner, talk about the children we had met, and thank all in attendance for their generosity. But it turned out that the American fund-raising organization did not have a not-for-profit permit to solicit funds legally in China. Who knows why this information had not come out sooner. It was your basic instance of Americans with good intentions but a certain amount of ineptitude. In any case, people from the Public Security Bureau came to the hotel the afternoon before the dinner and informed the organizers that it would have to be canceled. The American organizers pleaded. The PSB officials were at first adamant, yet after some negotiation allowed the group to hold the dinner—although the banners would have to come down and the ballroom would have to be partitioned, as if this were only a dinner and not a charity event. Any mention of soliciting money was strictly forbidden. This was most unfortunate, and a few people were mightily angry. We coped. The dinner went on as planned. We did not give speeches from the podium, but went from table to table to thank everyone for coming.

A number of reporters attended the dinner. They saw the event quite differently. The next morning, the Reuters and AP stories went something like this: "Police stormed and raided the hotel, tearing down banners, and prevented the author Amy Tan from going to the podium to speak about the situation of orphanages in China." By the next day, the story was picked up by maybe a hundred newspapers and television stations worldwide. In one televised report, old footage taken when I was promoting my latest novel ran strategically next to footage of a dying child in an orphanage, which had been filmed surreptitiously by a British crew for another program. With the manipulation of images, it appeared that I was expressing shock and outrage over the condition of orphanages in China.

Soon after, China shut the doors of its orphanages to prying Western eyes. The monies that should have gone for cleft-palate surgeries, for saving the lives of babies, were held up. The adoptions of Chinese babies by American couples were stopped. And I was banned from returning to China. The fact that real lives had been compromised bothered me greatly. In fact, it angered me. And my anger was directed not just at the officials who closed the orphanage doors to additional help, but at the Western media and those who had taken this event as an opportunity to rail against the conditions of the orphanages in the name of human rights. Their actions had not helped those babies; they imperiled them. What had gone wrong?

As Americans, we have an inordinate fondness for rights. Our country was founded on them; we enjoy the right to bear arms, to bear children, to bare our thoughts as we see fit. The right to life, the right to choose, the right to die, the right to speak out or remain silent. We argue ferociously for our rights in whatever way each of us interprets them. When we do it on our own soil, we are on solid ground. We have lawyers who can back us up. But when we argue for rights on behalf of people in another country, things get a bit tricky. They don't always go the way we intend. Doors might slam shut, and who knows what goes on behind them.

Look at South Africa, some will say. We criticized them for apartheid, imposed sanctions, really put the pressure on. What a success. But China is not South Africa. What works in one country, with a white ruling class, does not necessarily work in another. That's rule number one in foreign diplomacy school.

Yet when you are aware of human suffering, you can't simply stand by and say nothing. As we learned from the Holocaust, indifference is a murderer too.

So what should we do about human rights in China? My honest answer: I don't know what *we* should do. I only know what *I* should do. I think about my uncle in Beijing, the one who believes China is the most peace-loving country in the world. I think about what I would do if I had to tell my uncle to mend his ways and join me at the U.S. ambassador's house for dinner with Fang Lizhi. Would it do any good to shout at him, to threaten him, to stop calling him? That would be an effective way to start the equivalent of a war between us. With my uncle, I have to show my concern in subtle ways. I have to win his trust, spend more time with him. And yet I also know he probably won't change his mind about Fang Lizhi, about other dissidents still in jail, about the cultural destruction of Tibet. He is set in his ways. He thinks I don't understand China. And he's right in many respects.

I hope the politicians know much more. What I can do is give money for cleft-palate surgeries. I can fund fellowships so that foreign journalists can study in the United States and take fundamental ideas back to their own countries. I can provide assistance to Tibetan groups developing self-sustaining industries.

It's not enough, I know. But my right to complain and shout doesn't necessarily do a damn bit of good. In the meantime, I keep asking myself: What do I believe is right? What are my intentions? What are my responsibilities? How can my intentions match the hopes of those real lives I hope to affect?

· the opposite of fate ·

At the end of June 2001, after a four-month book tour that had taken me to forty cities across the United States, then to a dozen more in the United Kingdom, the Republic of Ireland, Australia, and New Zealand, I returned home to San Francisco. I lowered the shades, crawled into bed, and began the long rest I felt I deserved. I slept for nearly twenty-four hours that first day, and then another twelve to twenty at a time in the weeks that followed.

Even before the tour, I had been exhausted, always desperate for sleep. Any amount of activity felt overwhelming. Mail piled on my desk, and I had no motivation to sort through the debris. While on the tour, I was plagued with a constant headache, a stiff neck, a heart rate that zoomed to 130 at odd times, as well as middle-of-the-night insomnia and a moldering apathy, all of which I would blame on the constant change of hotels, the frequent-flyer miles, and the emotional upheaval of recently having lost my mother and my editor just two weeks apart.

Back at home, I told my husband, Lou, that I felt as if something in my body had broken. Something was not right. Weeks went by, and still I did not feel rested. If anything, I was more tired than ever, in part because I could sleep for only two or three hours before being awakened by a sensation I described as "Dolby Digital syndrome," a constant vibration within my body, which felt as though someone had installed in me a souped-up megabass system for stadium-strength rap music. Unfortunately, such symptoms do not match anything in the standard diagnostic criteria.

During the day, I could not concentrate long enough to write anything new and found myself looping around and around the same pages I had written months before. Writer's block too, however, is not a recognized medical malady. Reading had become a similar challenge with my waning attention span. By page three or four of the stories I started, I was unable to recall anything I had read, and had to begin anew. At dinner parties, I often could not keep up with fast repartee. I could not follow segues in conversation. Everyone I met seemed quick-witted to the point of intimidation. I nodded and laughed at the moments when I saw everyone else do so.

For reasons unknown to me, I was easily overcome with dread when I was alone. Small sounds startled me, made me leap and jerk, then imagine descendants of the boogieman from my childhood. I guessed that I was not acknowledging some deep-seated anxiety, and so off I went to consult a psychiatrist, the first time I had done so in nearly twenty years. The last one I had consulted had been pivotal in my life: he was a taciturn Jungian analyst who fell asleep during three sessions, and that had the effect of leading me to replace the sleepy doctor with a more lively fiction-writing workshop. With that, I began to write stories, a whole new career opened for me, and voilà, here I am, able to appreciate the absolute necessity of the doctor's falling asleep when he did. Had he been more attentive, I might have continued my other course in life. Naturally, I wondered what profound changes in my life the new psychiatrist would bring.

This psychiatrist remained awake. She listened, and thought I had posttraumatic stress disorder, aside from my long-seated depression. There were obvious elements in my life that might have accounted for that. For one, I had a mother who had often been seized by rages and despair. I had seen her dramatic attempts to end her life on numerous occasions during childhood, and instead of becoming inured to these episodes, I had grown up with an anticipatory angst, what people develop after a big earthquake, unsure as to when the next temblor will come along, yanking the ground from beneath them. As a teen, I had watched my father and brother waste away to skeletons from brain tumors, which my mother feared she, my other brother, and I were destined to have; I would hear this prediction echoed the rest of my life whenever I had a headache. Since we were doomed to die anyway, why not sooner than later? That logic led my mother once to vow to kill me as she pressed a meat cleaver to my throat for twenty long minutes.

In later years, I accumulated, as others might Hummel figurines, a variety of accidents, assaults, and acts of God. While I was in college, I was a passenger in a car without seat belts that crashed into a pole; I was thrown into the windshield, with the result the rearrangement of my face. While I was in graduate school, a robber pressed the muzzle of a gun against my temple and made me and my co-workers at a pizza parlor lie facedown in the meat locker; he promised to blow out our brains if we made a single sound, whereupon the woman lying beside me began to scream like an actress in a bad horror movie. The next year I entered a bloody room that smelled of nervous sweat, so that I might identify what items had been stolen by whoever had also tortured and killed a former roommate of Lou's and mine. Lou and I had slept in that same room the night before, and only by chance were we elsewhere the night of the crime.

Just before my first book debuted, I nearly managed to be published posthumously, when I came close to drowning in the Sea of Cortez. I had to be dragged back to shore and have salt water pushed out of my lungs. More recently, after forty inches of rain melted twelve feet of snow, mudslides the size of container ships ramrodded their way down the sides of our cabin in Tahoe, leaving Lou and me stranded next to a perilously rising river. To add to my sense of foreboding, there was the dark side of being published: the overly devoted fans and detractors, three of whom had expressed fantasies of killing me, one of whom had followed me onto a plane to tell me how he would do it.

In retrospect, it is no wonder I was jumping out of my skin at every little noise. I seemed to be a magnet for danger. Why was I so unlucky? Was this karmic payment for some carelessness in a past life? Were these signs that my demise was one breathless moment away? Or could it be that the reverse was true, that these calamities were proof, deliberately sent, that I was amazingly lucky, as invulnerable to weapons and villains as a comic-book action figure? I have fluctuated between the two views: incredibly lucky, incredibly unlucky, doomed to die soon, destined to overcome all. And until recently, I had accommodated an eventful life with high resilience and a low dose of antidepressants. Why was my body now expressing its outrage at these traumas?

The psychiatrist wisely suggested that I have a complete medical workup, so off I went to consult with my regular doctor. Wouldn't it be wonderful if it turned out I was merely deficient in one of those vitamins or enzymes without which one becomes nervous, weak-minded, and neurotic?

A week later, while I was in New York, my doctor in San Francisco called with the results of my blood tests. I was perfectly normal, she told me, except for one thing: my blood sugar was low. Well, no surprise there. I had told her years before that I was prone to "low blood sugar," especially when I was traveling or under stress. And besides, everyone had occasional hypoglycemia. It was the yuppie disease, and a bag of M&M's was usually the remedy.

"This is really low," my doctor said. "In fact, the number is rather alarming." Doctors tend to be unfazed when your limbs have nearly rotted off, so I wondered what could be viewed as "alarming."

She explained that the glucose reading was 27, a level that in most people would mean unconsciousness or at least inability to sit up and talk, whereas I had walked into her office the day the blood was drawn, and remained both conversant and vertical. My doctor ran through the possibilities that might account for the glucose anomaly, but dismissed most of them, including my having secretly injected myself with purloined insulin or eaten unripe ackee fruit from Jamaica. Finally, I heard her say she wanted to do more tests when I returned to San Francisco, so we could rule out a tumor in my pancreas and possibly my brain. Those two things, she hastened to add, were highly unlikely.

I remember that I forced myself to sound calm, almost unconcerned, when in truth I was the one who now felt alarmed. Could this be the fulfillment of the curse my mother had feared? At last, it was happening. I could sense it: I had a brain tumor, just as my father, older brother, and mother had had. Mine would make four, and four was the unluckiest number in Chinese, for the *si* for "four" is homophonous with the *si* for "death." Then again, this might not be a Chinese curse but a genetic one, a fate that lay within my family's DNA, encoded in a cell that was all too eager to turn ugly, proliferate like roaches, and squeeze its nest into the limited confines of my skull.

Confronted with all this, I did what any person with Chinese curses and bad medical news does these days: I consulted the Internet. While my mother had turned to the supernatural for its infinite wisdom, I found solace within the vastness of the World Wide Web. There I could continue the search for a diagnosis and cure with the help of Dr. Google, who guided me, nonjudgmentally, through a universe of astrocytomas and migraines, chemotherapy and miracle cures of charlatans.

My preoccupation with illness could be only short-lived, for the next day I had to go to the CNN newsroom in midtown Manhattan for a live interview related to the launch of *Sagwa*, an animated series on PBS based on a children's book I had written. I had struggled against fatigue to awaken before eight that morning. In the newsroom, I was sitting in a tall director's chair, earpiece inserted, lavaliere microphone hooked to my lapel, black monitor before me as visual focus so I could pretend to be talking face to face with my interviewer. On the TV monitors to my right, I saw images of pregnant models wearing scanty rave-style clothing that exposed their ballooning bellies from bra line to crotch. It was Fashion Week in New York, and in my opinion, someone had scraped the bottom of the barrel for that one.

"One minute to live," I heard a voice say in my earpiece. It was shortly before nine a.m. Eastern Daylight Time. This was the soft-news hour, when hardworking people in New York had already gone to their jobs, when alarm clocks on the West Coast were starting to sound, and mothers between those geographic points were preparing their children's breakfasts and were eager, I hoped, to learn of a new cartoon that would occupy the minds of their brilliant young progeny.

I was relaxed, an old hand at interviews, yet something did not feel quite right. People in the newsroom were talking in loud, tense voices. I knew that background sounds gave the impression of fast-breaking news, but this level of verisimilitude was ridiculous. People seemed gruff, even rude. I concluded that these were colleagues who disliked one another and were suffering job burnout. Listen to them yell at each other:

"What do you mean, you can't get him on the line? Then go and find him. Quick!"

"Where the hell is Aaron?"

"That's insane! This is absolutely insane!"

"Go down to the Port Authority, right now—I said right *now!*"

"All right, we got live feed! Everybody, here it is."

And I saw an image flash onto a dozen screens: a burning building.

I pulled off the earpiece, undid the lavaliere. From years of doing two-minute television interviews, I knew that just about anything—breaking news on political scandals, updates on O. J.

Simpson's trial, and certainly a local fire with live footage—would be deemed more important than an author plugging her own work. And then I noticed a bizarre element. There was a plane stuck in the heart of the building, and the building itself was not just any building with a city's downtown horizon behind it. It was one of the World Trade Center towers, and the horizon was the clear blue sky.

"It's a commercial jet," someone confirmed. "We have a witness." And I realized that the shouting in the newsroom had not been rude exchanges but tension bordering on chaos.

When another plane hit the other tower, I heard someone murmur, "This is war." I left my chair and walked to the greenroom, trying to fathom what this meant. What do you do when World War III has erupted and you're in a newsroom hearing about it? An intern came up to me and said, "I'm sorry, but we'll have to do this some other day." I nodded, although I knew there would be no other day, certainly not for this interview, and possibly not for anything else. Another woman grabbed me and said frantically, "Have you seen Aaron? We need Aaron in Hair and Makeup right away."

"Okay," I said, having no idea who this Erin woman was. Was she a paramedic? People were going about doing their jobs, enacting approximations of what they usually did, but making no sense in this altered context. I needed to go home and turn on the news to find out what was going on. But wait—these were the very people viewers turned to for that. To everyone's credit, no one in the newsroom was racing out the door or hiding under a desk in fetal position. Yet to judge from the stunned faces, the tearful curses, the sky was falling, and we were all going to die.

Of course, I was not close to death, not like those who worked in the towers and had escaped by accident, or God's grace, or whatever timely circumstance intervened and delivered them out of harm's way. It could have been a missed train, a daughter's earache, a decision to go downstairs to buy a new pair of reading glasses. As for me, I would be the answer to a trivia question that would never be asked: Which guest on CNN was preempted by the attack on the World Trade Center?

An hour or so later, I found myself walking along Seventh Avenue, trying to reach home to be with Lou. I was heading downtown against a stream of people moving uptown, their dusty bodies like figures from Pompeii come back to life. We all stopped when the second tower collapsed, descending like a runaway elevator into the earth. In my mind, I rode it the whole way down and felt in my chest the crush of lives.

For the next six days, while barricaded in our home a mile north of the site, I paced about with tightened sphincter muscles and gritted teeth, waiting for the next explosion, the next wail of fire trucks, the roar of F-16s zooming past our windows and then across the television screen. I felt lucky to be alive, but like those around me, I did not know how long that luck would last. I didn't know what would come next. The only thing any of us could do was pass the time as fate took its course.

When I returned to San Francisco, I sensed I had been given a reprieve from terror. The danger was far removed now. Or was it closer than ever? While I was no longer as focused on the uncertain future of the world, I had to turn to the uncertain state of my own body. Another blood test showed dangerously low blood sugar. And thus began a regime of tests to rule out the usual, and the unusual, suspects. There was a terrorist in my body, and I wanted it caught and removed.

Several times a week, I went to the hospital for tests—giving what felt like liters of blood and urine, as well as undergoing two CAT scans, an MRI, and a forty-eight-hour hospitalized fast. For most of my life, I had rarely gone to a doctor's office, let alone a hospital, save for an annual Pap smear and mammogram. I had not suffered from any prolonged illness. Flu symptoms lasted no more than twenty-four hours. I always managed to avoid colds, while my husband might catch two or three a year. I had been so confident of my health that I had only the barest of insurance policies, one that cost a few hundred dollars a year, and that accordingly covered only the most basic of emergencies, such as decapitation.

Now I was paying the price for arrogance about my good health. I had been thrown into the maze of hospital corridors and insurance forms, with every procedure automatically denied by a grand vizier who lived unseen behind an 800 number. To this magistrate of maladies, my symptoms did not exist unless I died from them. So for now, since I was still very much alive, the tests were unnecessary and not covered.

Some good news came early on. I did not have a brain tumor. There were fifteen "unidentified bright objects" in my frontal and parietal lobes, but that might be nothing more than the residue of age, I was told. So the curse was off, the images of my blank-eyed father and comatose brother receded.

I found myself wishing for a diagnosis, which in essence meant I was wishing for a disease. As the weeks passed, I grew impatient having to keep my life on hold until the next batch of test results arrived. I had to cancel lectures in Maryland and New York, an appearance for *The Washington Post*'s book club, a trip to Aix-en-Provence to honor Toni Morrison, a fête in New Delhi with Salman Rushdie and V. S. Naipaul—though who wanted to fly in this time of heightened security? Better to stay home, where I could stand on my toes, watching for the demise of the Golden Gate Bridge, waiting for the latest tests results. I was struck by how my sense of danger matched the new national climate. We were all anxious over the unknown terrorist who was awaiting us, in tall buildings, at monuments, in amusement parks. We all delayed going on vacation, taking airplanes, and crossing bridges. If anything, my disease served me well as a distraction from a larger uncertainty. Nonetheless, I wanted to secure a diagnosis, good or bad, and then move on with my life in some place other than a hospital waiting room with unread *Golf* magazines and elderly patients who looked genuinely unwell.

What if I had to spend the rest of my life being this lethargic and foggy-headed and not know why? What if I would never again have the energy to hike along the trails of Mount Tamalpais, or ski in races that didn't matter, or dance like a fool with The Rock Bottom Remainders? What if I had to struggle with each sentence I wrote, feeling as if I were writing with a terrible head cold and lack of sleep? What the hell was wrong with me? The cause had to be medical, for I wasn't unhappy with my life. I wasn't the sort who needed a psychosomatic ailment to compensate for a psychic wound. Yet no cause for my illness would turn up. Time after time, the tests came back as disgustingly "normal." To me, "normal" meant that I had *failed* the tests. I wanted numbers that were tangibly abnormal, anything that would explain the problems, lead to the correct treatment, and enable me to return to a truer normal, to be oblivious of my state of health. Soon the doctors would exhaust the possibilities, and if nothing was found, they would give me a benevolent look, tell me that I was quite healthy, and that I should discuss this further with my psychiatrist.

Somewhere in the parallel universe, where everything is absolutely known, was the elusive namable reason. Could the reason be changed? Could I do as Christians did when they went to China in the 1800s and conquer Chinese fate with religious faith? If I prayed for a less serious ailment, could I really change an already given cause? Was it possible to have symptoms to suit a dozen diseases and have God decide later which one, if any, it was? Hadn't He already decided what I had when He allowed the symptoms to arise? Or was He in charge only of reducing the medical sentence? How did prayer work, anyway? What were you praying to alter or affect?

And then one day, finally, after so many tests, a promising candidate surfaced as the source of my problems: a tumor on one of my adrenal glands, that set of organs above the kidneys that does not exist in most people's minds until something goes wrong. *A tumor!* So my mother was right once again.

The tumor, on my left adrenal, was a tiny little thing, a tad more than a couple of centimeters wide, called an "incidentaloma" because it was the kind of anomaly doctors find incidentally when searching for other problems. As the specialist explained, if you examine anyone's body long enough, you will find all kinds of bugaboos: cysts and scotomas, lesions and adhesions, calcification and clogs, thinning and thickening of cells, tissue, and arteries, and skin eruptions as varied as snowflakes, most of which are the usual detritus of commuting, fast food, and the vicissitudes of time. It sounded as harmless as finding loose change and popcorn stuck between the seat cushions in an old movie theater. A small portion of incidentalomas might require cleanup and removal, but for the most part, some degree of body weirdness and decrepitude was expected. And indeed, my doctor told me my tumor was probably benign, given its size, meaning it was probably not malignant.

In my posttraumatized state, "probably not" was not a reassuring prognosis. After all, did most people nearly die a dozen times? Did most people have three brain tumors among their immediate family members? The answer to both was "probably not," but look what had happened to me. The specialist went on to suggest a reasonable plan: I could wait and see, then have a CAT scan done every six months to check whether the tumor was growing. Or I could choose to have the left adrenal gland taken out now. Let's see, I said to myself, which would I rather do—gnaw my fingers down to the bone over the next six months, or convict and sentence the tumor right now, guilty on all counts? Off with its head, I said.

After the laparoscopy, I was given steroids to help me along until my right adrenal gland kicked back into service. As I recovered from surgery, I noticed that the Dolby Digital buzz and fast heart rate were gone. My doctor and I congratulated ourselves on having found the apparent culprit. But then the hallucinations began.

The night they first came, I had retired to bed early. Three hours later, I suddenly woke up, as I often did. I glanced at the clock. It was only twelve-thirty a.m. The light in the dressing area was still on, and I was about to get up to turn it off when I saw my husband standing in the doorway. "Lou?" I called out. He walked silently toward me until he reached my side of the bed. Oh no, bad news. I waited for him to turn on the lamp and tell me who had died. But he said nothing. Was he dumbstruck with grief? "Lou?" I said again, and as I reached for him, my fingers raked thin air, and the figure before me warped and then evaporated.

I jumped out of bed, certain now that Lou was dead and the vision I had just seen had been his ghost. I ran down the stairs and through the house, my dogs at my heels, calling his name until I found him, very much alive, watching television. So what had I seen? Was the hallucination the residual effect of being on morphine and anesthetized during surgery? Since my release from the hospital, besides steroids, I had been taking nothing more powerful than ibuprofen.

My doctors did not think the vision was a drug reaction. Yet they could not say what it was. With their kind but concerned looks, did they think I had the dreaded medical malady known as "loose screw"?

The hallucinations came once a week, then every few days, and eventually, daily. This was especially problematic when I was away from home and staying in a hotel. Since I had had stalkers and death threats, I could not automatically assume that the stranger I thought I saw lying next to me in the middle of the night was a phantom of my mind and not a flesh-and-blood lunatic (on one occasion years before, a *real* man, drunk and completely naked, had come into my hotel room from an adjoining door). To deal with the hallucinations, I trained my Yorkshire terriers to search hotel rooms before I entered. "Find bin Laden" became my cue, and their game was to dash behind doors and into dark closets, to zoom under beds and behind curtains in search of vermin in their mind and a villain in mine. When the odd people appeared to me at night, I would whisper, "Who's there?" and the dogs would instantly leap to attention, scan the room, sniff the air. When they settled back to sleep, so would I. That is, I would try to sleep after having seen a corpse lying next to me, or a pudgy poodle dangling from the ceiling, or two girls skipping rope by the side of my bed, or a woman in a white dressing gown standing in a garden, or a carnival barker playing a circus organ.

I began to track when the hallucinations occurred: always when I had just awakened from sleep. The hour did not seem to matter, whether it was midnight or seven in the morning. It did not seem to correspond to the degree of light in the room, or to my blood sugar levels, whether I was home or away, whether I had had wine at dinner or none for weeks. Some switch in my brain that controlled dreams now seemed to fail to turn off once I opened my eyes, and before me would spring forth the embodiment of my nightmares, the incarnation of my imagination. Had I been a science fiction writer, I would have been blessed with abundant material.

My bedtimes became even wilder, and not in the ways most people would find sexy and desirable. Along with having hallucinations, I began to act out my dreams. I ran in bed, I sat up, I talked. Since I often had dreams of being attacked, I would kick and thrash, push and pummel, and Lou would bear the brunt of those kung fu moves. Other victims of my assaults were a lamp, the sharp corner of my nightstand, and my pillow. I awoke with bruised fists. One night, while dreaming that a woman was about to stab me, I tackled her in my dream and in doing so dived out of my real bed and landed with full bodily force on my crown.

Then there were the bizarre acts I committed of which I have no memory. I purportedly threw laundry around our loft in New York, draping clothes over chairs, sofas, and tables in odd configurations, so that when I saw my rearranged rooms the next morning I thought a deranged interior decorator had broken in. The notion of ghosts also came to mind. Another time I apparently crammed several boxes' worth of tea bags into a small bowl. I thought Lou had assembled this odd presentation of herbal choices for future guests. And one night, while in a hotel in Pasadena, I reportedly called a friend at midnight and left a message in a woeful little-girl's breathy voice, asking whether my friend had seen Lou and my dog Bubba. The next day, after I refused to believe I had called her at such an ungodly hour, she played back the message for me. Listening to my recorded voice, I had the eerie feeling I had developed multiple personalities. Had I been a drinker, I would have sworn off alcohol.

I was worried that I was developing dementia, that I might be following in my mother's footsteps and have Alzheimer's disease; I gave Lou permission to place me in an assisted-care facility, should the time come. We revised our wills and set up a trust. I consulted a few more doctors. I saw a sleep-disorder specialist who found only that I did not have apnea. I saw a neurologist, who said I did not have signs of seizures. I was starting to wonder whether perhaps nothing was wrong with me but the general malaise of growing older and stranger. Did other people simply accept that their bodies broke down like automobiles the moment their warranties expired?

The psychiatrist believed that there was indeed something more. It relieved me greatly that she did not think I was crazy. She pressed me to have more tests done. The most troublesome problem now was my inability to work because of exhaustion and poor concentration. If anything, going to and from the hospital made it even less possible to write. I decided to stop seeing all doctors for a while and try to follow the British example: with a stiff upper lip, carry on.

As my problems worsened, I made light of them with my friends. "Good thing I'm a fiction writer and not your airline pilot," I would say. To them, I looked normal; they assured me I was suffering only from the forgetfulness common to all baby boomers. We all walk into rooms and wonder why we are there, they said. We can't remember names, and even our own phone numbers. We all have stiff muscles and aching joints. We all suffer from bad dreams, especially since September 11. We are all losing our hair.

Rather than feel comforted, I felt alienated, for that was not how it was for me at all, yet it would have sounded crazy to explain why not. Did most baby boomers lose their hair in clumps, so that their shower drains had to be unclogged almost daily as the equivalent of a small wig was extracted? Did my friends read e-mails, respond at length, then have no memory of doing either? Were they stunned to read unfamiliar pages of stories they had evidently composed? Did they leave the first letters off words when writing by hand? Did their speech become garbled, such that they substituted like-sounding but nonsensical words? And did they become lost in their own neighborhoods, unable to recognize familiar landmarks, too mortified to ask for help? When flustered by a distraction, were they overwhelmed, then disoriented? I would stand on the sidewalk, paralyzed with indecision, fully aware that I looked like a potential victim for a mugger as I glanced up and down the street, baffled. My salvation was to nudge my dogs to walk ahead of me on their leashes to keep me going in any direction until I could find my bearings. If we were close to home, they went in that direction. In New York once, without the dogs, I wandered aimlessly for an hour in a snowstorm, just two blocks from home, because that blanketing of white rendered the terrain unfamiliar.

Driving a car was no longer something I could do with natural ease. It became a mental chore, a test of my reflexes. I marveled that most people knew automatically not to brake at green lights but to do so at stop signs. Colors and foot movements became tricky, as did directions. People honked in exasperation at my mistakes. I stopped driving. I no longer left the house alone. Bit by bit, I learned to make accommodations to deal with my problems. But consequently, my life was becoming very small.

I have Madonna to thank for my diagnosis. In November 2002, Lou and I were headed to Miami for a reunion with my fellow bandmates in The Rock Bottom Remainders. The boys in the band thought it would be hilarious if I sang "Material Girl," badly—not that there was any other way I was capable of doing it. I had my doubts about singing this particular song, but I went ahead and purchased a new wig for the act, as well as a nylon bag with the Enron logo, both of which I found on eBay. My Material Girl would be a corporate-scumbag lady. On the plane from San Francisco to Miami, I studied the lyrics and listened to a karaoke version of the song on my CD player.

For the next six hours, I tried to commit the lyrics to memory. They were not profound—this was about a girl who liked to fool around but who was no fool when it came to money. Yet trying to hang on to the words was for me like trying to wrangle oiled fish. After six hours of study and karaoke-style practice, I still could not recall the first line without having the printed words in front of me. I reasoned that I was tired. Once in a hotel in Miami, I continued to practice, from nine p.m. until two a.m., at which point I tried a test neurologists use with Alzheimer's patients—counting backward from one hundred, subtracting seven each time. It was terrifying. I felt as if I were swinging on monkey bars, having to remember simultaneously which hand to release and which bar to grab, only I would hesitate too long in figuring this out and would fall between bars. I was sweating with frustration and fear. I noticed also that my left arm, which had been numb down to my forefinger, now developed an icy-burning sensation. I'd had a similar problem with my right arm two years before. In the morning, I still could not remember the "Material Girl" lyrics, and could barely move my left arm without the shock of exquisite pain.

Lucky for me, our band is known for being ludicrous, so it didn't matter that I had to read the lyrics stiffly to perform them. Yet even reading them was difficult, for in doing so, I had to sing, listen for musical cues of when to come in, and move my body in more or less rhythmic fashion. There was so much I had once taken for granted that I now struggled to do. My bandmates thought it went over hilariously well. I was mortified.

When I returned home, I made an appointment with another neurologist. This time I was determined to continue with tests until something came up. I had taken a look at an MRI report from more than a year before. What were those fifteen small "unidentified bright objects" on my brain? Were they *always* a normal part of aging? Could they relate to something else? And what about the burning in my arm, which an MRI showed to be synovitis? Why did I have synovitis first in my right arm and now in my left? The doctor agreed to prescribe more tests to rule out multiple sclerosis, lupus, and a squiggly word on a lab slip that I thought said "Lyme."

Until then it had not occurred to me to consider Lyme disease. Wasn't that something that was on the East Coast only? Then again, I was someone who bounced back and forth between coasts. In any given week, I might be in San Francisco, New York, or five cities in five different states. I recalled that I had found engorged ticks on both of my dogs, several times as a matter of fact, and even as recently as a few months previously, shortly after being in Washington, D.C. Upon seeing a wad of matted hair on my dog Lilli, I cut it off, and blood spurted onto my fingertips. Had I injured my dog? I brought the wad closer to my eyes, and the fleshy-looking piece began to move, legs bristling, combing the air in a desperate search for another patch of warm skin. I nearly vomited with disgust. Both of my dogs had received Lyme vaccines as a precaution, but I now took them to their veterinarian to be tested just in case.

Why had I never thought to test myself? The reason was simple: I had never seen the "bull's-eye rash" that everyone said was the defining sign of a tick gone bad. I had read about it in a newspaper or magazine. I thought that "bull's-eye" referred to a visible tick bite surrounded by a thin red ring about the size of a wedding band. But now, unsure as to what it looked like, I did a search for Lyme disease on the Internet. Up came a website with photographed examples of erythema migrans, the rash characteristic of the spirochete borrelia. My scalp prickled. *There was my rash.* I recalled it: a huge red splotch wrapping my shin, just below the sock line, about four inches in diameter. What was that? With my impaired memory, I tried to piece together clues. I remembered seeing the growing rash and thinking it might have been caused by a tick, but there was no red circle. So I assumed it was a spider bite. Now, after viewing these examples from the website and reading the descriptions, I knew that rashes did not necessarily develop the bull's-eye immediately or at all, and the bull's-eye itself was not necessarily a thin perfect band; it could be the remnants of the large rash as it cleared outward from the center. It might be better described as a cloudy halo, sometimes well demarcated, sometimes messily, appearing in some cases like the primordial outline of an unevenly submerged volcanic cone, as mine had appeared when it gradually faded over the month. In more than fifty percent of the cases, the website said, the patient never even saw the tick bite or the rash.

The most dangerous ticks, another website reported, were nymphs, so small as to be the size of the period in this sentence. They often went unnoticed. Now I recalled that at the center of my rash there had been a very black dot. I remembered its blackness, and that it was unusual. The dot was rounded and raised, so

I assumed it was a blood blister formed from my scratching at the rash. When it fell off, it left a pit with edges that continued to slough. Soon more rashes appeared on the sides of my lower leg, and then three more bloomed on my upper arm. I remember thinking I must have had an infestation of spiders that dropped down from my ceiling at night. But the website led me to new conclusions: As Lyme disease disseminates, the rash may appear on other parts of the body.

I then recalled that sometime later, the tops of my feet had gone numb, and I had wondered whether the rash had anything to do with it. I had mentioned this to my doctor during my annual checkup, and I remembered the approximate date of that appointment, November 1999, shortly before my mother died. In some quick tests of my ankle reflexes, which proved absent, my doctor had scratched along the top and bottom of my feet, which lacked normal sensation but strangely were also painful. She concluded that I had peripheral neuropathy but no other apparent neurological problems. I would keep a watch for other problems, but for now, we agreed, this symptom seemed only a curiosity, nothing to worry about.

Three years had passed since my feet had gone numb. As I scanned the websites on Lyme disease, I felt the heightened tension of reading the inevitable conclusion of a murder mystery. Here were all the clues, so obvious now: the rash, the exhaustion, the numbness, the stiff neck, even the hypoglycemia. Reading the list made me feel as if I were watching that old show *This Is Your Life*, in which sentimental details from someone's past were dredged up and paraded before the public: an old math teacher, a boy once dated, a first boss. But instead, these were the visitors from my past: thinning hair, rapid heart rate, hypersensitive hearing, palpitations, the sense of internal vibration (my Dolby Digital Syndrome!), stiff muscles, migrating joint pain, ringing in the ears, sensations of burning and stabbing, a crackling neck, synovitis, insomnia. Then came the cronies of late-stage borreliosis: such cognitive problems as slowed mental processing, geographic disorientation, lack of concentration, and even hallucinations, my visitors in the night.

A new question came to mind: When had I been bitten? Where, exactly? Had it been while I was walking the pastures in New Jersey, attending an outdoor dog show in early autumn? Was it during the spring when I was in upstate New York, visiting my editor, who was ill? Did it happen during the hot summer when I went to a writers' conference in Old Chatham, New York? Was it at the outdoor wedding in Dutchess County? Or had it been when I was hiking the grassy woodlands of Sonoma, Mendocino, or the Yosemite basin? Did it happen in China, Italy, Poland, or Czechoslovakia, places I had visited that had borrelia ticks of a different strain? It was impossible for me to know, because I had led such a peripatetic life recently. A tick that had attached on to me in one location could have been transported home with me to San Francisco.

Yet this was the question that came back to me throughout the day and in the middle of the night. I could not stop imagining the various scenarios, me blithely enjoying myself, walking along a grassy path on a gorgeous day, while the little vampire scurried up my leg. I wanted to envision it so that I could uselessly ask: "Why me?" Why had I, out of hundreds or thousands who might have passed that same spot, become the hapless meal for a nymph tick? What was I doing while the spirochetes were swimming in my bloodstream, using their corkscrew tails to propel themselves quickly into my tissue, my organs, my brain?

Because that tick bite had changed the course and quality of my life, I wanted to be able to capture the precise moment, see it as live feed on a CNN monitor. I wanted to play it back repeatedly, and the moments right before and after, as we do with all the great and terrible moments of our life, the ones that are both personal and universal, the seconds that changed our world forever, be they the birth of a child or the death of a loved one, the assassination of a great leader or the collapse of the World Trade Center towers.

I knew my doctors would advise against gorging myself on excess information, but I was desperate to know as much as possible about the parasite in my body. I searched the Internet again and found a support group, inhabited by a virtual underworld of longtime sufferers of Lyme disease. The recent posts came from the newly frightened, often the mothers of children whose perfect peach skin had been defiled by a tick and who were now listless and doing poorly in school. I had yet to be diagnosed, but I felt certain I had found my culprit.

In reading the posts, I learned my case was typical. I had spent a few years looking for a cause. I had had surgery and more than $50,000 of diagnostic tests. Some of the Lymies, as they called themselves, had been long undiagnosed—some for ten, twenty, even thirty years. Like many of them, I had been told Lyme disease was rare. There were only 139 new California cases reported in 1999, the year I was probably infected. *Reported* cases, the Lymies countered. They knew of a Lyme specialist in San Francisco who had treated five hundred patients.

Now what should I do? My virtual friends were more seasoned warriors than I, of both borrelia and ignorance in the medical community. They urged me to avoid the screening test most doctors gave, the enzyme-linked immunoassay, or ELISA. It had a ninety-percent specificity but only a sixty-five-percent sensitivity: this test delivered an unacceptable level of false negatives. In contrast, tests for anthrax were 110 percent sensitive, which meant some false positives. With a deadly disease, wasn't it better to err on the side of being overly inclusive? Yet the opposite was true of the screening test for borrelia. If you take the ELISA and it's negative, the Lymies warned, that is what your doctor will believe, and you will not be given the Western blot, the test given to those who test positive on the ELISA. The Western blot is a more sensitive test, they said, but the disease has to be diagnosed by someone who recognizes the whole panoply of history and clinical symptoms.

Unfortunately, few doctors took the time to be updated on the intricacies of such a clinical diagnosis. Why should they? They had never seen a Lyme patient. For the latest information, they depended on one-sheets that spelled out the basics: "Use the ELISA screening. If it's positive, it may be a false positive, unless you see the bull's-eye rash. For actual infections, ten days of antibiotics will suffice." Even newscast doctors received press releases with similar advice, and without questioning the source, they passed this along to viewers as sound advice. But the ten-day "standard" took as its basis a single study considered grossly flawed by many Lyme doctors who saw hundreds of patients each year. Ten days of antibiotics was a recipe for relapse, the Lymies said. That was like saying one Roach Motel was sufficient for any house, no matter how small or large, whether you had seen one roach recently or your house had been thick with them for years. If you don't believe undertreatment is dangerous, the Lymies told me, look at us. We are the fallout from this advice. We relapsed and were refused further treatment. We who were once professors, lawyers, carpenters, doctors, social workers, teachers, and busy mothers became bedridden, then lost our jobs, our homes, and sometimes our hope.

I felt I was hearing from people drowning in the River Styx. What sort of disease had I acquired? Was it Lyme that made these people suspicious and cranky? The Lymies demanded to know why the medical community had been so hasty, so determined to say short-term treatment was good enough. They pointed out that no one even knew for certain what the etiology of Lyme disease was until 1982. And in twenty years, there had not been enough research to know how to knock back borrelia's hydra-headed ways of invading the body and remaining entrenched in its favorite eatery, the brain.

Whether I had Lyme or not, I knew I was developing what some might call a "terminal illness," what one acquires sitting in front of a computer terminal, ingesting Internet information in megabyte doses. But I had to know who my terrorist was. I had to visualize what was now in my body. My enemy was a spirochete, a clever bacterium with a tail, four times more complex in its genetic structure than the spirochete that causes syphilis, for which patients are given *months* of antibiotic treatment. Like the frightening creatures of *Alien* moviedom, the borrelia spirochete is a smart bug that has the ability to transform itself into other forms, a cellular version of a wolf in sheep's clothing, able to hide and go unrecognized by antibiotics and the body's immune defenses. A changing arsenal of weapons was needed to knock it back, with treatment lasting years, if not a lifetime. Yet insurance companies, HMOs, and medical organizations had latched on to the notion that ten days of antibiotics was quite enough to defeat borrelia and restore patients to a pain-free, productive life. Their rationale for this parsimonious approach stemmed from concerns over antibiotic-resistant diseases that had developed worldwide from indiscriminate use of antibiotics. But acne patients continue to receive years' worth of antibiotics without any hassles. Acne was not a life-threatening disease, the Lymies pointed out, while chronic neuroborreliosis was.

The old-timers on this message board were a skeptical bunch. They did not trust most of the medical community, only those doctors they considered "Lyme-literate," the ones who saw hundreds of cases a year, as opposed to those who had seen only one or two, if any, in their entire years of practice. The Lymies exhorted me to find a Lyme-literate doctor, one who would order the tests by IGeneX, the lab that included all sixteen bands of the Western blot and more strains of borrelia, of which there are approximately three hundred worldwide, than any other lab.

But I was not as cynical as these Lymies. Not all doctors refused to consider Lyme. The new neurologist I was seeing had ordered the Lyme test without my bringing up the subject. He must have indeed considered it possible that I had the disease. Soon the test results would arrive, and I would have my answer.

The answer arrived: The tests were negative, all of them. I had been so sure I had Lyme disease. I still was. The Lymies' remarks about the poor sensitivity of the ELISA stuck in my mind. I called the specialist to say I had recalled important information that I had failed to tell him and my other doctors. I mumbled about the rash, the numbness, the stiff neck that led to my buying new pillows every week.

"I really doubt you have Lyme disease," he said. "It's extremely rare in California."

I hurriedly pointed out that I lived part-time on the East Coast, that I was often in Dutchess, Putnam, and Columbia counties of New York, which were known to have Lyme disease infestations. I had vacationed in Mystic, Connecticut, which is near Old Lyme, the town for which the disease was named. "I know that I tested negative," I said, "but I would like to take further tests, just to make sure."

And then my doctor surprised me. He said that the lab had not run the test for Lyme disease after all. They had tested me for syphilis, that other spirochete. But if it would make me feel more at ease, he could order the best test for Lyme, the ELISA. And if that was positive, we could do a spinal tap to make sure.

That evening I wrote an e-mail to the Lyme specialist in San Francisco who had been mentioned by Lymies on the Internet; considered by them among the top experts on the disease, he saw patients from across the country and one year had been voted as among the best doctors in San Francisco. At my appointment, I told him my symptoms, and instead of looking puzzled, this doctor nodded. "Quite common," he said. He looked at my MRI. "Characteristic," he noted. Nothing seemed too surprising or bizarre. He filled out a lab slip for the Western blot that would be run by IGeneX, the same lab the Lymies had recommended. In short order, I had my answer: the Western blot came back highly positive for Lyme disease, lighting up many bands. A scan of my brain showed hypoperfusion, also known as "clogged brain," which accounted for slowed processing and other damage, all typical of Lyme. My immune system showed abnormalities indicative of an immune system battling a chronic infection—a lymphocyte count of fifty-five percent, way over the high normal of forty-two percent. I also had abnormally low natural killer cells, a marker that this doctor had seen in almost every patient with late-stage Lyme disease. He wrote the name of my official diagnosis: neuroborreliosis, also known as neurological Lyme disease.

That day, I began taking megadoses of antibiotics. Two days later I was worse than ever. My brain felt as though it were swelling; I had a terrific headache. My joint pain had grown worse, the ringing in my ears was shrill, and my hands and feet were burning. I was exhausted, as though I were coming down with the flu. I told the doctor what was happening.

"That's good to hear," he said. The worsening of symptoms, the Jarisch-Herxheimer reaction, happens with very few diseases in response to antibiotics; one of them is syphilis and another—wouldn't you know it is Lyme disease. The fact that such a reaction occurs is a confirmation of the diagnosis.

After ten days, the antibiotics had not had much effect on ridding me of my symptoms. Thank God I was not with a doctor who stuck by the ten-day standard. But after eight weeks, some of the fogginess lifted and I had an amazing amount of energy—that is, a normal amount. I was elated. I cleaned my desk, rearranged furniture and changed bedding, drove to the hardware store for supplies, then returned to paint the garage, hang a bar in the closet, and hose down the terrace. Later I shopped for groceries, cooked a meal for friends, and washed the dishes—all ordinary chores I had not been able to do for lack of organizational skills, energy, and motivation. The next day I began to write again. A couple of weeks later the fog returned and once more I was easily tired and overwhelmed. When I tried to drive, I stopped at a green light and ran a red one.

As word of my diagnosis went around, a dozen people came forward to tell me that they too had been infected with Lyme disease. I had been initiated into a secret club. They included writers, a publisher, a publicist and his partner, a librettist, a veterinary technician, and the wife of a writer. I thought to myself: This is a rare disease? To judge from the numbers reported by the Centers for Disease Control, I should have seldom or never encountered another person who had this. Most of these people lived on the East Coast, where a tick bite is taken more seriously. A good many had been seen by savvy doctors who prescribed antibiotics without taking a screening test. The one who was not given early treatment lives in California and is also a writer. Like me, he had been unable to write. He has been battling the disease for six years. He has gone through various combinations of antibiotics, daily intravenous infusions, and painful shots. He is slowly getting well. "When the good days come," he said to me, "they are golden. Savor them. Write your heart out."

Finding the cause should have been the end of this story, yet I feel it is still close to the beginning. I am in it for the long haul, with treatment that will likely last for years. I won't feel safe until my brain scan and the blood tests on my immune system return to normal, until the Western blot is negative for Lyme disease, and the myriad symptoms are gone. Well, perhaps not all of them will disappear. I'm told I should expect to keep the joint problems as a souvenir.

Moreover, simply by having Lyme disease, I have been drawn into the medical schism over both diagnosis and treatment. I now know the greatest danger that borrelia has highlighted: ignorance.

I was ignorant and did not think the original symptoms were important enough to recount. The majority of doctors still believe that Lyme disease is extremely rare, yet each day I hear of more and more people who have it. The medical community believes without question that the ELISA is a fine diagnostic tool and that a short course of antibiotics is all that is needed. That, I learned, is the board position of the California Medical Association. Why did it issue such a dangerous precedent-setting recommendation? Executive staff there told me no proof exists yet that Lyme disease can turn into a persistent infection.

Where does that leave me? I have a persistent infection. And I am also, by nature, quite persistent. I persisted in finding the right doctor, finding the bug that got me. I will do what it takes to get well, ignorance and medical politics be damned. I am in charge of my body now. And thus for the first time I am certain I will get well. Even if I do not recover completely, I am grateful to have made a small improvement, for I am able to write again when the golden days quietly arrive. Writing comes with great effort. I have to think harder. But then again, the world is now a more difficult place for all of us. We all have to think harder.

For the time being, I can accept with aplomb and humor that I do indeed get confused and am not as quick as I once was. When I am disoriented, I know this is not panic born out of fear of the unknown. The terrorist in my body has been found. Yes, the world to me is still a scary place, but no more so than it is for most people. I am no longer governed by fate and fear. I have hope and, with that, a determination to change what is not right. As a storyteller, I know that if I don't like the ending, I can write a better one.

My mother and me.

The following have appeared previously, in slightly different form, in the following publications: "How We Knew" in *Harper's Bazaar*; "Last Week" (under the title "Family Ghosts Hoard Secrets that Bewitch the Living") in *The New York Times*; "My Grandmother's Choice" in *Ladies' Home Journal* and *Life*; "Fish Cheeks" in *Seventeen*; "Dangerous Advice" in *Ski Magazine*; "Midlife Confidential" in *Mid-Life Confidential* (Viking); "Joy Luck and Hollywood" in the *Los Angeles Times*; "Confessions" in *Confession* (PEN/Faulkner Foundation); "Pretty Beyond Belief" in *O, The Oprah Magazine*; "The Most Hateful Words" in *The New Yorker*; "My Love Affair with Vladimir Nabokov" (under the title "Amy Tan's Personal Best: *Lolita*") in *Salon*; "Inferior Decorating" (under the title "Tête-à-Tête") in *Elle Décor*; "Retreat to Reality" (under the title "Weekend Siege") in *Ski Magazine*; "My Hair, My Face, My Nails" in *Ski Magazine*; "Mother Tongue" in *The Threepenny Review* and *The Best American Essays 1991* (Houghton Mifflin); "The Language of Discretion" in *The State of the Language* (University of California Press); "Angst and the Second Book" (as "Angst and the Second Novel") in *Publishers Weekly*; "Required Reading and Other Dangerous Subjects" in *The Threepenny Review* and *Harper's*; and "The Best Stories" in *The Best American Short Stories 1999* (Houghton Mifflin).

All photographs courtesy Amy Tan.